S0-EEX-680

INTRODUCTION TO CRIMINAL INVESTIGATION

INTRODUCTION TO CRIMINAL INVESTIGATION

richard h. ward, d. crim.

John Jay College of Criminal Justice

formerly
Detective, New York City Police Department

ADDISON-WESLEY PUBLISHING COMPANY
Reading, Massachusetts • Menlo Park, California
London • Amsterdam • Don Mills, Ontario • Sydney

Copyright © 1975 by Addison-Wesley Publishing Company, Inc. Philippines copyright 1975 by Addison-Wesley Publishing Company, Inc.

All rights reserved. No part of this publication may be reproduced, stored in a retrieval system, or transmitted, in any form or by any means, electronic, mechanical, photocopying, recording, or otherwise, without the prior written permission of the publisher. Printed in the United States of America. Published simultaneously in Canada. Library of Congress Catalog Card No. 74-19703.

To my wife, Maureen
and my children,
Jeanne Marie and Jonathan Berkeley

preface

Probably no other aspect of police work is of more interest to the patrolman than that of criminal investigation. Despite this interest, however, few patrolmen are chosen to be detectives, and many of those who are probably should not have been. Unfortunately, the art and science of criminal investigation have not received the measure of academic attention they deserve, although there is a growing body of literature indicating that investigative effectiveness leaves much to be desired.

The contemporary investigator is faced with a most difficult task. To be successful he must not only be persistent and curious; he must also be equipped with the knowledge and expertise peculiar to his particular field. Many police administrators assume that because a patrolman makes a number of good arrests he will be a good investigator. Such is not necessarily the case.

This book provides a general introduction to the field of criminal investigation. Its purpose is twofold: first, to provide the student, or new practitioner, with the foundation necessary to be an effective investigator and, second, to create in the mind of the reader an awareness of the problems facing the investigator in today's complex society.

The primary focus is on the solution of crime by investigation. Certainly, no single work could possibly provide the avid student with all the material necessary for a complete understanding of the investigative field. It is the author's hope that this book will serve to whet the reader's appetite, and interest him in pursuing the works of other experts in criminal investigation. With this in mind, a short selected bibliography follows each chapter to provide a basis for further study.

The emphasis here is on basic criminal investigation; the techniques and tools necessary to accomplish the task are discussed with a view toward providing a systematic approach. The book has been designed for the investigator, but much of the material will be of value to the patrolman, especially in those departments in which he is responsible for some aspect of the investigation. A noticeable trend in police work has been toward the "team" concept, wherein the line units act as an operating team to carry out the police function. This approach places greater responsibility on the individual patrolman, and in such a case the book should be of value in assisting him to carry out the investigative function.

The rapid proliferation of programs in police science and criminal justice, especially at the community college level, indicates a growing interest in police professionalization. The concept of education requires more than training, and the text is in keeping with this tradition. In addition to the practical "nuts and bolts" aspects of criminal investigation there is an orientation toward the historical, theoretical, and methodological problems surrounding the discipline.

The problems of criminal investigation are manifold. Recent Supreme Court decisions in the area of individual rights place greater restrictions on the investigator, and in order to safeguard these rights he must be aware of the limitations involved. A number of breakthroughs in the area of technology provide the investigator with new tools. He must be familiar with these innovations, and know when to use them. The increased emphasis on scientific criminal investigation requires that the detective be more than familiar with its capabilities.

Beyond these aspects is the need for an understanding of the behavioral sciences, particularly psychology and sociology, and their relationship to individual behavior and the investigative role. An understanding of people and the processes of human interaction is central to the task because much of the investigator's work involves dealing with people. Unlike most professions, police work often entails an involvement with people who are likely to be hostile, frightened, antagonistic, or secretive. It is always the investigator's job to ferret out the truth.

All too often there is an assumption that each crime can be investigated in the same manner. If this were the case, there would probably be no need for specialization. Nevertheless, the trend in criminal investigation is toward specialization, and for good reason. The complexities of an urban environment virtually mandate this shift. The investigator must not only be familiar with the individual aspects of a particular crime, but must also have an in-depth knowledge of likely suspects and their specific traits. Thus, attention has been given to the characteristics of various crimes. The serious student will be able to extrapolate parallels from the material presented here in order to develop a better approach in the investigation of similar crimes.

Many chapters are followed by questions, and exercises designed to develop the student's awareness of the chapter's important elements. The reader is urged to develop his own powers of reason and logic, powers crucial to the investigative function. No book can provide the reader with experience, but an understanding of the fundamentals involved in an investigation make it possible to increase the probability of success. It is with this in mind that *Introduction to Criminal Investigation* was written.

acknowledgments

The number of individuals who contributed to the preparation of this manuscript, both directly and indirectly, would fill more than several pages. In addition to the advice and assistance of those who provided continual reviews, I am indebted to my former students at the John Jay College of Criminal Justice and the University of Missouri, St. Louis, who read the manuscript in earlier stages and made useful suggestions for its use as a practical text. I would hope that, through my use of the manuscript as a classroom text for over a year, many of the problems associated with current textbooks have been eliminated.

I owe a particular debt of gratitude to those with whom I have worked as an investigator, especially Detectives Frank Randise, Jim Cooley, and Bob Laino. Much of what is written here evolves from the continuing debate and discussion over investigative effectiveness, and many of the ideas presented are attributable to any number of my professional colleagues.

For contributions to the manuscript itself I am indebted to Dr. Gordon Misner (University of Missouri, St. Louis), who has always been a source of encouragement. Dr. Joseph Peterson (John Jay College of Criminal Justice) made numerous worthwhile suggestions, as did Noel Criscuola (University of Missouri, St. Louis). Major Fred Guenther, Sergeant Darrel Stephens, and Tom Sweeney, of the Kansas City, Missouri Police Department have always been quick to provide assistance. Lourn Phelps, former Chief of Police, Richmond, California, provided much useful information and assistance, and Lt. Gerald O'Connell of the St. Louis, Missouri Police Department offered many important suggestions for improvement of the manuscript, as did Prof. Robert Sheehan (Northeastern University).

Several of my former students at the Police College, Bramshill, England were also most helpful, but I am particularly grateful to Inspector George Dent, New Scotland Yard, for reviewing the book in detail and making some important comments. Steve Opara, a good friend and colleague, also made several important suggestions.

I am particularly indebted to my research assistant, Jayne Feeley, who devoted numerous hours to completion of the text, and who has been both a good critic and an invaluable aide. My thanks also to Laurel Angelos-Robles who typed the earlier drafts of the manuscript.

Donald Riddle, the president of John Jay College of Criminal Justice, deserves special thanks for his encouragement and friendship. It would be impossible to thank all of my colleagues at John Jay who provided assistance, but Gerald Lynch, Jim Curran, John Cronin, Ron McVey, Lin Henderson, and Claire Villarreal deserve special mention.

The staff of Addison-Wesley Publishing Company were particularly patient and helpful, and it has been a pleasure working with them.

The ultimate contribution to completion of the book was made by my wife, Maureen, and our children, Jonathan and Jeanne, who gave up time that should have been theirs. For this it is impossible to adequately say thank you.

For what success *Introduction to Criminal Investigation* enjoys, I am indebted to many, but for its failures I take full responsibility, hoping it will make some contribution to criminal justice literature.

New York, New York R.H.W.
February 1975

contents

Part I
BASIC CONCEPTS OF CRIMINAL INVESTIGATION

Chapter 1 **The history of criminal investigation**
Criminal investigation in the United States 5
The advent of scientific criminal investigation 8
Scientific criminal investigation in the United States 10
The contemporary detective 12
Questions for discussion 14

Chapter 2 **General aspects of the investigative function**
Internal implications of criminal investigation 16
External implications of criminal investigation 17
Elements of the investigation 18
Interviewing and interrogation 18
Information 19
The crime scene 20
Utilization of scientific evidence 20
Victims, witnesses, and suspects 21
Reports 21
Preparation for court 22
Summary 23
Questions for discussion 23

Chapter 3 **Preliminary investigation and the crime scene**
Conducting the investigation 25
The function of records 26

The crime report 28
The crime scene 32
Conclusions and theory building 39
Summary 40
Questions for discussion 40

Chapter 4 Photographing and sketching the crime scene
Crime scene photography 43
Persons 47
Places 48
Objects 49
Measurements and markings 49
Special photographic problems 50
Videotape and motion pictures 51
Crime scene sketching 51
The measured field sketch 52
The scaled sketch 54
Special sketching techniques 54
The use of sketches 54
Questions for discussion 55
Exercise 55

Chapter 5 Scientific evidence and criminal investigation
Recognition and collection of physical evidence 58
Casts 61
Chemical 63

Documents 77
Fingerprints 79
Firearms 87
Weapons 92
Instrumentation 92
Photographic 93
Tool mark comparison 93
Physical matches 93
Summary 94
Questions for discussion 95
Exercises 95

Part II
THE INVESTIGATIVE FUNCTION

Chapter 6 Interviewing and interrogation
Interviewing 100
Situation 100
Setting 102
Clientele 103
Language 107
Method 107
Interrogation 108
Situation 109
Setting 109
Clientele 110

Language 111
Method 111
Summary 113
Questions for discussion 113
Exercises 113

Chapter 7 **Informants and information**
Informants 115
The confidential informant 116
Management of the confidential informant 118
The "one-time" informant 119
The involuntary informant 120
Verification of informant statements 120
Information 121
Government sources of information 122
Private sources of information 123
Public sources of information 124
The utilization of information 125
Summary 126
Questions for discussion 127
Exercises 127

Chapter 8 **Information analysis and theory building**
Internal aspects of the investigation as a science 130
Chance 130
Imagination 131

Intuition 133
Reason 134
Observation 136
Strategy 137
Developing and testing theories 138
Theory building 139
Summary 142
Questions for discussion 143

Chapter 9 Crimes and their patterns: crimes against the person

Criminal homicide 146
Physical evidence and criminal homicide 146
Establishing the case 147
Premeditated murder 148
Murder during the commission of a crime 150
Murder as the result of a physical assault 151
Summary of criminal homicide investigations 152
Robbery 153
Robbery investigations 158
Sex crimes 160
Rape 160
Sexual deviation 161
Child molestation 162
Summary 162
Questions for discussion 163
Exercises 163

Chapter 10 Crimes and their patterns: crimes against property

Larceny and theft 165
- Commercial and business larcenies 167
- Theft 168
- Credit card and check thieves 169
- Counterfeiting and forgery 170
- Confidence games 174
- Pickpockets 176
- Auto theft 177
- Other forms of larceny 178

Burglary 179
- Burglary types 180
- Property identification and recovery 183
- Pattern analysis 183
- Primary and secondary witness information 184
- Physical evidence 184

Burglary of safes 186

Summary 187

Questions for discussion 188

Chapter 11 Legal aspects of the investigative function

Criminal law and the investigator 189
- Admissions and confessions 190
- Searches and seizures 191
- Search warrants 193
- Executing a search warrant 194

Electronic surveillance and wiretapping 195
Informants 197
Surveillance 197
Lineups and identification 198
Summary 199
Questions for discussion 201
Exercises 201

Part III
SPECIAL INVESTIGATIVE TECHNIQUES AND PROBLEMS

Chapter 12 **Undercover and surveillance operations**
Undercover operations 205
Surveillance 207

Chapter 13 **Narcotics and dangerous drugs** 215

Chapter 14 **Ghetto or inner-city investigations**
Approaching the problem 230
Minorities and investigation 231
The inner-city investigation 232
Summary 232

Chapter 15 **Organized crime**
The structure of organized crime 236
Combatting organized crime 236
Summary 241

Chapter 16 **Relations with other agencies and organizations**

Jealousy 243

Professional rivalry 244

Bureaucratic red tape 244

Poor interagency relations 245

Summary 245

Chapter 17 **The role of the criminal investigator in contemporary society** 247

Bibliography 253

BASIC CONCEPTS IN CRIMINAL INVESTIGATION

part I

CHAPTER 1

the history of criminal investigation

Criminal investigation, as a specialized form of police work in the United States, has its roots in the very origins of European criminological history. The concept of utilizing specialists to investigate crime can be traced to early times. Marcus Lucinius Crassus of Rome, for example, is said to have used intelligence operatives to gather evidence for use in the law courts. In later years Frederick the Great employed "agents" to provide him with information.[1] Toward the end of the eighteenth century, there were 50 or more detectives in London.[2] However, the formal use of detectives is probably best exemplified in the history of France, where the Sureté (Security) was formed in 1810. An innovative attempt by Paris officials to cope with a rising crime rate, this new organization was headed by Eugene Francois Vidocq.

Vidocq had an interesting background. As a former criminal, he had established a reputation for his ability to escape from French prisons. The celebrated French "criminal" maintained that crime could only be fought by former criminals, and many of his detectives were recruited from behind prison walls. At the height of his career, he was to employ some 24 former inmates as investigators.

France's first "detective" distinguished himself as a pioneer in criminal investigation. Jurgen Thorwald, author of *The Century of the Detective,* points out that Vidocq was a master of deception.

> He would "assign" his men to prison using fake arrests, even going as far as to simulate escapes and deaths. In this way Vidocq developed an extremely sophisticated informational system concerning the underworld. He developed a unique record system containing drawings of known criminals, their *Modus Operandi* and their criminal records.*

Vidocq's endeavors produced amazing results and in one particular year, with the help of 12 men, he was credited with arresting 812 criminals.[3] His resignation

---

*Reproduced with permission from Jurgen Thorwald, *The Century of the Detective.* New York: Harcourt, Brace and World, 1964, p. 4.

in 1833 was prompted by the hiring of a new Prefect of Police who rebelled at the idea of his entire investigative force being made up of former criminals. During his tenure Vidocq amassed enormous archives which are said to have contained five million items of information related to criminal investigation.

While Vidocq and the Sureté represent the more popularized genesis of criminal investigation, they are not the first investigative force. As early as 1725, Henry Fielding, then a London Justice of the Peace, saw the need for a formal police service to cope with the rising crime rate in London. It was not until 1750, however, that he saw his idea become a reality. Known as "The Bow Street Runners" or "Thief Takers," this group of men is viewed by many students as the earliest detective force in the world.[4]

The Bow Street Runners achieved a modicum of success, but their reputation was often marred by a willingness to cooperate with criminals and, in some instances, even to commit criminal acts themselves. Despite a proclivity to lawlesssness, the group (which never exceeded 15 members) provided London with the only civilian criminal police for 90 years. Fielding's efforts on behalf of criminal investigation included publishing the names of wanted men in local newspapers, as well as the establishment of a criminal records system.

As a result of the industrial revolution which started in England about 1760, the cities began to grow rapidly, slum conditions developed, and crime continued to rise. By 1829 Sir Robert Peel, the Home Secretary, recognized the deficiency of the present forms of policing (the Bow Street Runners, the Merchant Police, and Parish Police) and published "An Act for Improving the Police In and Near the Metropolis." Known as the Metropolitan Police Act, the study called for a formal police service. Peel introduced his proposal to Parliament, his recommendations were accepted, and he was named to head the new organization.

By 1910 a number of scholars within the field of criminal investigation had begun to emerge. Among them was Hans Gross, whose *Criminal Psychology* remains a classic. In this book Gross discusses the impact of psychology on crime, covering such subjects as depositions of witnesses, perception, superstition, probability, sensory illusions, inference, and sexual differences. Gross was born in 1847 in Austria, and after pursuing his studies at Vienna and Graz, qualified as a lawyer in 1869.[5] He served as an examining magistrate and a professor of law at the University of Graz, and authored "a considerable number of volumes bearing on the administration of criminal law and upon the theoretical foundations of the science of criminology."[6]

On December 7, 1829, London's first police force was established with 1000 men. By 1842 it became apparent that something more than uniformed police was needed; thus, 12 policemen were assigned to plainclothes duty and given rooms at 4 Whitehall Place, also known as Scotland Yard. The exploits of Scotland Yard were chronicled by Charles Dickens some ten years later. Dickens, in the person of his hero Inspector Bucket, introduced the words: "I am Bucket of the detectives.

I am a 'detective officer'. " Thus, the word detective was introduced into the common language and public consciousness.[7,8] The exploits of Scotland Yard have since become legend.

CRIMINAL INVESTIGATION IN THE UNITED STATES

The use of specialized criminal investigators developed slowly in the United States. While, in 1636, Boston was the first city to establish a *night watch,* it was not until 1833 that Philadelphia established the first daytime, paid police force. In 1838, Boston established a day force of six men, and in 1844, New York had day and night police forces.

Prior to 1845 criminal investigation was often performed by constables in Boston. This work was in addition to their regular duties, and more often than not in quest of a reward offered for the recovery of property, rather than as an effort to apprehend the criminal.[9] However, Boston had established a 33-man force by 1846, including three detectives. "The detectives were assigned to the central office, together with several headquarters officials, the marshal himself, and the two deputies."[10]

"Roundsmen" in New York, who appeared on the department's payroll in 1836, are sometimes considered that city's first detectives, but it was not until 1857 that New York's Board of Police of the Metropolitan District adopted a resolution authorizing the assignment of 20 policemen from the Metropolitan police to be designated "detectives."[11,12]

Allan Pinkerton is considered by most scholars as Chicago's first detective. He was appointed by Mayor Boone in 1849 and, according to one account, he was not only competent, "he was original, unique."[13] Pinkerton did not remain in the city's employ for long; about 1850, with an attorney named Edward Rucker, he established a "General Detective Police Business in Illinois, Wisconsin, Michigan and Indiana" which attended to "the investigation and depredation, frauds and criminal offenses; the detection of offenders, procuring arrests and convictions, apprehension or return of fugitives from justice, or bail; recovering lost or stolen property, obtaining information, etc."[14]

Despite his move from the public scene, Pinkerton did contribute to the beginning of criminal investigation in the United States, and often cooperated with local sheriffs and police agencies in matters of mutual concern. Pinkerton has been credited with initiating a number of investigative techniques in the United States, including the use of daguerrotypes (early photographs) and facsimiles of suspects' handwriting.

In 1860 Chicago established its first detective unit.[15] As John Flinn, author of the *History of the Chicago Police,* points out, during the early years of the detective department men were usually chosen from the ranks of patrolmen although "some of the officers . . . were appointed without having served a day on the force; but there was always some good reason for such an appointment . . ."[16]

In New York, the Detective Division had grown to include 62 detectives by 1873, and in 1875 the force was divided into two branches: the Headquarters detectives and the Ward detectives. The Headquarters detectives were responsible for crimes assigned by the superintendent of police; the Ward detectives (two in each of the city's 31 precincts) were responsible for crimes committed in their jurisdiction.

Between 1878 and 1885, Boston had established a rule which "declared that frequent changes in detective personnel were to be expected, and that demotions were not reflections on the individuals involved."[17] Corruption during the formative years of investigative operations became common, and was virtually an accepted practice in many police departments; Boston's attempt to deal with it was probably more successful than the attempts of other cities—due in no small part to the efforts of the Chief of Police.[18] Boston's experience with corruption came to a head in 1870 when the city's Aldermen issued a report denouncing the detective system and, in doing so, abolished the detective bureau, serving notice that they would institute a system "which would better meet the demands of law and justice."[19]

Thomas Byrnes was named to head the detectives of New York in 1880. Byrnes' approach to criminal investigation proved to be effective in many respects, and his success in curtailing crime in the Wall Street area earned him many friends. His fame was widespread and, in addition to collaborating on a number of books, he authored one of his own, *Professional Criminals of America,* which was published in 1886. Byrnes' vivid descriptions of such criminals as Aleck the Milkman, Piano Charley, Brummegan Bill, English Paddy, the Peoria Kid and others, seem somewhat novelistic today, but his "collection" of underworld characters may be viewed as one of the first attempts to disseminate information to both law enforcement agencies and the private sector.

Byrnes was eventually promoted to Chief Inspector of the department, but was later forced to retire under a cloud of suspicion. As James Richardson, author of *The New York Police: Colonial Times to 1901,* writes:

> The detective was involved in intricate and tension-producing relationships with criminals, the public, and his fellow police officers. It was not easy for a detective to be both effective and honest. When stolen property was involved, the easiest way for the detective to get it back was for its lawful owner to compound with the thief, promising him immunity for other crimes or a percentage of the reward offered.*

The detective's close relationship to the criminal population and his ability to make "deals" created a situation in which corruption occurred easily. Byrnes came under

---

*Reprinted by permission from James Richardson, *The New York Police: Colonial Times to 1901.* New York: Oxford University Press, 1970, p. 207.

pressure of the Board of Commissioners in 1895, largely as the result of Theodore Roosevelt's distrust of him.

Byrnes' ties with the past, and an admitted worth of $350,000 (to the Lexow Commission, which was appointed by the State Senate to investigate corruption) were enough to force him to retire.[20] Despite his financial disclosures he was still regarded as a hero by many New Yorkers. Jacob Riis considered him one of New York's best policemen.[21]

During Byrnes' tenure the detective division received its share of publicity, both good and bad. His establishment of the Wall Street Squad earned praise in the newspapers, but increasing hostility between the uniform force and detectives was seen as hampering the overall effectiveness of the department.[22]

During the last quarter of the nineteenth century the concept of specialized criminal investigators continued to grow. By 1886 Chicago had two black detectives, William Smith and William Greene, who specialized in handling investigations in Chicago's black community.[23] In 1878 Boston mandated the investigation of all suspicious or violent deaths by a medical examiner. Medical examiners replaced the old coroner system, and policemen acted as assistants, calling in the detectives where murder was indicated.[24] In 1883 Chief Austin Doyle, citing the large number of passenger trains (850) entering and leaving Chicago, and the numerous prisons within 100 miles of the city, stated that "A competent and efficient detective force is needed to watch the movements of professional criminals . . ."[25]

By the turn of the century virtually every major city in the United States had some form of investigative unit. During these years detectives were usually generalists, although there were some assigned to specific crime categories. Detective selection was usually based on recommendations of field commanders or, as was often the case, through political "pull." Thus political patronage resulted in many appointments to the detective division. Guile and wit were the chief tools of the investigator during the early years, as were informants and the use of "third degree" methods.

The use of State Police investigators did not grow until after World War I. One organization, the Texas Rangers (founded in 1835), had a long history of involvement in criminal investigation. Massachusetts formed a state investigative unit in 1865, and Connecticut formed one in 1902. The primary responsibility of these units was the investigation of vice. Coal strikes in Pennsylvania formed the catalyst which brought the Pennsylvania State Police into being in 1905.

On the federal level, there were a number of investigative units formed to deal with specific crimes. In 1836 Congress authorized the Post Office Department to hire agents to investigate postal matters. Counterfeiting brought the establishment of the Secret Service, and in 1868, 25 detectives were hired by the Internal Revenue Service. The Department of Justice was formed in 1870, largely as a result of the problems facing the nation after the Civil War.

In 1905, President Theodore Roosevelt, recognizing the need for a centralized investigative agency concerned with violations of federal laws, instructed his Attorney General, Charles Joseph Bonaparte, to establish a force of trained detectives known as the Bureau of Investigation. The early years of the Bureau were fraught with incompetence and charges of criminality. One of the early heads of the Bureau was William J. Burns, who later formed the Burns Detective Agency. In 1924, President Calvin Coolidge appointed Harlan Fiske Stone—who later became Chief Justice of the Supreme Court—as his Attorney General. Stone removed Burns and appointed a young lawyer, J. Edgar Hoover, in his place, giving Hoover a mandate to "clean" up the Bureau.

Hoover was just 29 years old at the time, but he was a visionary and his ultimate success in making the Bureau famous is now legend. In the early days of the organization he was faced with the problem of gaining acceptance. "He worked slowly and let the achievements of his organization speak for him."[26]

Meanwhile, on the local level, the concept of criminal investigation began to gain acceptance as a professional approach to the crime "problem." The gains of scientific evidence were finally beginning to see some light in the United States.

THE ADVENT OF SCIENTIFIC CRIMINAL INVESTIGATION

The inadequacy of criminal investigation systems in the middle of the nineteenth century was becoming more and more of a problem.[27] The vast files and records that had been amassed by such men as Vidocq and Fielding served little toward identifying criminals with past records. Many of these criminals were prone to giving fictitious names, and their identification ultimately depended on the memories of investigators and clerks.

In July of 1879 an obscure clerk, Alphonse Bertillon, who was working in the Sureté, came upon the idea of measuring various anatomical features as a means of identification. Bertillon was familiar with the work of Quetelet, who maintained that no two persons had identical physical measurements, but he did not know that years earlier the Director of Louvain Prison had given consideration to the idea of measuring prisoners for future identification. Bertillon spent much time developing a system of measurement and in October of 1879 he sent a report to the Prefect of Police in Paris. He received no reply, but continued to develop his theory. Finally, he was called before the Prefect where he was told not to annoy his superiors with such ludicrous notions.

Upon the appointment of a new Prefect, Bertillon once again set out to prove his theory. With the assistance of a number of his father's friends who persuaded the new Prefect to give the theory a chance, Bertillon was finally permitted to try his radical approach to criminal investigation. He was given three months to prove that his idea would work. Fortunately he was able to come up with an identification in this short period of time, and the science of anthropometry was born. The concept known as anthropometric measurement caught on fast and was used throughout Europe, and even in parts of the United States, until 1914, when the use of fingerprints became the accepted method of identification.

As early as 1877 the idea of fingerprinting, as a means of identification, was recognized. Although they were being used in a number of ways, little or no consideration was given to the use of fingerprints on a large scale for the identification of criminals. For some 20 years William Herschel had been taking fingerprints in connection with his post as an administrative official in India, and his letter to a prison official in 1877 probably represents the first attempt to apply the use of fingerprinting to criminology. Unfortunately, little or no attention was given to his revelation.

In 1880 Henry Faulds, a Scottish physician who was instructing medical students in Tokyo, wrote a letter to *Nature,* a popular science weekly published in London, pointing out the value of fingerprints for criminal investigation and identification. Upon reading Fauld's letter, Herschel corresponded with *Nature* stating that he had been working with fingerprints for some 20 years. Faulds, however, ignored the claim and began to campaign for the acceptance of fingerprints in police work.

Faulds' efforts produced little in the way of acceptance, but in 1888 Francis Galton, the son of a London manufacturer, was dispatched to France by the Royal Institute to observe the Bertillon method of criminal identification. Already considered an expert in anthropometry, Galton was becoming skeptical about its scientific basis. His dissatisfaction caused him to recall the letters of Faulds and Herschel, which had been published eight years earlier.

In a lecture on May 25, 1888, Galton pointed out the existence of a method of identification other than the Bertillon system "probably as effective, if not more so: fingerprinting."[28] Galton subsequently went on to study the science of fingerprinting and in 1892 published a book entitled *Fingerprints.*

Prior to publication of his book Galton had written at least one article about fingerprints and in 1891, Juan Vucetich, a 23-year-old policeman in Buenos Aires, was given a magazine containing the article. Previously he had been ordered to set up a system utilizing the anthropometric method, but soon after reading Galton's work he began taking fingerprints in addition to physical measurements. Shortly thereafter he had developed a classification similar to Galton's, not mentioned in the article, and had carried the system further by coming up with the idea of counting papillary lines. Unfortunately, he was unaware of the gains he had made, or how far ahead he was of methods on the continent.

While Vucetich developed his system in almost complete anonymity, the British Inspector General of the province of Bengal, Edward Henry, was struggling with the classification system problem. The son of a doctor, he had come to India in 1873 where he entered the Indian civil service. By 1891 he had attained the position of Inspector General of the Police, and shortly after introduced the Bertillon system with some success. However, like Galton and Vucetich, he saw many drawbacks to the system. In 1893 he read Galton's book, and began to work on the classification problem.

Eventually he established five basic patterns and, in doing so, developed a method whereby it was possible to classify millions of fingerprints so that they could be retrieved in minutes. His discovery marked the beginning of a new era in criminal investigation and identification and, to this day, stands as one of the most significant contributions to criminal investigation. Eventually, fingerprinting would be used throughout the world, and probably nowhere has it been organized so efficiently as in the United States.

SCIENTIFIC CRIMINAL INVESTIGATION IN THE UNITED STATES

As early as 1857 New York had established a "Rogue's" portrait gallery, and in less than a year it included about 700 photographs of known criminals.[29] Byrnes had established the morning "parade" or lineup, and the Bertillon system of identification was then in effect.

In 1904, Detective Sergeant Joseph A. Faurot, who had become interested in fingerprinting while working in the identification section, was sent to London for an examination of Scotland Yard's methods. By the time Faurot returned from London, the department had changed commissioners and the new commissioner, upon hearing Faurot's proposal, told him to forget fingerprinting. The sergeant, however, did not give up and began to compile his own collection of fingerprints.

A break came in 1906 when Faurot, while on patrol, discovered a man sneaking out of a hotel room. The suspect protested his innocence, claiming he was a British citizen and that he was just leaving his "lover's" apartment. Faurot mailed the suspect's fingerprints to his old teacher, Chief Inspector Collins, and it was not long before a record arrived showing him to be a notorious hotel burglar who was wanted in England.

The sensation caused by the identification caused the newspapers to take an active interest in Faurot's work. However, it was not until four years later that another case of importance arose. His identification of the murderer of a young girl through the use of fingerprinting renewed public interest in the sergeant's work, but wide acceptance of fingerprinting was still some time in the future.

In 1911, Faurot became the first person in the United States to introduce fingerprinting in a court. His testimony in a burglary case caused the defendant to change his plea from not guilty to guilty. During the following years fingerprinting gradually became an accepted practice, but it was not until 1928 that New York State held that fingerprinting was legal—rebutting the arguments of many that it was against their civil rights.

On the federal level, J. Edgar Hoover had been campaigning for the establishment of a central identification unit, and in 1930 Congress authorized such a

Bureau. Formation of the Bureau of Identification marked the United States as a leader in the field of dactyloscopy (fingerprinting). The Bureau has grown to house the largest collection of fingerprints in the world.

Despite major gains in the United States in the field of scientific criminal investigation over the past 100 years, one finds that virtually all major breakthroughs originated and were developed in Europe. Thorwald points out that although by 1930 forensic medicine was an accepted and popular practice throughout Europe, "The United States . . . still evidenced a certain backwardness."[30] The concept of the coroner system, disbanded in Boston and New York in favor of medical examiners, remained popular.

Forensic toxicology gained little in popularity, although there are a number of cases on record which indicate that the field began to grow toward the end of the nineteenth century.

In one important field, however, the United States not only pioneered but also produced one of the most effective tools ever designed for scientific criminal investigation. The advent of the comparison microscope marked a milestone in forensic ballistics. An attempt was made by Charles E. Waite in 1920 to catalog information relative to the differences between firearms. After some three years work, Waite found that no two firearms were alike in every detail. Unfortunately his tests were limited to arms of American manufacture, and he soon found that a great number of those firearms used in crimes were made in foreign countries. Waite spent the next year covering Europe, where he compiled a vast array of information relative to firearms made outside the United States. Shortly after his return he was instrumental in providing information which led to the arrest of a suspect in a murder case.

Waite realized that his method could only provide a description of the weapon a bullet came from by make, and did not necessarily prove that the bullet came from a particular firearm. He realized that differences in manufacture and toolmaking made each weapon unique, but he was unable to develop a method of proof. He took his case to Max Poser, a specialist in applied optics and microscopy at the Bausch and Lomb Optical Company, who developed a special microscope designed for holding and measuring bullets and their markings.

Introduced to this problem by Waite were a number of other scientists, one of whom was John Fisher, a physicist who had an interest in firearms. Fisher devised what he termed a helixometer, capable of examining the barrels of rifles and pistols; he also developed an instrument in the form of a microscope, which made it possible to measure the lands, grooves, and twists of barrels.

Philip O. Gravelle, a student at Columbia University, was interested in microscopy and photography, and Waite introduced the young man to his research. Gravelle experimented with thousands of bullets and made comparisons of their characteristics with the weapons from which they were fired. Recognizing the possibility of human error in making comparisons, Gravelle designed an instrument using two microscopes mounted side by side—the comparison microscope. This enabled the observer to compare two bullets simultaneously.

Another of those interested by Waite was Calvin Goddard, a medical doctor who had shifted to the field of ordinance. Goddard was soon to become the leading authority in the field of forensic ballistics. His use of the comparison microscope enabled him to make identifications hitherto unheard of, and his contributions served to pioneer further research in the field of forensic ballistics.

Goddard devoted the rest of his life to the field of scientific criminal investigation. He gave up his private laboratory in New York to become the director of the Scientific Crime Detection Laboratory on the campus of Northwestern University, where he worked until 1934. In 1938 the laboratory at Northwestern was purchased by the Chicago Police Department for $25,000.[31]

Scientific evidence had finally come into being as an accepted tool of criminal investigation. During the following years cities throughout the United States began to add crime laboratories and, if a city did not have a lab, the FBI. provided its services with one of the most advanced laboratories in the world.

THE CONTEMPORARY DETECTIVE

With the introduction of scientific evidence, detectives had another tool with which to work. Unfortunately, the acceptance of scientific evidence has not been widespread and, in many cases, is only used when a "major" crime has occurred. Studies have shown that the presence of physical objects at crime scenes is not uncommon;[32] yet retrieval attempts are seldom made. Thus the field of scientific criminal investigation has not attained the degree of use or effectiveness it might.

The concept of specialized criminal investigation has achieved a great deal of popularity over the past 25 years. In fact, the use of specialized detectives assigned to a particular crime category has further developed the field. O. W. Wilson, a pioneer in the development of police administration, was an early advocate of specialized investigators.

Despite the rapid technological growth in the United States during the past three decades, the function and methodological approach to criminal investigation has changed little. Indeed, much of the change has resulted from Supreme Court decisions, which have served to promote procedural change and to some degree, have placed restrictions on the use of technological advances such as wiretapping and electronic eavesdropping.

The moral question aside, it becomes apparent that the prohibited use of various techniques "outlawed" by the courts restricts criminal investigation. All too often, the law enforcement reaction has been to cry "foul," and fail to develop new and better methods which are acceptable to the courts. Nevertheless, a thorough understanding of the investigative function, and a constant desire to improve can go a long way toward overcoming the various problems with which the investigator is confronted.

NOTES

1. Donald Schultz and Loran A. Norton, *Police Operational Intelligence.* Springfield, Illinois: Charles C. Thomas, 1968, pp. 5–10.

2. J. J. Tobias, *Against the Peace.* London: Ginn and Co., 1970, pp. 63, 64.

3. *Ibid.*

4. Gilbert Armitage, *The History of the Bow Street Runners.* London: Wishart, 1932.

5. Hans Gross, *Criminal Psychology.* Montclair, N.J.: Patterson Smith reprint, 1968, p. xi.

6. *Ibid.*

7. Jurgen Thorwald, *The Century of the Detective.* New York: Harcourt, Brace and World, 1964, p. 38.

8. It should be noted that the word "detective" was not coined by Dickens, but has its origins around 1852.

9. Roger Lane, *Policing the City: Boston 1822–1885.* Cambridge, Mass.: Harvard University Press, 1967, p. 57.

10. Lane, *op. cit.,* pp. 60–61.

11. *Spring 3100.* New York City Police Department, Nov., 1968, p. 38.

12. Robert Cordella, "The Detective Division: New York City Police Department," unpublished Master's thesis. Bernard M. Baruch School of Public Administration, the City College, City University of New York, p. 16.

13. James D. Horan, *The Pinkertons: Detective Dynasty That Made History.* New York: Crown Publishers, 1967, p. 23.

14. *Ibid.,* p. 25.

15. *Chicago Police Star.* Chicago: Chicago Police Department, January, 1966, p. 6.

16. John J. Flinn, *History of the Chicago Police.* Chicago: Police Book Fund, 1887, p. 371.

17. Lane, *op. cit.,* pp. 204, 205.

18. For an account of Chief Savage's approach to corruption, see Lane, *op. cit.,* pp. 142–156, 205.

19. Lane, *op. cit.,* p. 156.

20. Much of this money was the result of investments made on "tips" given to him by friends on Wall Street. See James Richardson, *The New York Police: Colonial Times to 1901.* New York: Oxford University Press, 1970, p. 210.

21. Jacob Riis, *The Making of an American.* New York, Macmillan, 1901, p. 339.

22. See Cordella, *op. cit.,* p. 21, and Richardson, *op cit.,* p. 212.

23. Flinn, *op. cit.,* pp. 390, 394.

24. Lane, *op. cit.,* p. 205.

25. Flinn, *op. cit.,* p. 219.

26. Thorwald, *op. cit.,* p. 261.

27. See, for example, J. J. Tobias, *op. cit.,* p. 65.

28. Thorwald, *op. cit.,* p. 38.

29. Richardson, *op. cit.,* p. 122.

30. Thorwald, *op. cit.,* p. 261.

31. *Chicago Police Star, op. cit.,* p. 7.

32. See, for example, Brian Parker, "Physical Evidence Utilization in the Administration of Criminal Justice." School of Criminology, University of California, Berkeley. Study funded by the National Institute of Law Enforcement and Criminal Justice. No. N10032.

QUESTIONS FOR DISCUSSION

1. In France much of Vidocq's success is attributed to his being a former criminal. What implications or impact might result from such an approach in the United States, and how are criminals used in the investigative process?

2. Throughout the history of American law enforcement, appointment to the detective division has often been through "political" patronage. What impact might this have on the investigative function?

3. While the United States has been slow to adopt the concept of scientific criminal investigation, in recent years there has been increasing interest in and involvement with the crime laboratory. Nevertheless, its use in the "average" crime remains minimal in many police departments. In what areas has the crime laboratory been most effective, and what are its deficiencies?

SUGGESTED READINGS

Byrnes, Thomas, *1886 Professional Criminals of America.* New York: Chelsea House Publishers, 1969.

Ellis, Havelock, *The Criminal.* New York: AMS Press, 1973.

Langford, Nathaniel Pitt, *Vigilante Days and Ways.* New York: AMS Press, 1973.

Pinkerton, Allan, *Professional Thieves and the Detective.* New York: AMS Press, 1973.

Thorwald, Jurgen, *The Century of the Detective.* New York: Harcourt, Brace and World, 1965.

CHAPTER 2

general aspects of the investigative function

The primary function of the criminal investigator is to gather information, determine the validity of this information, identify and locate the perpetrator of the crime, and provide evidence of his guilt for a court of law. Inherent in this function is a responsibility to protect the innocent.

The means by which the investigator carries out his function may be classified in two ways: internal and external.

> *Internal* refers to the process of logic, expertise, intuition, experience, and knowledge that he brings to the investigation.
>
> *External* refers to the tools, scientific aids, additional personnel, and other resources that he brings to bear on the investigation.

Thus the internal aspects of criminal investigation depend in great measure on the capabilities of the individual investigator. Indeed, most cases today are handled by the lone investigator. The external aspects involve the investigator's ability to utilize resources that are available to him. In many investigative operations this ability is seriously lacking.

In the past, criminal investigation has often been classified as an art rather than a science, because it involves precepts and advice rather than laws and rigid theories. With the rapid advances in technology and the behavioral sciences a new era has dawned, and the investigator will find that, from a scientific standpoint, much information in both theory and practice has become available to him. Unfortunately, too few investigators are aware of these advances.

The nature of the investigative function is to solve crimes. Generally, when we think of solving a crime there is a tacit assumption that one has been committed. In some police departments the investigator is employed to investigate, discover, and apprehend suspects while they are in the act of committing the crime. In fact, at least one recent study indicates that this approach may be more effective in apprehending the criminal.[1] However, for the most part, this book is devoted to the investigation of a crime *after* it has occurred, and generally after it has been reported.

Because the function of the investigator is to solve crimes, an evaluation of his effectiveness should depend on his ability to do so. Nevertheless, the investigator who solves the most crimes is not necessarily the better investigator, and any evaluation must give consideration to the types and categories of crime he is investigating.

In order to measure the effectiveness of a detective, at least two criteria should be employed:

1. The number of cases handled versus the number solved. In order for a case to be considered solved, there is a tacit assumption that either an arrest has been made, or a warrant has been issued for the suspect.
2. The types or categories of cases assigned to the detective. Since some cases will be more difficult than others, this is an important factor.

In the first category an objective measure may be employed, but in the second some form of rating scale or subjective measure is necessary. Since the better investigator is likely to be assigned the more difficult cases, the second criterion protects him from an unfair evaluation.

At the outset it should be made clear that all crimes cannot be solved. However, it is reasonable to assume that, except in unusual circumstances, a certain percentage of cases assigned to an investigator will be solved. There is little doubt in the author's mind that the percentage of crimes *actually* solved by investigation is woefully small. The President's Crime Commission notes that in 1965 78% of reported serious crimes against property were never solved.[2] In some measure this may be attributed to such factors as department policy, heavy caseloads, paperwork, and a lack of manpower. Nevertheless, the poor training and education offered to investigators in most departments has a significant impact on their effectiveness on duty.

Under ideal investigative circumstances, which is to say that the investigator has the time, expertise, and tools necessary to accomplish the task, a much greater percentage of crimes could be solved. The assumption throughout this book is that these circumstances exist, and that the investigation can be carried forward and closed with the apprehension of the guilty party. With this in mind, a discussion of the internal and external implications of the investigation follow.

INTERNAL IMPLICATIONS OF CRIMINAL INVESTIGATION

In conducting the investigation, the investigator may call on his own expertise in a particular case. Much of this expertise is based on experience, but knowledge developed through education and training is also an important factor. Much of his reasoning will be based on logic; he must ask himself two questions: "what happened?" and "why did it happen?" The determination of what happened may be linked to the *corpus delecti,* or the fact that a crime has been committed. Until this fact is established the investigation may be meaningless.

Once it is established that a crime has been committed, the investigator turns to the question, "why did it happen?" This leads to two important considerations: the type or category of crime committed and the motive for the crime.

Certainly the most important aspect of an investigation is the capability of the investigator. Much of the process of criminal investigation requires interviewing and interrogation. Essentially, this involves gathering information, assigning it some value, sorting it, and finally utilizing it to develop facts.

At the outset, the investigator must be aware that, due to any number of reasons, not all information is factual. The person may be lying, he may have forgotten, or his perception may be at variance with reality. Also, the underlying reasons behind a person's supplying information may have a bearing on his statements. He or she may be a relative or friend of the suspect who is understandably likely to be biased.

The investigator's task is to determine which of the statements are true. In doing so he brings his skills to the forefront. Generally, he must depend on his own reasoning, but in some instances he may turn to an external source such as the polygraph or lie detector for help in substantiating statements.

Generally, the discovery of these facts offers no problem to the investigator, for they are readily apparent. However, he must be careful not to assume that a particular set of events, or apparent facts, is not subject to question. Not questioning his observations, no matter how factual they seem, is probably the most glaring error an investigator can make.

Once a determination of *what* has happened and *why* it has happened is made, the investigator turns to the question of *who* did it. This may represent the most difficult aspect of an investigation. Here the investigator must rely on his ability to put the pieces of the puzzle together. Although often he will be frustrated by dead ends and false clues, patience and perseverence are necessary to reach the goal.

In developing the facts in a case the investigator need not rely on his capabilities alone, and should be ready to call for assistance whenever it is warranted. This "call for assistance" is viewed as the external function of the investigation.

EXTERNAL IMPLICATIONS OF CRIMINAL INVESTIGATION

The investigator is not without assistance, if he chooses to utilize it. In most police departments the use of external assistance is limited because the investigator either is not aware of its existence or decides not to use it. Studies indicate that the use of scientific evidence in the investigation of the "average" crime is relatively rare. Thus, in the "sensational" and much publicized crime the laboratory is often called in, but in the usual felony, such as robbery and burglary, it is used comparatively little. The trend in criminal investigation appears to be toward the utilization of scientific evidence, but the investigator must be more aware of the capabilities of the laboratory before he can make adequate and efficient use of it.

In addition to the crime laboratory, the investigator has access to any number of other aids and tools which can assist him. A number of large police departments now have computers, from which information can be retrieved in seconds. State and federal agencies also have a computerized retrieval capacity that would have been thought impossible a few years ago. Many such agencies maintain a computer data bank containing biographical and historical information on individuals which can be of immense value in the development of a case. The investigator should familiarize himself with the capabilities of the computer and develop a working relationship with the personnel assigned to these units.[3]

Probably no other resource has been ignored as much as the patrolman. All too often, the investigator regards himself as being far above the patrolman in rank and ability. The lack of coordination between the patrol force and the investigative operation has become endemic in American policing. Often the patrolman will have information that may be of value to the investigator, but because of an innate hostility or organizational deficiencies which might exist, he may not come forward. It is incumbent on the investigator to develop strong ties with the patrol force, on an individual basis wherever possible, and he must be willing to see that the patrolman who supplies information or assistance is rewarded. This cooperation is also necessary with other operating agencies in the area of criminal justice. A good working relationship with these agencies may save hours and even days of the investigator's time.

Finally, the investigator's working relationship within his own unit is of utmost importance. Interoffice rivalry impedes working toward a common goal. While the spirit of cooperation in an investigative unit may be a responsibility of the supervisor, a good investigator can strengthen the relationship by supplying information and assistance where it is needed.

ELEMENTS OF THE INVESTIGATION

In order to develop a better understanding of the integral parts of an investigation some mention should be made in a general context. A number of the following points are developed in later chapters, but an initial understanding of them will be of value to the reader.

INTERVIEWING AND INTERROGATION

Much of the investigator's work involves interviewing and interrogation. Interviewing differs from interrogation in that during the interview the individual is generally cooperative and answers questions as truthfully as possible. Of course, the individual may be feigning cooperation, but this is the exception rather than the rule.

Interrogation, on the other hand, generally refers to the questioning of a hostile or uncooperative subject.

Both interviewing and interrogation are skills that can be developed with experience and an understanding of human behavior. A good investigator must be able to interview and interrogate, since much of his success depends on the ability to elicit information that is of value. Most investigators can get the subject to talk, but not all can secure information that is valuable in an investigative sense.

Recent Supreme Court decisions, especially in the case of *Miranda* v. *Arizona,* which specifies the individual rights of a suspect, have placed restrictions on the process of interviewing and interrogation. Nevertheless, the investigator should be aware that, despite limitations, he is not prevented from asking questions, and the capable interviewer can still operate within the bounds of legality. The Court has not denied the investigator a right to interview, and knowledge of the ruling in this decision is imperative. The development of good interviewing techniques makes it less difficult to work within the framework of the law. Furthermore, the *Miranda* restriction involves suspects, not witnesses.

INFORMATION

Information may be defined as the knowledge produced from people and things. The purpose of interviewing and interrogation is to gather this information. In fact, the entire process of criminal investigation involves the collection and use of information.

Information may be gathered from any number of sources. (Indeed, even the fact that a person refuses to speak during an interrogation may provide information.) The crime scene, objects, and actions of persons are but a few.

In an investigation information may be classified in one of three ways: (1) information of direct value; (2) information of indirect value; and (3) information of no value. Information of *direct value* is that which has a direct bearing on the case: the crime itself, statements of the suspect, victim, or witnesses, and physical evidence (such as fingerprints) which has been collected. Generally, this will be of direct value either to identify, exclude, focus suspicion or provide a basis for further information.

Information of *indirect value* is that which is ancillary to the crime. In this category, statements, background information (such as criminal history), and the history of relationships (such as antagonism between the victim and suspect) may be of value in formulating theories.

Information of *no value* is that which provides nothing of importance to the investigation. In virtually every case there will be information that proves to be useless and often misleading, such as anonymous tips, irrelevant clues, and witnesses with poor perception. This category probably represents the most difficult for the investigator, for what may seem to be of no value at one point, may have a direct bearing on the ultimate result of the investigation. For this reason the investigator, in determining the value of information, must not entirely discard that which he thinks to be of no value. One suggestion is to maintain a separate file, or place such information in the rear of the case folder. In this way, he may find it valuable to peruse it when the investigation has slowed or come to a dead end. In any event, he should be careful not to discard such information.

The utilization of information depends on the capabilities of the investigator. It is the detective's task to develop as much information as possible about a case. His experience and observations in collecting information should enable him to apply it to the case in a logical manner. In developing information the first logical step requires a visit to the crime scene.

THE CRIME SCENE

The crime scene is simply the location where the offense occurred. Generally, the crime scene will involve one place, although there are a number of crimes, such as kidnapping and rape, which may involve two or more locations. It is incumbent on the first officer to arrive at the scene of the crime to perform the first necessary aspect of the investigation: to safeguard the location as soon as possible. The investigator arriving on the scene should not move blindly into the area, but should gather as much information about the crime as possible, and then initiate a systematic survey of the area. This initial survey should not be to collect evidence, but rather to develop a mental image. Where possible, the scene should be photographed and sketches should be prepared.

Too many crime scenes are disturbed by curious superiors, patrolmen, or investigators, and it is not uncommon to find meetings, press conferences, and the like being held in the middle of an area that might contain much physical evidence. The investigator is responsible for conducting the investigation, and where the rules are being violated he should politely request that such intruders leave the scene.

UTILIZATION OF SCIENTIFIC EVIDENCE

Once the scene has been safeguarded, photographed, and sketched, and witnesses have been interviewed, the investigator should conduct a search for evidence. In some departments he may call on the services of the crime laboratory or evidence technicians. In any event he should take part in the search and be able to testify as to where and what kind of evidence was obtained. In the average case the investigator may decide not to request the services of the laboratory. However, he should conduct a thorough examination of the scene, and should have enough familiarity with evidence collection to be able to spot anything which may be of value to him.

Once collected, care must be taken to identify, safeguard, and preserve such evidence, and it should be delivered to the laboratory without delay. In some instances a continuing investigation will preclude the investigator's personally delivering it, but in order to maintain the link between evidence and the scene he should carry out this function himself whenever possible. Evidence that is not destined for the laboratory should be handled in much the same manner, except that it should be placed in a locked property room.

The development of criminalistics, or forensic science as it is coming to be known, has broadened the investigator's capabilities. Unfortunately, most investigators have little familiarity with this aspect of the investigation, and their major reliance has been on a search for fingerprints.

The forensic scientist can be the link between success and failure in an investigation. While much of his work occurs in the background, a good working relationship is of immense value.

VICTIMS, WITNESSES, AND SUSPECTS

Once the crime scene has been secured, the investigator should interview the victim or witnesses. If there are two or more victims they should be interviewed separately. Notes should be taken, and it is usually wise to gather as much detail as possible during this initial stage. Because notetaking may be cumbersome and may have an effect on the subject, a number of departments have equipped their investigators with small tape recorders. Such an approach is ideal in most cases. During the initial interview the investigator should attempt to answer the following questions: When?, Where?, Who?, What?, How? and Why? Once they have been answered, a more detailed interview can begin.

In most instances it is advisable for one investigator to interview all the witnesses, rather than dividing the interviews among two or more investigators. If this is feasible, the second investigator should be on hand to help recall detail and, where necessary, help clarify points.

During this period the investigator is often faced with gathering a large amount of information in a short period of time. For this reason, the first round of interviews should generally be limited to the particular aspects of the crime. Background and historical information can be filled in later.

If the suspect has been apprehended and has been warned of his rights, the investigator should make an effort to secure a statement. Very often the direct approach is the best, and the suspect should be asked, "What happened?"

The techniques of handling the victim, witnesses, and suspects is discussed in greater detail in a later chapter. Suffice it to say that many an investigation has been thwarted by improper handling of such persons at the outset.

REPORTS

Reports are an important aspect of any investigation and should be prepared with care. Tape recorders are invaluable for this procedure, and all efforts should be made to curtail the amount of paperwork. The investigator generally handles numerous cases, and it should be recognized that not all facts can be committed to memory. The goal of the investigation is to bring the perpetrator of the crime to court and provide evidence that will convict him. Any number of cases have been dismissed or the defendant has been found not guilty through the inefficiency of an investigator in not keeping adequate records. The investigator who assumes at the outset that the case will not be solved is making a drastic mistake. In fact, these are the cases in which a thorough report may prove to be invaluable should information be discovered at a later date.

While there is some disagreement as to report style, it is generally held that there should be at least two forms, one for the original complaint and one for supplementary investigations. In some departments ancillary data, such as the crime laboratory report, may also involve different forms.

All reports should be serially numbered and readily identifiable. In addition to supplying the necessary information, they should be legible, accurate, and capable of being used by other investigators. Thus, except in unusual instances, codes and symbols should not be used.

There is no need to discuss the security of reports; security procedures should be carefully followed. Nevertheless, reports should be available to any investigator who can demonstrate a need to use them.

PREPARATION FOR COURT

The ultimate goal is to bring the case to a court of law. If the investigator has followed the procedure outlined here, is familiar with elements of the crime according to the penal law or code, and has communicated his findings to the prosecutor, he is then ready to help present the case.

If the suspect has been arrested, he will be taken before a magistrate or judge for arraignment. If he has not been arrested, the district attorney may decide to take the case before a Grand Jury for an indictment. When an indictment, or true bill, is handed down, a warrant will be issued. Generally, these are the two most common ways in which a suspect is brought before the court. The procedures to follow in bringing a case to court are discussed in a later chapter.

The investigator should remember that his role is that of an *impartial* participant in the court, and while his case is presented to the prosecutor, he has a moral, as well as a legal obligation, to present *all* the facts and information, omitting nothing.

In addition to a thorough understanding of the penal law or code, the investigator should be familiar with Supreme Court decisions and lower court decisions that may have an impact on the case. He should also familiarize himself with courtroom procedure.

SUMMARY

The preceding chapter offered a brief description of those elements and characteristics that make up the investigative function. At the heart of any successful investigation is a dedicated individual who takes the time and makes an effort to follow the correct and legal procedures. He cannot do so if he is not properly equipped, intellectually and through proper training and education. He must also have at hand the resources necessary to accomplish the task. These factors represent the foundations of criminal investigation.

NOTES

1. Peter W. Greenwood, *An Analysis of the Apprehension Activities of the New York City Police Department.* New York City Rand Institute, 1970.

2. A report by the President's Commission on Law Enforcement and Administration of Justice, *The Challenge of Crime in a Free Society.* Washington, D.C.: Government Printing Office, 1967, p. 97.

3. For a discussion of the capabilities of the computer, see Paul M. Whisenand and Tug T. Tamaru, *Automated Police Information Systems.* New York: John Wiley and Sons, 1970.

QUESTIONS FOR DISCUSSION

1. Discuss the difference between the internal and external aspects of criminal investigation. How can the investigator develop his internal capacities? What types of cases are more likely to involve external assistance, and why?

2. What is the difference between interrogation and interviewing? What is information, and how should the investigator view it?

3. Who has overall responsibility for the investigation? Why is it important that responsibility be placed?

SUGGESTED READINGS

International Association of Chiefs of Police, *Criminal Investigation.* Library of Congress, 1968.

Leonard, V. A., *Criminal Investigation and Identification.* Springfield, Ill.: Charles C. Thomas, 1971.

Liebers, Arthur, and Carl Vollmer, *The Investigator's Handbook.* New York: Arco Publishing Co., 1962.

O'Hara, Charles, *Fundamentals of Criminal Investigation.* Springfield, Ill.: Charles C. Thomas, 1956.

CHAPTER 3

preliminary investigation and the crime scene

The investigation of virtually every crime begins with the basic premise that, while most crimes may be dissimilar in fact and occurrence, the steps employed in their solution are generally similar. Naturally the degree of effort, both internal and external, will vary according to the nature of a particular case. Thus sound principles of investigation must be followed in order to bring a case to successful solution and ultimate conviction of the perpetrator of the crime.

Departmental policy should place responsibility for investigation, from the initial report through investigation and prosecution. Responsibility begins with initial contact or assignment, and a mistake by anyone in the process can result in seriously impeding a case, or even destroying it entirely. For this reason, everyone in the department must be familiar with sound investigative techniques.

Generally, the first person to arrive at the scene of a crime is the patrolman. It is his responsibility to do the following:

1. Aid the victim.
2. Arrest the perpetrator, if he is still on the scene.
3. Detain the victim, suspect, and witnesses.
4. Safeguard the crime scene.
5. Communicate with superiors or investigators, and apprise them of the situation.
6. Make a written record of the facts, answering the following questions: When? Where? Who? What? How? and Why?

Once these steps have been carried out, the investigation may proceed.

CONDUCTING THE INVESTIGATION

In order to bring a case to court, the investigator must satisfy two essential elements:

1. Proof that a crime has been committed. This is known as establishing the *corpus delecti.*
2. *Legal* proof that the accused is connected to the crime.

It is important that a complete record be maintained to help to establish these facts. While each patrolman is equipped with a notebook or memo book, recent technological advances may make it advisable to equip each with a small cassette recorder, especially if patrolmen are responsible for the initial investigation. This not only facilitates interviewing, but also makes it possible to record a narrative description of the crime scene at the earliest moment and precludes errors that may arise as a result of incomplete or sketchy notetaking. Each investigator should also be equipped with a recorder, and the department should provide a transcribing service.

In addition to this equipment, each patrol unit and investigative team should be equipped with a camera. Utilization of small, inexpensive cartridge cameras enables a speedy visual recording of the crime scene or victims in cases where it may not be feasible to secure an evidence technician rapidly, or where his presence is not required. Examples of this include cases in which the victim is likely to be sent to a hospital (assault cases); where inclement weather such as rain or snow may damage the scene; or where departmental policy is to refrain from calling in a technician (house burglary). While the patrolman is generally the first person on the scene, and is responsible for making preliminary written notes, he should avoid entering the actual crime scene area for photographs and recordings until the responsible investigator has given him permission, and in no case should he remove or reposition evidence or alter the scene in any way. If an evidence technician is available, the crime scene *must* be preserved until he has completed his task. If a homicide is involved the body should be left in place until the arrival of the medical examiner.

THE FUNCTION OF RECORDS

A complete record of the case must be maintained, for this will supplement every phase of the investigation. The functions of records include the following:

1. Provide the basis for an ongoing investigation
2. Eliminate duplicity
3. Provide for examination, supervision, and continuity
4. Serve as a "memory jogger" for the investigator
5. Provide newly assigned investigators with background information
6. Act as a basis for future reports
7. Provide a means for developing inconsistencies in witness testimony
8. Serve to develop leads
9. Provide for logical development of the investigation
10. May be used in court

In order to provide adequate records, the investigator should take accurate and complete notes. These should be entered in a bound or looseleaf notebook (not on "scrap" paper), with statements of witnesses recorded verbatim on separate sheets of paper.

All records must be identifiable, and should include the case number, the name of the officer, and the time, place, and identity of persons interviewed. Unless the person being interviewed has been the subject of an earlier interview, further identifying data, such as the person's address, should be included. If there are two or more persons of the same name, or if the name is common, it is often advisable to include some further descriptive phrase, such as "brother of victim," or "witness to crime." All information or statements should be included in the record, and data which may serve to weaken the case *must* be included.

If a tape recorder has been used it is advisable to have transcripts made at the earliest convenience. In some instances, due to workload constraints or repetitious tapes, this may not be feasible. However, all tapes should be retained until after the case has been adjudicated in court—and even then it is advisable to store them for a reasonable time in the event of appeal—or for a reasonable time after it has been decided to close the case for inactivity. Generally, and except in unusual cases, a period of six months to one year should be sufficient for the retention of tapes. If a tape is to be destroyed, however, it should be checked to ensure that any relevant information lacking in the written file is recorded.

Each case should be assigned a separate file and number; if a case has some relationship or similarity to another investigation, it should be cross-referenced. In addition, it is advisable to maintain a crime index file to provide the following information:

1. Crime category by type, i.e., residential burglary, factory burglary, etc.
2. Location by street or address
3. Victim or complainant's file by name
4. Perpetrator or suspect file by name
5. Perpetrator or suspect file by physical description
6. Witness file by name

These files should also be cross-referenced, and should include any available photographs of perpetrators and suspects.

In addition to written and recorded information, the use of sketches and photographs is an invaluable aid. (Recording of this material is discussed in greater detail in Chapter 4.) Particular care must be employed in identifying graphic information, for it is likely to be used during a trial or in the preparation of exhibits.

Undoubtedly there will be some question concerning the storage of records, for each case is likely to generate a relatively large file. For this reason, consideration might be given to the use of a computer system for both storage and retrieval.

Virtually all the records previously discussed can be stored in a computer, and perhaps more important, can be retrieved quickly.

THE CRIME REPORT

The crime report is a written record of the case. Generally there should be two forms, one for the initial complaint and one for supplementary reports. While there is no standard form for crime reports throughout the United States, the following information is essential and should be included.

Initial Complaint. The initial complaint acts as a basis for further reports; therefore it should be accurate, concise, and above all, complete. Headings should be provided for:

1. *Complaint number.* Generally complaints will be recorded chronologically, beginning with each new year.
2. *Investigative case number.* In departments where not all crimes are referred for investigation or disposal by the investigative unit, but may be investigated and closed by the patrol force, it is advisable to maintain a record of all cases in the investigative unit. If a chronological system is used, it may be advisable to precede the number with an "I," which indicates an investigative case. The primary benefit of this approach is to provide a ready reference of the investigative unit's workload.
3. *Date and time of report.* This should be the date and time that the report is actually taken, whether it be in the field or by telephone.
4. *Date and time of occurrence.* Since it may prove important later in checking alibis or for court, this information should be as accurate as possible. If the exact time is unknown, indicate the parameters, e.g., between 6:00 P.M. and 9:00 P.M.
5. *Complainant's full name, address, and telephone number.* If the complaint originates in a business or store, the home address and phone number of the owner or manager should also be included.
6. *Complaint classification.* The more serious violation should be listed first if there is more than one crime involved. It is also advisable to list the Penal Code citation where applicable.
7. *Location of the offense.* This information should be specific, including the type of building (private residence, factory, grocery store).
8. *Manner in which complaint is received* ("on scene," by telephone, by letter, or through other referral).
9. *Description or information about perpetrator* (including criminal record number if available).

10. *Value and nature of property stolen and/or description of injury* (including description, serial numbers, etc. and/or type of weapon used).
11. *Individual and unit or department taking the report* (precinct number, or squad, whenever applicable).
12. *Unit or squad and individual to which report is assigned* (as well as distribution information, i.e., Chief of Police, District Attorney).
13. *Specific description.* This should include a concise narrative version of the offense.
14. *Status of case.* A space in the upper righthand corner of the report should be available for determining the immediate status of the case. If the case is "Open," the space should be left blank. A "Closed" stamp can be used when a case has been completed. It may also be advisable to utilize two "Closed" stamps, one being "Closed-WR" to indicate that the case has been solved, and another being "Closed-NR" indicating that the case has not been solved. This method facilitates records searches.

Supplementary Investigative Reports. This report is used in follow-up investigations, generally by the investigator assigned to the case, although others involved in the case should be required to file supplementary reports of their activities to provide other information. Although this report should be simplified to eliminate redundancy in administrative detail, the following information should be included:

1. Complaint number, and case number where applicable
2. Crime classification
3. Complainant's name
4. Time and date report made
5. Time and date of occurrence
6. Name of investigator assigned to case
7. Name of investigator submitting report
8. Subject of report: a concise statement of the nature of the particular report, e.g., "Interview with witness: John Smith."

All reports should be filed according to crime classification, and a chronological record should be maintained listing the complaint number, the complainant's name and telephone number, the investigator assigned, and the status of the case.

Maintenance of the Case. Generally, only two designations should be used to describe the status of a case: "Active" or "Closed." In some instances it may be necessary to develop a "Pending" classification for crimes which have not been solved, and in which the investigation has terminated. However, this classification should not be used hastily, since it tends to increase both supervision and maintenance problems. For this reason, the "Closed–No Results" category is deemed more advisable. If further information is discovered a case can always be reopened.

In any event, all "Pending" cases should be reviewed periodically by a supervisor as well as the investigator assigned. Except in homicide cases, where it may be the policy of the department to keep them open indefinitely, those cases that show no progress over a reasonable period of time should be closed.

Once a complaint has been assigned to an investigator, he should be responsible for submitting supplementary reports as the investigation proceeds, as well as periodically if it has slowed.

It is important that the investigator adhere to the principles of good report writing. Whenever an opinion or subjective judgment of the investigator is advanced, this should be indicated in the report. In other words, quite often the investigator will develop a theory or idea on the basis of information he has received or worked up. If this is not *proven* to be *factual,* the statement should be preceded by the phrase, "In the investigator's opinion . . ." Generally such observations will appear as the last paragraph of the report, for they are or should be based on the preceding material.

If the statement of another person is used, it should be preceded by an identification of the subject. It is also advisable to capitalize the surname, i.e., "Mr. Joseph SMITH stated that . . ." (Figure 3.1 illustrates one particular approach to a supplementary report.)

In compiling the case folder relevant reports should be placed chronologically in time, but an effort should be made to place them in such a manner as to provide continuity.

Care should be taken to remove irrelevant or miscellaneous reports which have no direct bearing on the case. As stated earlier, it is often advisable to keep such reports at the rear of the file. These might include interviews with residents that proved unsuccessful, anonymous tips that have been investigated and found false, and reports of physical evidence that have no direct bearing on the case, such as the discovery of the victim's fingerprints at the scene.

The investigative record should be designed to provide a functional approach. While some authors recommend removing irrelevant data completely, it is virtually impossible to determine how necessary certain information may be in a trial, or whether it may prove valuable at a later date. For example, it may be important to prove that a thorough canvass of the neighborhood was conducted, or that the victim's fingerprints indicate he was in a location other than where he claimed to be.

Termination of a case should be for one of two reasons: first, when the case has been solved and the offender brought to trial, and second, where all leads have been exhausted and a case review indicates that nothing will be accomplished by keeping the investigation open.

FIG. 3.1 Example of supplementary report

On June 24, 1971, at 2:30 PM the undersigned interviewed the witness Mr. John SMITH, 245 Alamo Drive, at his home. The subject was previously interviewed on June 21, 1971 by Patrolman John EVANS (see Supplementary Report dated June 21).

Mr. SMITH stated that he was standing approximately thirty (30) feet from the deceased when he heard him say, "I don't give a damn about you." At this point the unidentified perpetrator removed a revolver from beneath his coat and shot the deceased twice. He then fled through the front door of the store. Mr. SMITH stated that he then called the police and attempted to aid the victim. Mr. SMITH further stated that he did not know the perpetrator, had never seen him. He described him as being a male, white 22–24 years, wearing a brown overcoat, khaki trousers, and black shoes. He further stated that he would be able to identify the perpetrator if he saw him again.

In the earlier interview Mr. SMITH stated that he would not be able to identify the perpetrator.

In an interview with Mr. George SANDERS, 8020 Crescent Lane (see Supplementary Report dated June 22, 1971), a brother of the deceased, Mr. SANDERS stated that his brother (the deceased) and Mr. SMITH had an argument on the morning of June 21st, and SMITH said, "Leave me alone or you'll be sorry."

Mr. SMITH stated that he never made such a statement.

In an interview with Mrs. Joyce SMITH, 930 Grange Avenue, the former wife of Mr. SMITH (see Supplementary Report dated June 22, 1971), Mrs. SMITH stated that her husband owned an unregistered pistol. She described the weapon as being a revolver. (See sketch attached to Supplementary Report of Mrs. Smith's interview.)

Mr. SMITH denied ownership of any weapon and stated: "My wife is out to get me."

It is the investigator's opinion that Mr. SMITH is a prime suspect. However, pending further investigation, no action is advisable at this time. CASE ACTIVE.*

---

*Some departments advise against citing opinions in crime reports, as this may prove detrimental in court. Generally, the use of opinions in reports is likely to depend on the number of investigators assigned to a case.

The case should not be terminated if it has been solved but the suspect is still at large. If the suspect has died, or is in another jurisdiction and a decision has been made not to extradite, the decision to terminate a case should be based on the ultimate probability of future prosecution. This also holds true for persons who have been incarcerated for another crime.

The deciding factor should be the probability of continuing the case successfully. Whenever this is unlikely or impossible, the case should be closed.

The investigator should recognize that case maintenance is a means to an end, not an end in itself. The purpose is to provide the investigator and other officials with a logical approach to crime investigation and solution. A case should not be judged on the merits of how much paperwork is involved, but rather on the quality and success of the investigation.

THE CRIME SCENE

Probably no other aspect of a case is as open to error as the investigation of the crime scene. Therefore great care must be taken in the protection of the area. To begin with, valuable physical evidence is all too often not only overlooked by investigators, but also discarded because of a lack of expertise. While it is not necessary for a good investigator to be familiar with the manner in which tests are conducted or the finer points of handwriting and fingerprint identification, it is essential that he be able to discern information which can be analyzed fruitfully by the crime laboratory.

Certain crimes virtually mandate a crime scene search. These include arson, assault, burglary, homicide, rape, robbery, and auto theft, especially if the car had been used in another crime. Generally, wherever a struggle, an entry, or a specific crime location is involved, the scene should be protected. Further, if weapons, tools, or other implements are a part of the crime, they should also be protected. The success of the investigation may depend on such action.

For the purpose of investigation crime scene information can be divided into four categories. An understanding of these categories will aid the investigator in the logical development of the case. They include:

1. Evidence left by the criminal at the scene.
2. Evidence imparted to the criminal by the scene.
3. Location and position of materials affected by the crime.
4. Information or evidence that is ancillary to the crime.

Evidence left by the criminal at the scene may be classified in five ways: (1) Body material (blood, hair, semen, tissue, etc.); (2) Impressions (fingerprints, tool marks, foot prints, tire marks, etc.); (3) Trace evidence (paint traces, tobacco, fibers, soil, etc.); (4) Weapons, firearms, tools; (5) Personal property (clothing, jewelry, matches, cigarettes, etc.).

Evidence imparted to the criminal by the scene includes: (1) Victim's body material (blood, tissue, hair, etc.); (2) Impressions (wounds, scratches, auto damage, etc.); (3) Trace evidence (soil, paint, fibers, etc. on perpetrator or his property);

(4) Weapons, firearms, tools (for comparison with evidence at scene); (5) Personal property from scene (victim's property or other evidence that would link perpetrator to scene).

The location and position of materials and other objects may be used in reconstructing the crime and determining the actions of the perpetrator (e.g., method of entry). The investigator should be concerned with the exact location of objects, weapons, disarranged furniture, and other articles.

Information or evidence that is ancillary to the crime might include letters, notes, recordings, or other articles that will provide the investigator with background information.

In beginning an investigation of the crime scene the investigator should keep in mind three factors: *purpose, process,* and *physical evidence.* The *purpose* of the crime scene search is to establish the *corpus delecti,* the *modus operandi,* and the identity of the perpetrator.

The *process* involves proceeding in a systematic, planned manner, rather than by intuition. Intuition has no place in the investigation of the crime scene, for such an approach creates disorganization and increases the probability of overlooking items. By proceeding in a systematic manner each step is taken one at a time, and every avenue is thoroughly explored.

Physical evidence is the primary goal of a crime scene search. It should be kept in mind that physical evidence is often overlooked or destroyed through carelessness or a misinterpretation of the scene.

If more than one man is conducting a crime scene search, overall responsibility should be designated. The supervisor's role is to assign and direct the personnel, thereby assuring a systematic approach to the search. If the department employs a crime evidence team or technicians, steps must be taken to coordinate their activities with those of the assigned investigator. For this reason, evidence technicians should *not* enter the scene until the investigator has arrived and had an opportunity to make his initial survey. When adequate personnel are available, the following individual roles should be assigned: note taker, photographer, sketch artist, evidence collector, interviewer.

Search of the crime scene should involve the following steps, in order:

1. During the initial survey and appraisal, the investigator should curtail his desire to move rapidly into the crime scene to make individual notations. He must first make an overall observation, followed by individual observations made in a systematic manner. Remember that from a psychological standpoint we are often likely to see what we want to see. For this reason, it is wise to practice making observations of various locations in your everyday routine. Once the initial appraisal has been made, photographs of the entire scene should be taken. The investigator should then move carefully into the area making general observations, and recording the most general and basic information.

2. After the initial appraisal has been made, all crime data should be recorded, compiling notes, photographs, sketches, and measurements prior to the physical search. A logical and careful procedure must be followed in permitting individuals to enter the scene. (For example, the photographer should precede the sketcher into the area.)

3. The physical search, wherein a detailed survey is undertaken, should be planned in advance. This may involve any one of a number of possible approaches, but the overall consideration is toward a complete examination of the scene. Uppermost in the searcher's minds should be the realization that the success of the case rests on the evidence uncovered during the search. Generally, one of the following six categories of search may be chosen. The one chosen depends on the particular nature of the crime scene, i.e., indoors or outdoors, large area or small area. Physical limitations, such as terrain, objects, or equipment, may also determine category choice.

a) *Grid.* A relatively thorough approach, the grid search is ideal for covering relatively large areas with a number of men (Fig. 3.2). The search area is blocked off in the form of a rectangle or square, and the searchers proceed along a parallel path from one end to the other. If two searchers are working, it is advisable to have them alternate paths. A number of variations of this approach may be used (Fig. 3.3). If the search area is cluttered with grass, weeds, or other objects it may be advisable to return along the path, and then move to an adjoining section. Once

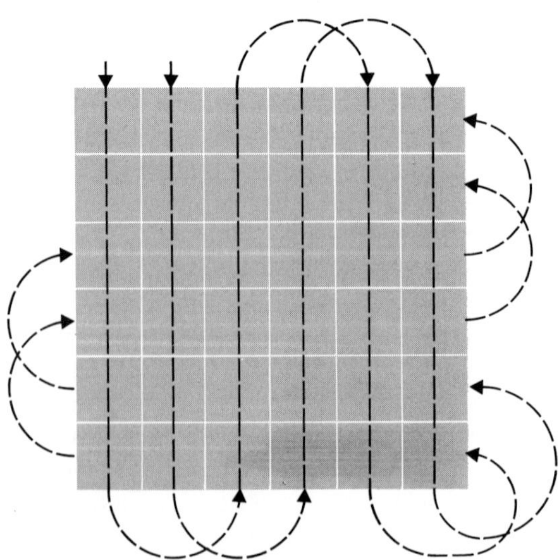

FIG. 3.2 The grid method of search.

the area has been covered in a horizontal direction, the searchers then proceed to cover it in the same manner along a vertical plane. This is probably the best approach to use whenever conditions permit.

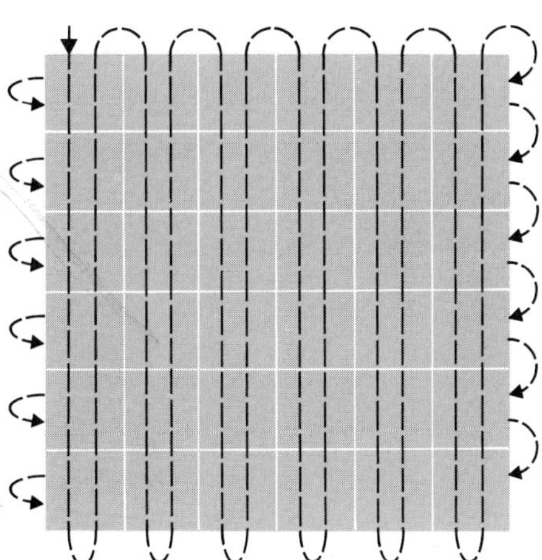

FIG. 3.3 The double grid method of search.

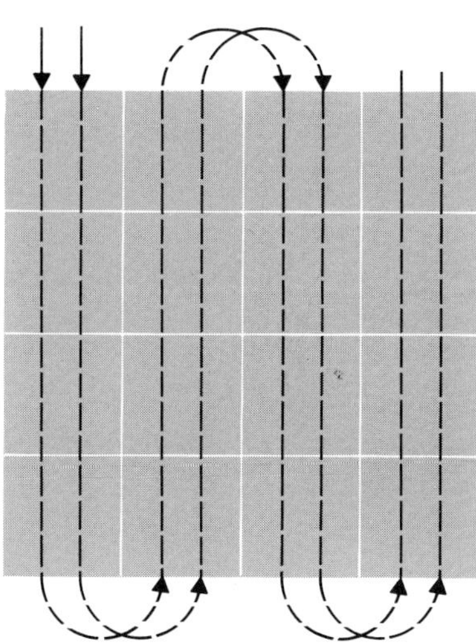

FIG. 3.4 The strip method of search.

b) *Strip.* The strip method (Fig. 3.4) is similar to the grid, but less thorough; generally it should only be used if the grid method is unfeasible. This method can be used effectively if the area to be covered is large and relatively open. Although any number of personnel may be employed, the strip method may also be used by one individual in a limited area, such as one room.

c) *Zone.* This method involves dividing the area to be searched into squares or sectors and assigning an individual or individuals to each sector (Fig. 3.5). The zone

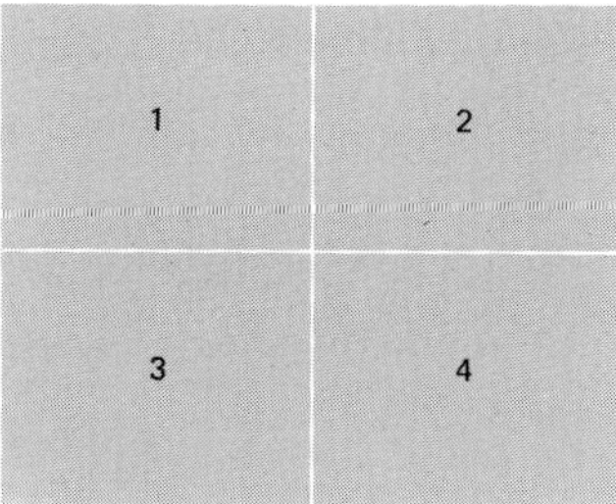

FIG. 3.5 The zone method of search (outdoors).

approach is generally effective indoors, where a room may be divided into such sections as floor, walls, and ceiling (Fig. 3.6). Needless to say, one should search the floor before beginning a search of the ceiling and walls. If the zone approach is used outdoors, it is likely to be ineffective unless used in conjunction with one of the other methods.

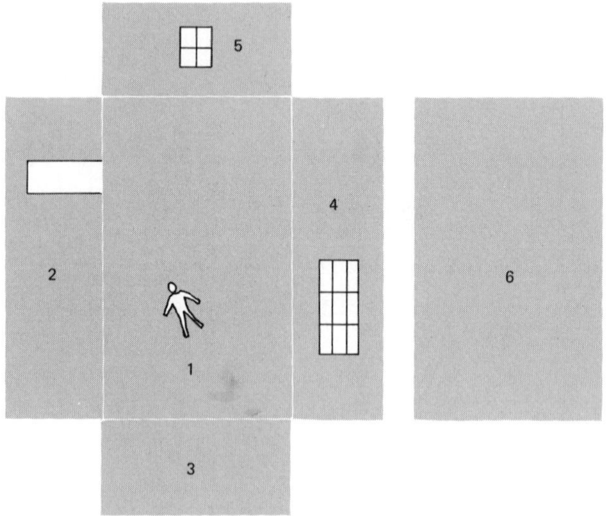

FIG. 3.6 The zone method of search (indoors).

d) *Spiral or circle.* In this method the searcher or searchers may begin from the center of the scene, or from the perimeter, and move in a circular path (Fig. 3.7). This approach has some value in a small area, but the wider the circle the greater the likelihood of overlooking evidence.

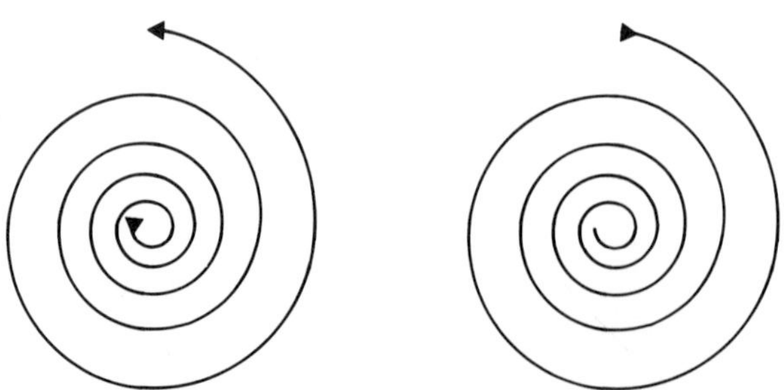

FIG. 3.7 The spiral, or circle, method of search.

e) *Link.* This method may be used when the crime scene involves two or more locations, such as different rooms, buildings in close proximity, or an outdoors area, and when manpower constraints preclude an exhaustive search. It is also of value in a preliminary search, when the investigator is attempting to reconstruct the crime. Essentially, this approach involves "following" the crime, and making a detailed inquiry at each location where it is apparent that some physical action took place (Fig. 3.8). The primary drawback to this approach is that the investigator may overlook evidence between the primary sites. Nevertheless it can be of extreme value if the crime involves a great degree of movement, such as kidnapping, burglary, rape, etc.

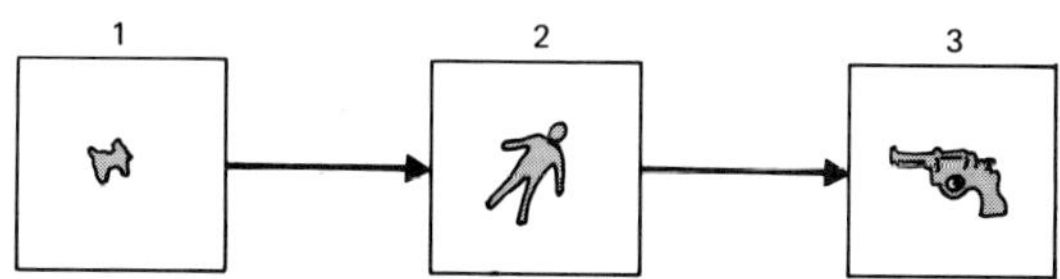

FIG. 3.8 The link method of search.

f) *Wheel.* The wheel method involves locating the searchers at the center of the scene and having them move out in spokelike directions (Fig. 3.9). The drawbacks to this method are many; thus it is not generally recommended. The two major disadvantages are that the searchers may ruin evidence while congregating, and that, as they move out, the distance between them rapidly becomes wider, making it easy to overlook evidence.

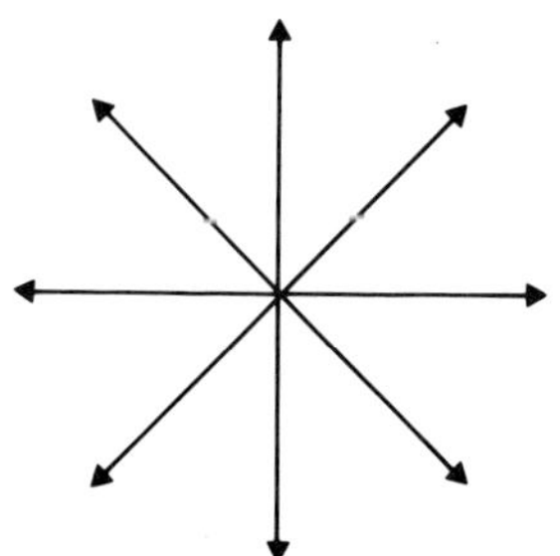

FIG. 3.9 The wheel method of search.

Conducting the Search. Photographing, sketching, and the techniques of evidence collection are covered in detail in later chapters. However, a discussion of the basics involved in the crime scene search should enhance the investigator's effectiveness.

A crime scene search should not be conducted unless the proper equipment is on hand. Generally, each investigator should be equipped with a complete evidence collection kit similar to that which will be discussed in detail in Chapter 5. If such a kit is not available the investigator should secure, at the very least, a flashlight, a magnifying glass, and rubber gloves.

Once the preliminary aspects of the crime scene investigation have been completed and the method of search selected, participants should be briefed. The supervising investigator should *not* assume that searchers are familiar with the case. Quite often an investigator will be occupied with another aspect of the case, such as interviewing a witness, and will not be aware of recent developments. Thus prior to the search all facts should be reviewed.

The extent of the search will depend on a number of factors, including available resources, the seriousness of the offense, and the potential for solution. If the crime is a serious one, the investigator is likely to have adequate assistance. However, it should be noted that many crimes go unsolved because the investigator made a hasty judgment concerning the probability of solution. For this reason it is advisable to conduct a crime scene search in any case where there is doubt.

Basically, the searchers are looking for two types of evidence: first, anything that may be out of place, added, removed, marked, touched, or struck (examples might be damaged furniture, articles left, absence of dust, scratches, fingerprints, or bullet holes); and second, any object or impression that might possibly be linked to the crime, such as fingerprints, palm prints, bullets, or cigarettes.

The mechanics of the search itself involve proceeding slowly along a path in the prescribed manner. If an object is found to be out of place, this is carefully recorded and photographed. If an item of evidence is discovered it is recorded, photographed, collected, and tagged. Once this has been accomplished, the search proceeds.

Each crime scene has certain characteristics, and the manner in which the search is conducted often depends on the investigator's initiative. For example, at an indoor crime scene it is wise to examine "out of the way" places (such as beneath table tops and chairs) for fingerprints. Windows, the edges of doors, dishes in the sink, books, papers and pamphlets, pictures, the insides of drawers, and cartridges are all likely to exhibit trace material. In one case with which the author is familiar an impression was obtained from a bar of soap which the perpetrator had used for washing up after the crime.

It is virtually impossible for the perpetrator to enter a scene and not leave some physical trace of his presence. Searchers should take care not to overlook the obvious. Cigarettes, matches, hairs, fibers, and impressions may be difficult to locate, but they are likely to be present. Garbage, closets, laundry bags, and the like should be carefully scrutinized. Discarded food containers and other material may also yield valuable information.

Outdoors the investigator is often faced with a more difficult problem. However, it should be recognized that the perpetrator is more likely to be careless about his actions when outdoors. In addition to leaving footprints and other impressions, he is likely to discard material or objects that will aid in tracing and/or linking him to the crime. Automobiles and other vehicles are ideal locations to collect evidence, if the investigator uses his initiative. Again, be careful to explore the "out of the way" places, behind the mirror, under and between the seats, the doors, the trunk, and the dashboard.

Much of the success involved in crime scene searches can be attributed to the internal orientation of the investigator. His knowledge, tenacity, and ability to approach the scene and its related clues logically, are of primary importance. In many instances the discovery of one piece of evidence means that a related object is likely to be present. (A simple example is the discovery of a .45 caliber bullet, and the probability that a shell casing might also be present.)

The manner in which the scene is explored can lead to the development of various theories. For example, has the scene been "staged"? Was the method of entry and exit consistent with the physical nature of the building? Was the search systematic or haphazard? What kind of property was removed? Is the victim's story plausible in view of the crime scene? The investigator should not hesitate to ask himself these questions, for they will aid him in developing a theoretical approach in later stages of the investigation. Of course, this does not mean that he should jump to conclusions, for things are not always as they appear to be.

CONCLUSIONS AND THEORY BUILDING

Once the reports have been made, victim and witnesses interviewed to the satisfaction of the investigator, and the crime scene search completed, it is natural for the investigator to formulate his initial theory or theories. Indeed, this process generally begins once the investigator is assigned to the case, although it is especially important that he keep an open mind throughout these early stages of the investigation.

Conclusions must be avoided until all the facts have been analyzed yielding a preponderance of evidence, which is then used to formulate the conclusion. In essence, this means that the conclusion should be one that is consistent with the facts, and one with which a reasonable man would agree. Ultimately the case must be presented to a prosecutor, who must agree with the conclusion presented, then to a judge or jury, who decides on the facts which led to the conclusion.

In a later chapter, the techniques of theory building are explored in depth. Suffice it to say, the investigator must use care in this phase of the investigation.

If he "jumps the gun" and makes an accusation that later proves to be wrong, he has aided the guilty party in establishing reasonable doubt.

Scientific evidence must be analyzed by the crime laboratory, and the investigator should await the results. The background of the victim and witnesses should be checked, both for previous history and reliability of information. If a suspect is present or has been identified, his background, as well as the reliability of his statements, should be investigated. The fact that a man has been accused of a crime should not satisfy the investigator. Granted, in many cases it may be incumbent on the investigator to make a summary arrest. Nevertheless, this should not terminate the investigation.

The value of a theory is in applying a logical approach to a problem. Thus, if the investigator has developed a theory, his next step should be an attempt to prove it wrong. The scientific approach to any problem involves an attempt to negate the theory. Once the elements of the crime have been established, the investigator should attempt to prove that the person could not possibly have committed the crime. If he cannot do this, he has increased the probability that the person is guilty.

On the other hand, if he attempts to weigh the evidence in such a manner as to prove the suspect guilty, it is likely that his personal bias would have an impact on the ultimate conclusion.

SUMMARY

We have now discussed the procedures to be followed in the preliminary investigation, including conduct of the investigation, the need for and function of records such as the crime report and supplementary report, maintenance of the case, crime scene searches, and the development of theory.

Preliminary investigation is the basis for continuance of a case. Without a thorough approach at this point, the case may be doomed to failure. Thus the investigator's responsibility begins here and continues throughout. His internal capacities and the utilization of external services provide the basis for a successful investigation. For this reason, it is imperative that he be familiar with the procedures for taking notes, keeping records, and conducting the crime scene search. Furthermore, his ability to supervise and direct others is of the utmost importance.

QUESTIONS FOR DISCUSSION

1. Why is it important that a methodological approach be taken in protecting and examining the crime scene? Discuss the actions that the first policemen on the scene should take.

2. What is the value of reports and records to the investigator? Discuss the ways in which they can be used in the investigation.

3. What are the different methods of crime scene search? Discuss the favorable and unfavorable aspects of each.

SUGGESTED READINGS

Inbau, Fred E., Andre A. Moenssens, and Louis R. Vitullo, *Scientific Police Investigation.* New York: Chilton, 1972.

Nelson, John G., *Preliminary Investigation and Police Reporting: A Complete Guide to Police Written Communication.* Beverly Hills, Calif.: Glencoe Press, 1970.

Svensson, Arne, and Otto Wendel, *Techniques of Crime Scene Investigation.* New York: American Elsevier, 1965.

CHAPTER 4

photographing and sketching the crime scene

Since photographs and sketches of the crime scene provide the investigator with essential information concerning the investigation, the police photographer and artist have become more and more valuable in the field of law enforcement in recent years. In the larger departments the investigator generally has access to these technicians. Nevertheless, every investigator should have some knowledge of the capabilities and limitations of photographs and sketches, as well as an understanding of the techniques involved in their preparation.

CRIME SCENE PHOTOGRAPHY

Although photography can be a complex matter involving a wide range of expertise, the investigator's basic knowledge should include a grasp of the techniques necessary to photograph the crime scene, specific items and objects, and fingerprints. The more complex and specialized photography is left to an expert in the field.

Photographers provide a permanent visual record of the scene and particular aspects of it that are of importance. Although "a picture is worth a thousand words," photographs do not eliminate the need for accurate written records.

Photographs may be used:

1. To refresh the investigator's memory.
2. To provide a new "slant" on the case.
3. To brief newly assigned investigators.
4. To record as evidence.
5. To illustrate details of a scene.
6. To provide proof of an injury or wound.
7. To make comparisons.
8. To present in court.

The use of photographs in an investigation is limited only by the ingenuity of the investigator. Quite often a thorough examination of a photograph will reveal something that was overlooked in the original search of the scene. This may include such things as position of furniture, foreign objects or damaged items. Photographs may also be used to develop theories, compare tool marks and tracings, or to understand the *modus operandi* of the perpetrator.

While the type of equipment available to the average investigator will depend on the resources of the department, each man should be issued an inexpensive cartridge-type camera, and have access to a fingerprint camera. These may be assigned to an individual or to a team, but it is essential that they be continually available so the investigator need not contact a property clerk each time he wants a camera. There are a number of adequate fingerprint cameras available which provide instant examination, and virtually eliminate the possibility of error (see Fig. 4.1). It should be noted that the more complex the equipment, the more difficult it will be to operate, thus the greater the likelihood of error. Furthermore, in some instances the investigator may have to testify in court concerning the type of camera he used and its particular characteristics.

An important use of photographs lies in their presentation in court when the case is brought to trial. Generally, photographs are admissible evidence in court, but certain criteria must be observed. To begin with, the photograph must be a true representation and not at all distorted. The use of color photography presents a number of problems, primarily due to color distortion. Thus in assault cases it is often advisable to photograph the victim with both color and black and white film. Finally, each picture should be recorded for later identification.

In photographing the crime scene, the photographer should move from the general to the specific. It is important that the scene not be disturbed until it has been photographed completely. For this reason, sketches are not made until after the initial photographs have been taken.

Before taking photographs the following information should be recorded:

1. Case number.
2. Investigator assigned.
3. Photographer's name.
4. Date, time, and location.
5. Weather conditions.
6. Type of camera, focal length of the lens, and special equipment, such as a special lens.
7. Type of film.
8. Type of illumination.

FIG. 4.1 A fingerprint camera is used to photograph fingerprints before they are removed from the bottle. This precaution not only makes it possible to prove that the fingerprints were on the bottle, but also provides a record in the event they are destroyed in removal.

Each photograph should be recorded as it is taken, and the following notations made:

1. Description of the scene or object, i.e., general view, victim.
2. Position of the camera.
3. Direction camera pointed.
4. Distance to subject.
5. Any other specific information which does not apply to all photographs such as use of wide angle lens or filters.

In photographing the general crime scene, the goal is to provide as accurate a picture as possible. The distance from the actual scene will depend on a number of factors, but it should be kept in mind that too great a distance makes the photograph indiscernible, and too small a distance makes it difficult to comprehend the "total" scene. The number of pictures taken will also depend on various factors, but in the average case a minimum of four general scene photographs should be taken. The photographer should take these at the four compass points if possible. (See Fig. 4.2.) Small rooms may require additional photographs which overlap so that a total view is ultimately exposed. If possible, it is advisable to take a picture from above, although such photos are subject to distortion. Outdoors the photographer may use a vehicle or the window of a house to provide an angle photo; indoors a ladder may be used.

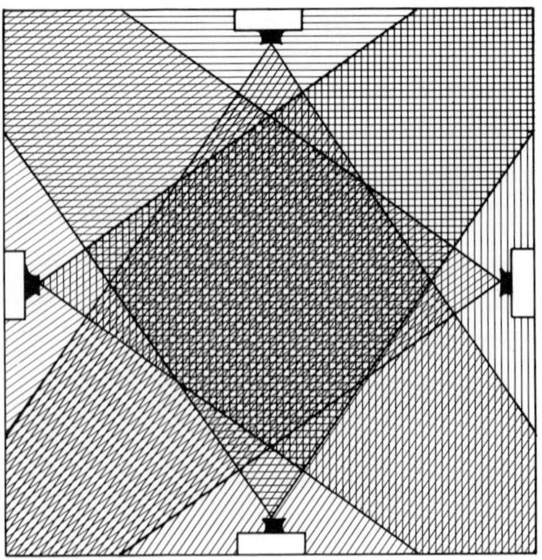

FIG. 4.2 Four-corner compass photography. Note that an overlap occurs in each of the photographs taken.

In order to reduce measurement error it is advisable to take a second series of photos with measurement markings present. These markings would include distance from camera to objects, as well as distance between objects. Remember that the general crime scene photograph is used to determine the relationship of objects to the scene, a particular pattern (such as movement), or the boundaries of the crime scene.

The boundaries of the crime scene should be set by the investigator in charge. As a general rule, the crime scene may be defined as any area in which an approach or departure was made, a search was conducted (burglary), an assault occurred, or a subject was present. In the case of a house or an apartment, the investigator should not assume that the crime scene is limited to one room; outdoors, a careful analysis of the area should be conducted before setting boundaries.

Good crime scene photography will tell a story and the investigator should be able to arrange the photos in a sequence which will enable him to portray the crime.

Once the general view photography has been completed, specifics or close-up photography can begin. Here again, if a sequence of events has been discovered, it is advisable to move through one step at a time. For example, in a burglary case, a general view of the house should be taken from outside first, followed by the necessary general views indoors. Close-up photography should begin with the means of entry, first outside, then inside. Any specifics such as tool mark striations should be taken with a suitable camera. The photographer should then proceed to the first place the burglar went, if this is evident. In some instances this may not be clear, but a logical examination will reveal his probable moves.

Specific or close-up photography requires care, patience, and imagination. The goal is to produce photographs that are of value. Pictures of fingerprints or tool marks are of little or no value if they are out of focus, and distorted photos of the victim or evidence may lead the viewer to the wrong conclusion. This form of photography is used to record objects in detail and their relationship to other aspects of the crime. In a general sense specific photography can be classified into three categories: (1) persons (victim, suspect, witness, wounds, etc.), (2) places (areas or locations), and (3) objects (material, weapons, traces, and impressions).

PERSONS

A common error made by many investigators at the crime scene is to photograph only the victim. However, it is often advisable to photograph witnesses and the suspect, if he has been apprehended. Such photos may be used later to determine the physical state of such individuals at the time of the crime. Furthermore, in any number of instances a witness has turned out to be the perpetrator of the crime. Staged photographs (those in which the witness is asked to recreate the scene) are also likely to have immense value in a later reconstruction of the crime.

The Victim. In homicide cases the victim should be photographed *in situ* (in place), whenever possible. In most instances the body has been moved by persons attempting to render first aid; thus this fact should be noted. Full-length photographs of the victim should be taken at various angles, and at least one should indicate the relationship of the body to a "landmark." If the wound or wounds are apparent, photographs should be taken at the angle which best portrays them. If possible, a photograph should also be taken from the direction in which the wound was inflicted. It may be necessary to move the body in order to accomplish this. After the body has been removed from the scene, additional photographs of the area should be taken.

In assault or accident cases, the photographer should attempt to get pictures of the wound or injury, although in most cases the fact that the victim was administered first aid will preclude this. Herein lies the value of equipping each patrol car with a small camera so that pictures may be taken immediately. If the victim has been taken to a hospital, it is often possible to obtain pictures while the person is being treated. In all cases, the victim's face should be photographed from the front and both sides.

Witnesses. Photographs of witnesses may be used at a later time to identify individuals, to note their physical appearance, and to link them to the scene. Once the crime scene photography, sketching, and search have been completed, it may be advisable to reconstruct the scene, asking the witnesses to stand where they were during the crime and to enact any position or movements they made. In addition to aiding the investigator in understanding the crime, such photos may be used to refresh a witness' memory at a later time, or to point out inconsistencies.

Suspects. A photograph of the suspect at the crime scene may be used later to indicate his physical appearance, his apparent state of mind, and any wounds he claims to have suffered. Here again it is advisable to reconstruct the scene, asking the suspect to reenact his actions and movements. These photos may prove invaluable in determining the truth of his statements, as well as their plausibility.

PLACES

Specific photography is often used to indicate a particular location, such as the window through which an entry was made or a bureau that was searched. These photos should provide the investigator with information on the perpetrator's or victim's actions. Also the arrangement of particular objects or items may be photographed to show their relationship to each other and the crime scene. This will often aid the investigator in establishing the *modus operandi.* The type of photographs taken will depend on the particular scene and the nature of the crime; suffice it to say that care should be taken in assuring accuracy.

OBJECTS

Object photography may be broken into two classes, the first being made up of objects or items of a general nature for identification, and the second of physical evidence which will be examined scientifically. In some instances there will be an overlap, for many items will be photographed to provide a record of their relationship to the scene and later analyzed by the crime laboratory. Weapons are a prime example; a firearm will be photographed at the scene and later examined by a ballistics expert. Emphasis in the first category should be on identifying the object clearly and portraying any peculiarities it may exhibit. Examples of this are overturned furniture, objects out of place, or weapons and their positions. At least two photographs of each object should be taken from different angles. Evidence in the second category should relate specifically to traces and impressions. Generally, any physical evidence that will be forwarded to the crime laboratory, and is photographed to preserve or identify it, will fall into this class. Fingerprints, tool marks, blood, hair, paint scrapings, and the like are further examples.

Generally, a special camera is used to record this form of evidence. The important factor is clarity, for the photograph may be used either for proof that the evidence existed (in the event it is destroyed while being removed), or for direct comparison purposes, as in examining tool marks. The utilization of photographs in the analysis of scientific evidence is discussed in the following chapter. However, it should be noted that in some measure this form of specific photography can be quite complex and requires more than average skill. The investigator charged with this responsibility should practice taking pictures of fingerprints, blood droppings, and other impressions. Quite often it may be necessary to use indirect lighting to bring out various impressions; and in the case of latent fingerprints too little or too much powder may negate taking a usable photo.

If it is possible to photograph trace and impression material larger than it actually is this should be done; however it is advisable to place a small ruler at the periphery of the vision finder in order to indicate perspective. If the object or item to be photographed is relatively small, at least two photographs should be taken. The first should be taken at a distance which permits identification of it in the area, and the second should be taken for close-up clarity.

MEASUREMENTS AND MARKINGS

The use of measurements has been discussed generally throughout this chapter, but some specific comments are of value. Markings may be used to depict a particular item or to show the location and position of persons or things that may have been removed.

In general, a second set of photographs using some form of discernible ruler or measure will enhance the value of the photography, for it removes any question of the relationship between items in the photograph. In general scene photos, a card may be used indicating the distance from the camera to a particular object as well as the distance between objects.

In accidents, or cases where the victim has been removed from the scene, it is common practice to draw a chalk mark indicating the position of the body. Some departments use paper silhouettes. Tire skid marks may also be identified in this manner. If there are bullet holes at the scene, it is often advisable to draw a circle around each point of entry. However, care should be taken not to circle the area too closely; this may result in ruining fragment or powder tracings.

Finally, in some instances, and especially if more than one photographer is working, an identification card may be placed in an area outside the primary scene, identifying the photographer and any other pertinent data. This should not conceal any part of the primary scene. A set of photographs *without* any additions should be taken. This will preclude any contention that the scene has been altered by foreign objects.

SPECIAL PHOTOGRAPHIC PROBLEMS

In recent years the development of various types of color and special black and white film has resulted in problems involving their presentation in court. The decision to use color film should be based primarily on its acceptance in court. In some instances, it may be of value to use both, but this will increase the costs. Color pictures have a distinct value, but in assault and homicide cases they may be deemed too graphic for presentation.

The use of special black and white film may result in varying tones and shades, which might have an impact upon their accuracy in presenting the actual scene. Experimentation and consultation with experts will provide the best answers to this problem.

In order to provide continuity in the chain of evidence, data should be kept on each roll of film, including the names of the photographer, the person who delivered the film to be processed, and the person who developed it. The developer should keep a record of the means used to develop the film. Finally, it is advisable to keep the negatives in a secure place, properly recorded; and they should not generally be given to the investigator. This precludes any allegations that the pictures may have been altered or removed from evidence.

Special photographic techniques employed, such as the use of magnifying equipment, wide angle lens, and filters, may have to be explained in court, and the photographer should be familiar with any criticism that may arise as a result of their use, and the precautions taken at the scene to avoid error.

The utilization of enlargements, both to further the investigation and to provide graphic evidence in court, can be extremely valuable. However, care should be taken in their preparation to avoid distortion. Unless a special grain film is employed, enlargements are likely also to result in an extreme loss of detail.

In homicide cases there may be instances where the identity of the deceased is difficult to establish, due to either the destruction of facial features by the perpetrator or decomposition due to the environment. In such cases photographs of any identifiable markings, such as tattoos or scars, should be taken.

VIDEOTAPE AND MOTION PICTURES

Although still photography remains the most accepted form of police photography, some consideration should be given to the utilization of videotape and motion picture cameras. In recent years the cost of using such equipment has come within the realm of the average-sized police department. Furthermore, use of this equipment is within range of the investigator's capabilities.

Needless to say, the use of moving pictures adds a new dimension to criminal investigation. In addition to a complete "running" view of the scene exactly as the observer sees it is a whole range of possibilities in the area of reconstruction. Further, the use of such films in court will enhance the value of still photographs and make it easy to place them in proper perspective.

The choice of equipment will depend on a department's budget. However, videotape equipment is now being used in a number of departments for criminal investigation. This equipment permits the recorder to offer a narrative description of the scene as he is working and allows participants' actions and statements to be recorded in a reconstruction. The use of videotape to record confessions has also proven valuable.

The use of motion pictures in criminal investigation has generally been limited to recording the movements and actions of suspects in a continuing investigation. However, motion pictures serve a similar purpose to that of videotape. Most investigators are overlooking an important tool which could be extremely valuable at the crime scene.

CRIME SCENE SKETCHING

The crime scene sketch is an integral part of the investigation, providing the investigator with a graphic portrayal of the scene and offering certain capabilities which are not possible with photographs. Essentially, the sketch is an *accurate* depiction of the relationship among various aspects of the scene. Generally, there are three types of crime scene sketches: (1) the general or rough sketch, (2) the measured field sketch, and (3) the scaled sketch.

These sketches may be prepared by one man, or several, depending on the resources of the individual police department. In most cases the assigned investigator should prepare his own sketch of the scene, regardless of the availability of a department artist or draftsman. The equipment necessary for preparing the sketch depends on the type of sketch being prepared. However, each investigator should be equipped with pencils, paper, a straightedge, and a compass. Graph paper is also useful in preparing field sketches.

THE MEASURED FIELD SKETCH

The most important of the three types of sketches, the measured field sketch is used to complete the final or scaled sketch. It should be an accurate portrayal of the scene, including an indication of direction and measurements between objects. The key to successful sketching is simplicity; unnecessary details should be omitted. However if there is some doubt about the importance of an item it should be included.

In preparing the sketch, the artist should be assisted by another person who can call out measurements. Measurements should reflect the accurate position of objects. This can usually be accomplished by a "two point" measurement; at least one set of measurements should be made from an immovable object, such as a wall or tree. A steel tape should be used for measurements indoors, and if the user is proficient a wheel-type measure may be utilized outdoors. Compass direction should be indicated by an arrow signifying "magnetic north."

In taking measurements objects should *not* be moved, and point-to-point markings should be indicated. In illustrating various objects, a key or legend should be used; this may involve the use of either numbers or simulated drawings. Generally, numbers should be used for items of evidence; however, if some item requires specific identification but is not considered evidence, letters may be used.

Sketches are generally two-dimensional; in the case of rooms, where the walls are included, a two-dimensional view can be constructed as in Fig. 4.3.

In drawing the scene the artist may estimate the distances, rather than draw to scale; however, the exact measurements must be indicated in the sketch. An accurate scale, in which each inch is equal to a number of feet, will be constructed later. The size of the sketch will depend on the scene itself. It is advisable to keep the sketch on a single sheet of paper if possible. Graph paper greatly facilitates entering measurements and reduces the probability of recording errors.

Each sketch should contain the following information for identification purposes:

1. Title of sketch, and location.
2. Crime, and case number.
3. Artist's name.
4. Assigned investigator's name.
5. Date and time sketch prepared.

In no case should a sketch be altered by anyone other than the original artist; this includes adding material that may have been omitted.

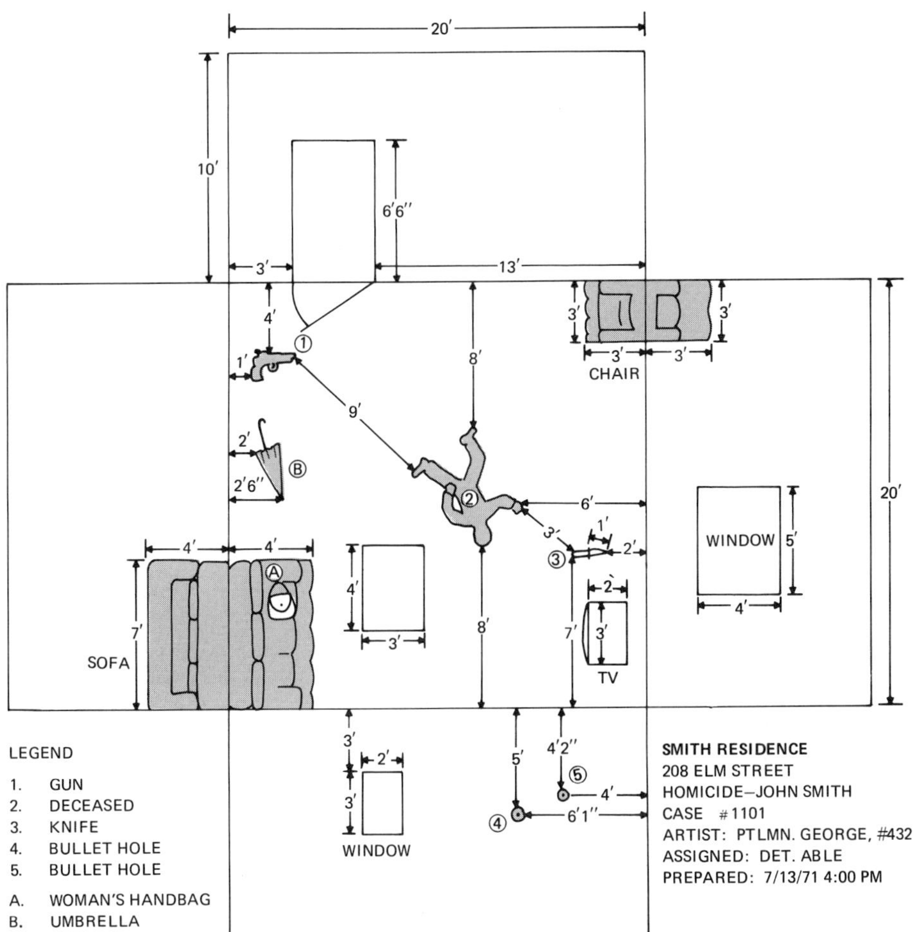

FIG. 4.3 Field sketch.

THE SCALED SKETCH

The scaled sketch is the final sketch, and is usually prepared by an artist or draftsman. It is designed for use in court, and represents an exact scaled replica of the crime scene. Some departments prepare the sketch without illustrating distances, thus reducing unnecessary cluttering of the sketch. A ruler can then be used to illustrate distance. The important aspect of this sketch to the investigator is its accuracy which, in turn, depends on the completeness and accuracy of the field sketch.

A scaled sketch need not be prepared until the case has reached the point of going to trial. The investigator should keep in mind that, since a scaled sketch is based on the field sketch, the defense attorney may wish to introduce the latter as evidence. For this reason, care should be taken to see that the field sketch is not mutilated, altered, or destroyed.

SPECIAL SKETCHING TECHNIQUES

Although sketches are generally two-dimensional, it may be advisable in many cases to prepare special sketches portraying certain important additional aspects of the case. This may involve three-dimensional sketches or diagrams indicating such things as the trajectory of a bullet, the path of an automobile, or the movements of a perpetrator. Those familiar with the assassination of President Kennedy will recall that sketches of this nature aided greatly in the investigation.

While this form of sketching can become quite sophisticated and is generally beyond the capabilities of the average investigator, he should recognize its value and familiarize himself with its attributes.

THE USE OF SKETCHES

While crime scene sketches are most commonly used as visual aids in courtroom presentation, the investigator should be aware that they can be of assistance during the investigation. Combined with photographs, sketches may be used to analyze the scene or to determine the relative probability of various aspects concerning the scene.

Sketches might also be used to refresh the memory of the investigator or witnesses, as well as to develop a clearer understanding of the occurrence. For example, participants may be asked to indicate their positions and movements during the crime, as well as those of others. If a sketch is used, the individuals can be asked to trace their actions on separate sketches. A comparative analysis of their sketches may then be used to develop inconsistencies that might not seem apparent in a verbal description.

In some crimes, the positions of objects or items may be inconsistent with the statements of witnesses or may indicate a "staged" scene. Examples of this occur sometimes in apparent suicides: What may appear to be suicide may in fact be murder. Thus, the position of weapons, furniture, or other items may be improbable and readily apparent in sketches. The distance of the chair from the deceased in a hanging may prove to be very important; in many such cases this is not recorded because the investigator assumes that a suicide has taken place. However, later examinations may reveal that murder is a possibility. In such cases, an adequate sketch can be an invaluable aid.

Body position may also prove important in homicide cases, the sketch being used to trace apparent movement or theoretical movement. The use of overlays also proves valuable in such examinations.

If a sketch has been prepared for use in court, the investigator should familiarize himself with all its various aspects. He should be familiar with the key or legend, as well as various distances and other items that may be the subject of cross-examination. In some instances it may be advisable to prepare "insets" or sketches of special aspects of the crime scene to clarify particular points.

Finally, the use of diagrammatic sketches illustrating position, movement, or trajectory can be prepared to clear up any misunderstanding that might result in the jurors' minds concerning a complex incident.

QUESTIONS FOR DISCUSSION

1. How can photographs be used in an investigation? Discuss the limitations of the use of photographs.

2. What information should be recorded when taking photographs and preparing sketches? Discuss the way in which sketches can be used to augment photographs.

3. In what ways can specific or close-up photography be used? Discuss the techniques involved in this form of photography.

4. In what way can videotape or motion pictures be used at the crime scene?

EXERCISE

1. Each student should prepare a measured field sketch of a room in his home.

SUGGESTED READING

Sansone, Sam J., *Modern Photography for Police and Firemen.* Cincinnati, Ohio: W. H. Anderson, 1971.

CHAPTER 5

scientific evidence and criminal investigation

Despite an increasing awareness of the importance of physical evidence, studies indicate that few investigators utilize science to its fullest capacity as an investigative tool. Indeed, with the exception of narcotics analyses and in some instances fingerprint comparisons, the crime laboratory contributes little to criminal investigation. The fault does not usually lie with the laboratory but rather with the investigator, who often fails to collect physical evidence that may prove valuable.

This deficiency can be attributed in some measure to a lack of expertise on the investigator's part. The utilization of evidence technicians has caused many investigators to conclude that the responsibility for scientific evidence now lies elsewhere. Nothing could be further from the truth. The investigator is charged with overall responsibility for the case; the employment of evidence technicians and the crime laboratory should be classified as external services designed to *assist* the investigator. For this reason, the investigator must have a thorough knowledge of not only the techniques involved in evidence collection but also the capabilities of the crime laboratory and the services which it can provide.

At the outset, a distinction between physical evidence and scientific physical evidence should be made. Essentially, all physical evidence may be defined as any *tangible* matter having some substance which relates to a crime or crimes. Physical evidence may be used to provide the following:

1. Proof that a crime occurred.
2. Proof that a particular weapon or instrument was used in the crime.
3. Proof of a particular occurrence.
4. Proof that links a suspect to the scene or that links evidence to a suspect.
5. Proof of the manner in which the crime was committed.
6. Proof of the identity and possible location of an individual.
7. Proof in the form of circumstantial evidence which can be used in court.

Generally, the difference between physical evidence and scientific physical evidence lies in its handling. Any evidence that is forwarded to the crime laboratory for analysis, comparison, or testing may be classified as scientific evidence.

Evidence is the proof which is legally presented at a trial through the use of witnesses, records, documents, and concrete objects.[1] In a later chapter the role of evidence in legal proceedings will be discussed. However, at this point the emphasis shall be on physical evidence—its collection, preservation, and analysis. The investigator must keep in mind, though, that evidence is used to establish proof, and proof may be defined as the belief or conclusion arrived at by a consideration of the evidence.[2]

Great care must be taken in the handling of physical evidence to prevent its alteration or destruction. Evidence must also be properly recorded, and the "chain of custody" maintained. Thus, from the time of discovery of each piece of evidence, a record must be kept listing every person who handled the evidence, as well as its place of storage and the duration. Evidence should not be kept in the investigator's private locker, automobile, or home, but should be stored in a locked cabinet or room set aside for this purpose. Access to the property locker should be limited. Many a case has been lost in court due to the lack of evidence "integrity."

RECOGNITION AND COLLECTION OF PHYSICAL EVIDENCE

Evidence may be collected from the crime scene or from persons or places removed from the scene. The ability to recognize evidence develops through training and experience. Properly equipped, the investigator should have no problems recognizing evidence, although studies have shown a lack of "internal" preparation or lack of expertise on the part of many investigators. While it would be impossible to list everything an investigator should look for at the crime scene or in pursuing the investigation, each crime does generally exhibit certain types of evidence. This typology is discussed in greater detail in a later chapter on individual crimes; our emphasis here is on general evidence collection.

To begin with, each investigator should be equipped with an evidence kit. If evidence technicians are used, this kit may be reduced to a relatively small size, containing only certain essential items. However, a complete kit should be available whenever required. The essential items to be included in the investigator's kit and those for a complete evidence collection kit are listed in Fig. 5.1.

The manner of storage will, of course, depend on the number of items included. Nevertheless, a kit should not be so unwieldy or heavy as to make its use difficult. If a kit is separated, materials should be stored in terms of their relationship to each other, and the probability of their use. For example, since the camera is used frequently, it should not be stored with heavy tools or incidental material; fingerprint equipment should be more accessible than casting material. While such an approach may seem inane to some, the investigator familiar with crime scene search techniques recognizes not only that time is valuable but also that inaccessible equipment results in a scattering of materials in unpacking and a greater probability of loss or misplacement.

FIG. 5.1 Evidence Collection Kit

The following items should be included in the investigator's kit:

1. Photographic equipment
   a) General use camera
   b) Specifics camera for photographing fingerprints and other trace material
   c) Film, illumination equipment, light meter, etc.
2. Fingerprint materials
   a) Powders, brushes, lifting tape, transfer paper, fingerprint cards (for taking elimination prints)
3. Magnifying glass and mirror
   a) A dentist's mirror may be included for examining inaccessible locations, such as beneath auto bodies for serial numbers
4. Flashlight
5. Measuring instruments
   a) Ruler, 18 inch, metal
   b) Steel tape measure, 50 feet
   c) Compass
6. Recording materials
   a) Graph paper, note books, evidence tags
   b) Pens, pencils, chalk, crayons
7. Tools
   a) Screwdriver and pliers
8. Tape
   a) Transparent, electrical, and colored
9. Storage material
   a) Envelopes, pill boxes, bottles, flat cardboard
   b) Cord, tape, labels, rubber bands
10. Tweezers, scissors, forceps, and picks
11. Paper towels, rubber gloves

In addition to the above, a complete evidence collection kit should be available containing the following items:

1. Floodlamps, ultraviolet lamp
2. Casting materials
3. Tools
   a) Hammer, sledge hammer, shovel, pry bar, saw
   b) Wrenches, pliers, lock cutter
4. Additional photographic equipment
   a) Movie camera
   b) Heavy tripod
5. Additional packaging equipment
6. Narcotics field test kit

The ability to differentiate between evidence and extraneous materials at the crime scene involves an understanding of evidentiary law, criminal law, which relates to the specific offense, and the capabilities of the crime laboratory. In addition, the investigator must be able to apply abstract theory in imagining and reconstructing the crime, asking such questions as: What happened? How did it happen? Why did it happen? What is not apparent? What should I be looking for?

When a piece of evidence is discovered, it must be collected and marked for future identification. However, care should be taken not to destroy any trace evidence that may be on the item. Trace evidence or latent evidence (which refers to hidden or undeveloped material) is often obliterated at an early stage by someone marking an item for identification. Weapons are a prime example; quite often a firearm is picked up before being examined for latent fingerprints. If there is any doubt the item should be protected in a prescribed manner, and its identity recorded on a tag, label, or the container in which it is placed.

Evidence destined for examination by the crime laboratory may generally be categorized in one or more of the following ways:

1. Casts (including plaster, moulage, and silicone).
2. Chemical (blood, fibers, glass, paint, residue, stains, semen, poisons, alcohol, and narcotics).
3. Documents (handwriting, restoration, typewriter, and other mechanical impressions).
4. Fingerprints.
5. Firearms.
6. Weapons.
7. Instrumentation (spectrographic, chromatographic, x-ray diffraction).
8. Microscopic (hair, fibers, paints, residue, stains, microcrystalline).
9. Photographic.
10. Serological (blood, semen, stains).
11. Tool mark comparison.
12. Physical matches.

Evidence referred to the crime laboratory may be examined in various ways. An understanding of these tests will aid the investigator in recognizing the value of evidence, as well as in providing for its preservation. While an in-depth analysis of the types of equipment and tests involved in the crime laboratory is beyond the scope of this book, the investigator should be familiar with the general procedures involved in the utilization of physical evidence.

The method employed to collect evidence will often depend on the type of laboratory examination to which it will be subjected. If the evidence may be subjected to more than one examination, the investigator should keep this in mind.

The following points are designed to familiarize the investigator with evidence collection techniques.

CASTS

A cast involves reproduction of an impression in its three-dimensional form. Closely related to casts are molds, which may be defined as the reproductions of *articles* or *shapes* in three-dimensional forms.

Impressions that are likely to be the subject of casts are foot and tire prints, tool marks, tooth bites, and other depressions that are created by an object coming into contact with a relatively soft surface, such as dirt or wood. Molds may be taken of such objects as weapons, tools, tire and shoe prints.

Casts and molds are used to make scientific comparisons and to maintain a replica of any evidence (such as foot and tire prints) that may be destroyed by the environment. A comparative analysis of impressions found at the scene of the crime can be used to link the suspect to the crime. Virtually all impressions display distinctive characteristics similar to fingerprints, that may be matched against the original item. Increased wear on the object may result in certain physical changes to its surface. But these drawbacks can usually be overcome by a trained criminalist. The most common forms of casts are those made of foot and tire prints. Examination of these prints at the scene might reveal a wealth of information. For example, the direction in which an auto was moving or the speed at which it was traveling can be determined by observing tread and skid marks. The size and weight of an individual, as well as whether or not he was walking or running (and in some instances, whether or not he was carrying a heavy object) may be approximated by analyzing footprints. The individual's gait can be indicative of a limp or an injury, and marks in the area might reveal that he was pushing or pulling an object. The investigator should examine the scene carefully before preparing casts. Of course, photographs of the impression should be taken before casting begins.

Casts may be constructed of plaster of Paris, moulage, modeling clay, or any similar substance. The choice of material will depend on the particular impression. The most common form of casting is with plaster of Paris (see Fig. 5.2). Each evidence collection kit should be equipped with the following items: various casting materials (plaster of Paris, clay, etc.), spray gun, shellac, mixing materials (pail, cup, spatulas), plastic spray, alcohol, and casting frame material.

Preparation of the cast is relatively simple; however, the following guidelines should be adhered to:

1. In soft material either shellac or a plastic spray should be used to provide a base. (Aerosol hair spray with a lacquer base may be used.) This material should not be sprayed directly, but rather indirectly, into the impression.

2. On surfaces which are likely to adhere to the casting material, a thin film of oil should be sprayed over the area.

FIG. 5.2 A plaster cast should be removed carefully after it has had sufficient time to dry. It should be handled by the edges, taking care not to chip or crack it. (Courtesy of SPRING 3100, New York City Police Department.)

3. A detaining frame of wood, sheet metal, or cardboard may be needed to prevent excessive spreading of the casting material.

4. The amount of casting material used will depend on the impression, but a thickness of at least two inches is desirable. The consistency should permit easy pouring, but should not be thin enough to saturate the area.

5. The material should be poured not directly into the impression, but over a tongue depressor or spoon to prevent marring. The cast may be reinforced with thin wire, twigs, or similar material. Care should be taken to see that this material does not settle to the depression.

6. When the plaster has dried somewhat, it should be marked for identification on the upper surface.

7. The time necessary for complete drying will depend on the amount of material used. The investigator should assure himself that the cast is solid before removing it. Once it has been removed, it should be allowed to dry for several more hours, after which it can be washed.

A silicone rubber material may be used to make casts if the surface in which the impression has been made is durable, such as wood or metal. This is accomplished by merely pressing the material into the impression.

Molds of objects often require greater expertise, and should usually be delivered to the crime laboratory for handling.

The original cast or mold represents a "negative" reproduction, and in some instances it may be desirable to construct a "positive." This is accomplished by using the original mold or cast to make another. In this way a replica of the original instrument or impression is constructed.

CHEMICAL

Chemical analysis may be conducted on various kinds of material collected at the scene. Generally, this evidence is referred to as trace material (blood, semen, fibers, stains, etc.). Instrumentation, or the use of scientific tools, is often used in connection with chemical analysis, and this is discussed in a later section. Essentially, chemical analysis is conducted to determine the various properties of material, either to identify a questioned substance or to compare the properties of two substances.

Blood. One of the more common chemical traces found at the crime scene is blood. This evidence can provide the investigator with information concerning the crime, the victim, and the perpetrator, as well as the events surrounding the crime. For example, blood drops may indicate the direction of travel, the height from which they fell, and the direction from which the wound was directed. Blood typing can be used to eliminate a suspect or to narrow the number of suspects.

While it is generally assumed that blood is easily recognized, the investigator should be aware that in many cases this may not be true. Dried blood often takes on another color, or its mixture with another chemical or material may make it unrecognizable. The investigator should not depend too heavily on color to determine whether or not a stain is blood.

If blood is in its liquid state, it should be removed with an eyedropper and stored in a sealed test tube for immediate delivery to the crime laboratory. An attempt should be made to deliver the entire article to the laboratory if blood has saturated an item. If this is impossible (such as on rugs), a piece of the item should be cut out. If the blood is moist, part of it should be stored in a test tube, and the remainder should be allowed to dry, placed in a proper receptacle, and delivered to the laboratory. Careful packaging is essential in order to preserve stain patterns, and to assure that during the transference of the evidence to the laboratory, unstained portions of the material are not contaminated with stained portions. If dried blood has been discovered, the article on which it appears should be delivered for analysis if possible. In any case, scrapings should be taken and placed in a sealed test tube. Because heat and cold affect blood, an attempt should also be made to keep the specimen at normal temperatures and out of direct sunlight.

Any specimen of blood at the crime scene may be from either the perpetrator or the victim. Thus, a record of where the blood sample was obtained should be kept. In searching the crime scene it is often advisable to look for evidence which the perpetrator used to protect his wound or to clean up. An examination of the garbage and sink may turn up blood traces. Also, matter beneath the fingernails of the victim is likely to produce blood traces. Keep in mind that if a physical struggle ensued, there is a strong possibility that blood is present, although an effort may have been made to clean the scene. Cracks in the floor or behind baseboards, beneath tables or chairs, or the trap in a sink may contain such samples. Luminol can also be used in detecting hidden traces of blood. This chemical test involves spraying the reagent over the surface to be tested *in the dark.* If blood is present a bluish-white luminescence is visible.

Blood drops should be examined prior to collection, in an effort to determine whether or not they might reveal information of any value. The direction at which blood drops strike a surface can be ascertained by observation. Blood striking a surface at a direct angle will generally be circular in pattern, with spokelike splashes emerging from the center of impact. Blood striking a surface at an oblique angle will usually be rounded at the direction from which it came, with the splashes pointing out in a singular direction opposite the angle from which it came. The height from which the blood struck the floor can sometimes be determined. The surface area which the blood strikes is a crucial factor, and tests on the same surface are of primary importance in any determination of height characteristics of blood drops. Figures 5.3 through 5.16 are illustrative of the wide range of blood drop patterns, and point up the need for scientific examination in this area.

Blood patterns may also be used to determine the movements of individuals at the scene, their proximity to each other, the direction of assault, and the location of the assault.

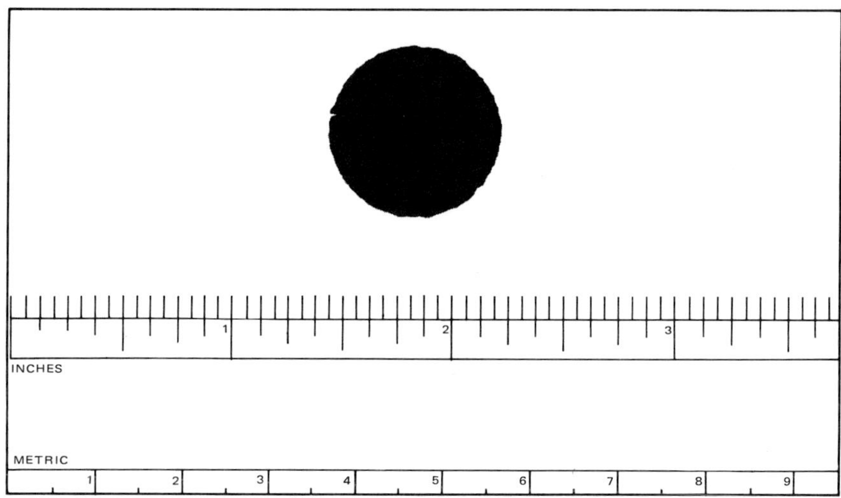

FIG. 5.3 Bloodstain from a single drop of human blood that struck a hard, smooth, glossy cardboard surface after falling 80 feet. (This figure and other blood stain patterns shown in this chapter are reprinted courtesy of the National Institute of Law Enforcement and Criminal Justice, from their pamphlet *Flight Characteristics and Stain Patterns of Human Blood,* November, 1971.)

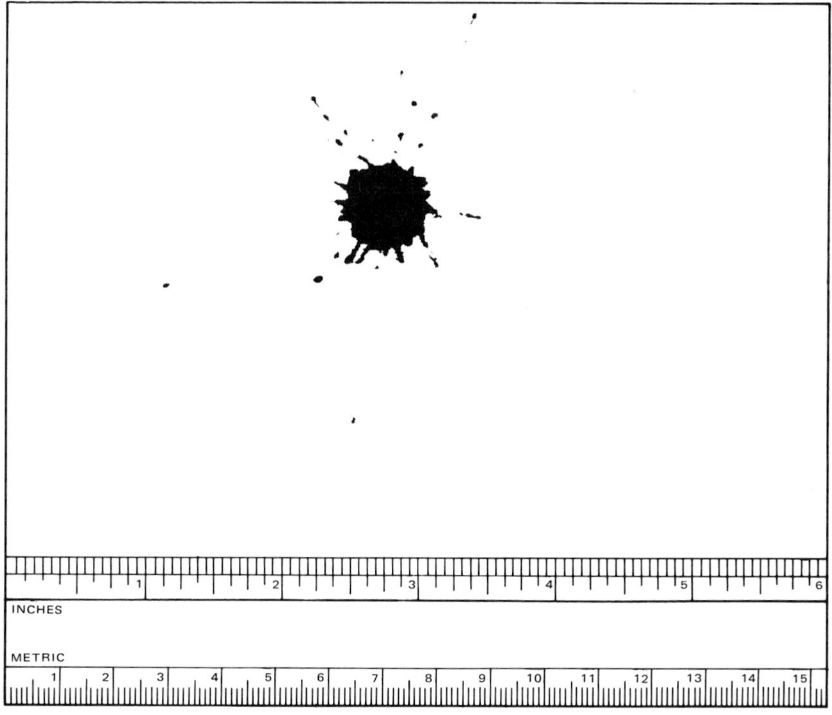

FIG. 5.4 Bloodstain from a single drop of human blood that struck a blotter after falling 18 inches.

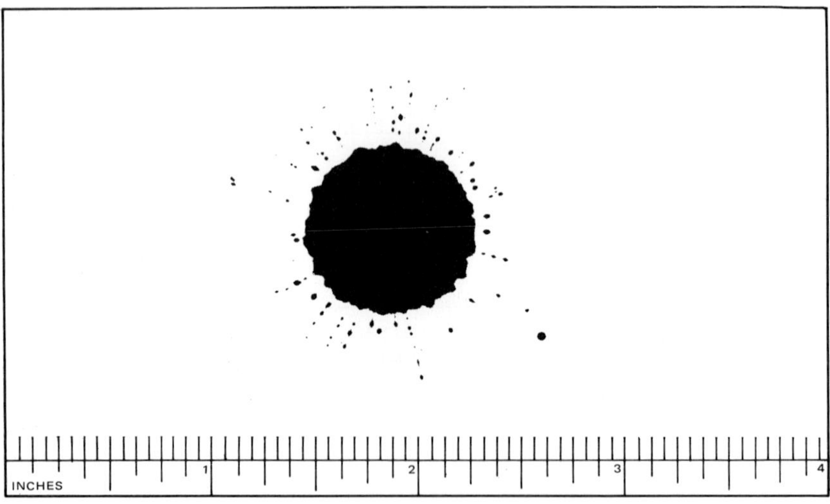

FIG. 5.5 Bloodstain from a single drop of human blood that struck a hard, smooth cardboard after falling 68 feet.

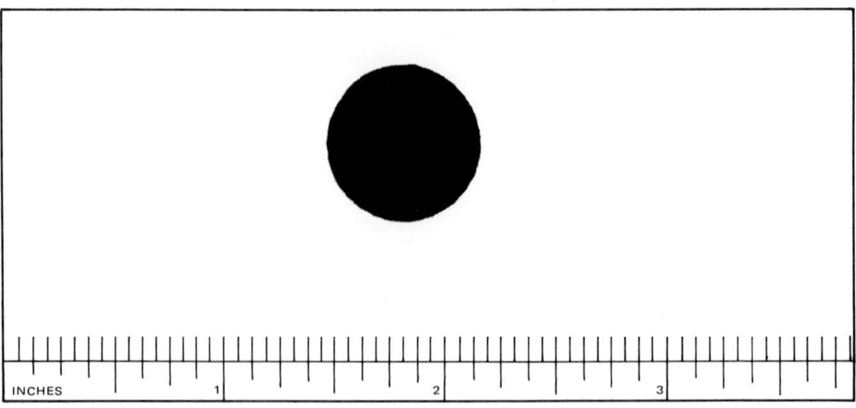

FIG. 5.6 Bloodstain from a single drop of human blood that struck a sheet of polyethylene plastic after falling 42 inches.

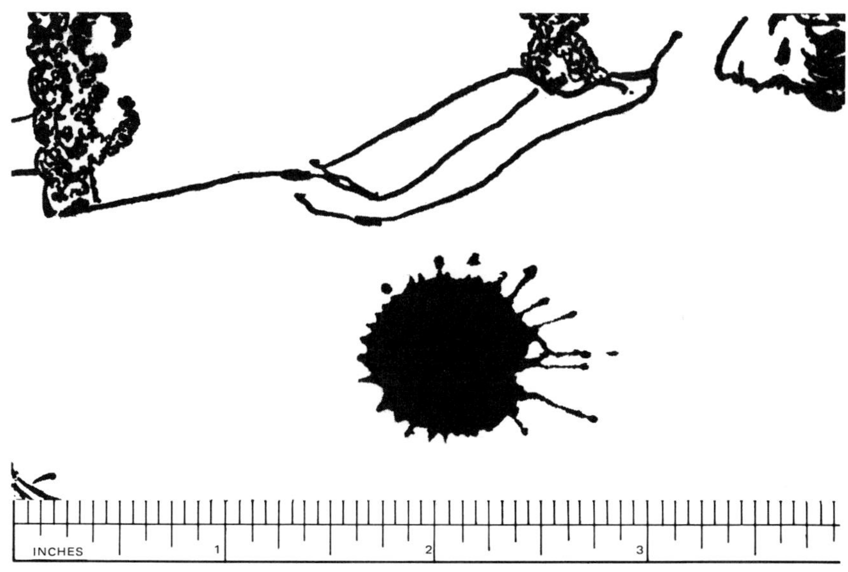

FIG. 5.7 Bloodstain from a single drop of human blood that struck a newspaper after falling 42 inches.

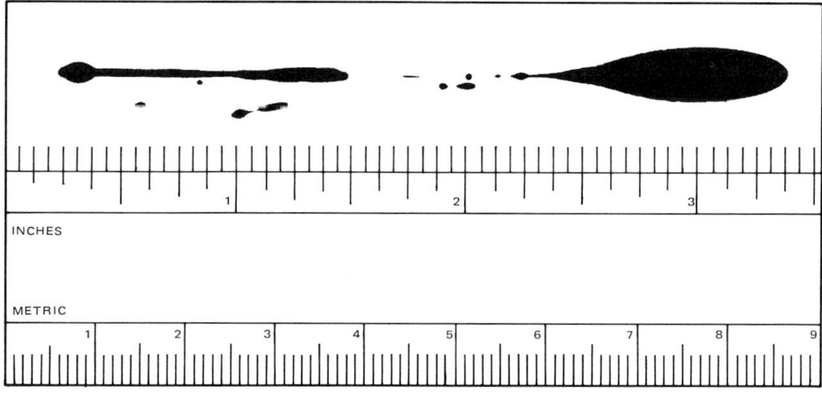

FIG. 5.8 Bloodstain produced by a drop of human blood striking a hard, smooth cardboard with a horizontal motion of about 10 feet per second at an angle of approximately 16 degrees.

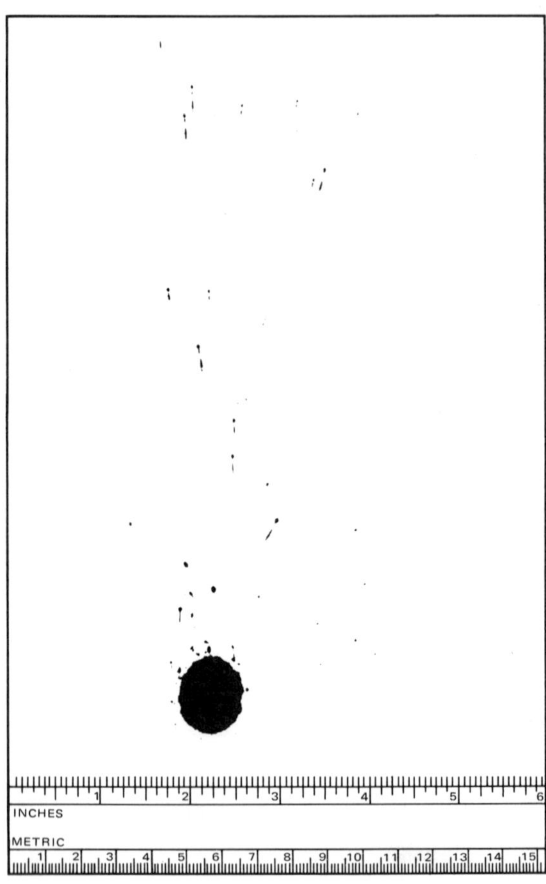

FIG. 5.9 Bloodstain produced by a drop of human blood striking a hard, smooth cardboard with a horizontal motion of about four feet per second at an angle of approximately 56 degrees.

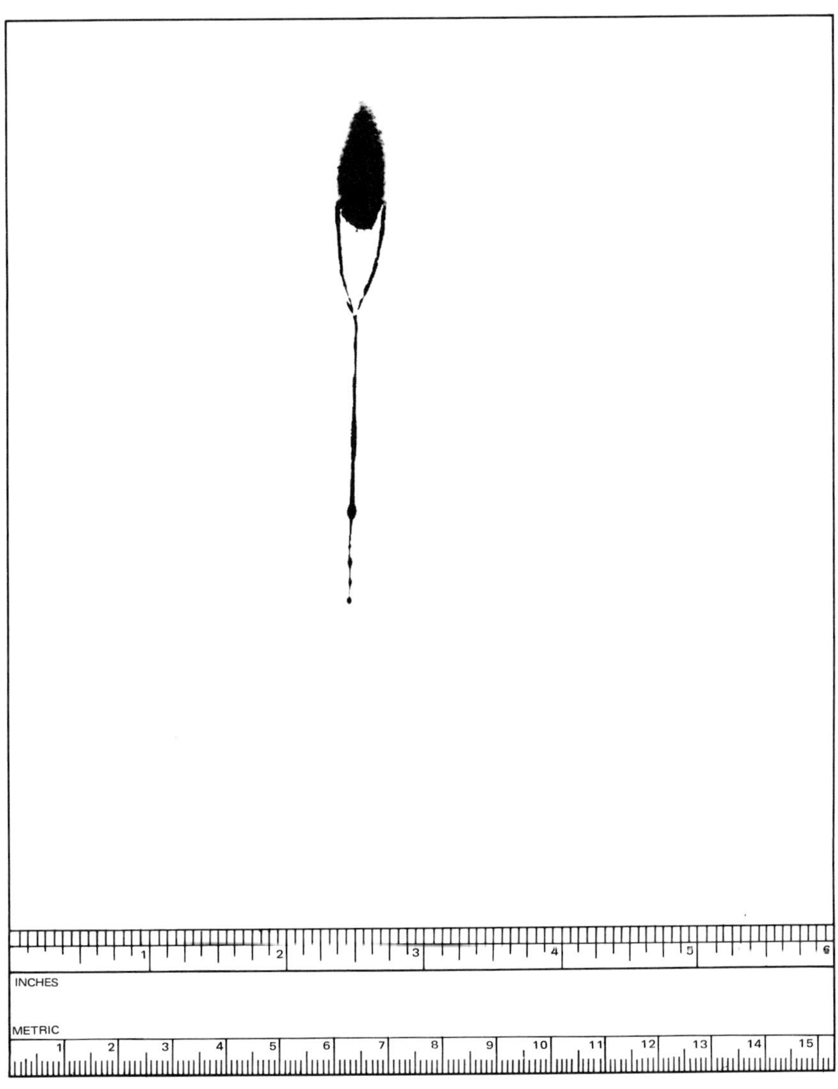

FIG. 5.10 Pattern of a single drop of human blood that fell 42 inches and struck hard, smooth cardboard at 20 degrees.

FIG. 5.11 Pattern of a single drop of human blood that fell 42 inches and struck hard, smooth cardboard at 10 degrees.

FIG. 5.12 Pattern of a single drop of human blood that fell 42 inches and struck a soft blotter at 30 degrees.

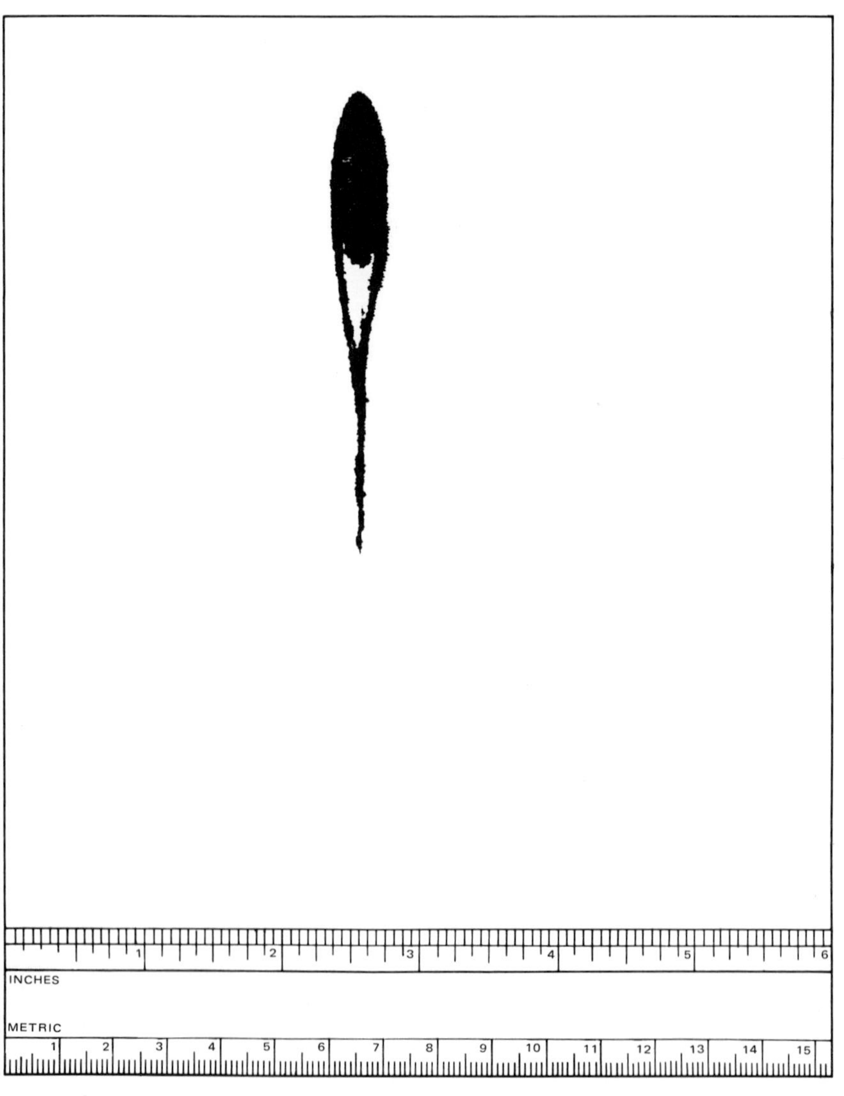

FIG. 5.13 Pattern of a single drop of human blood that fell 42 inches and struck a soft blotter at 20 degrees.

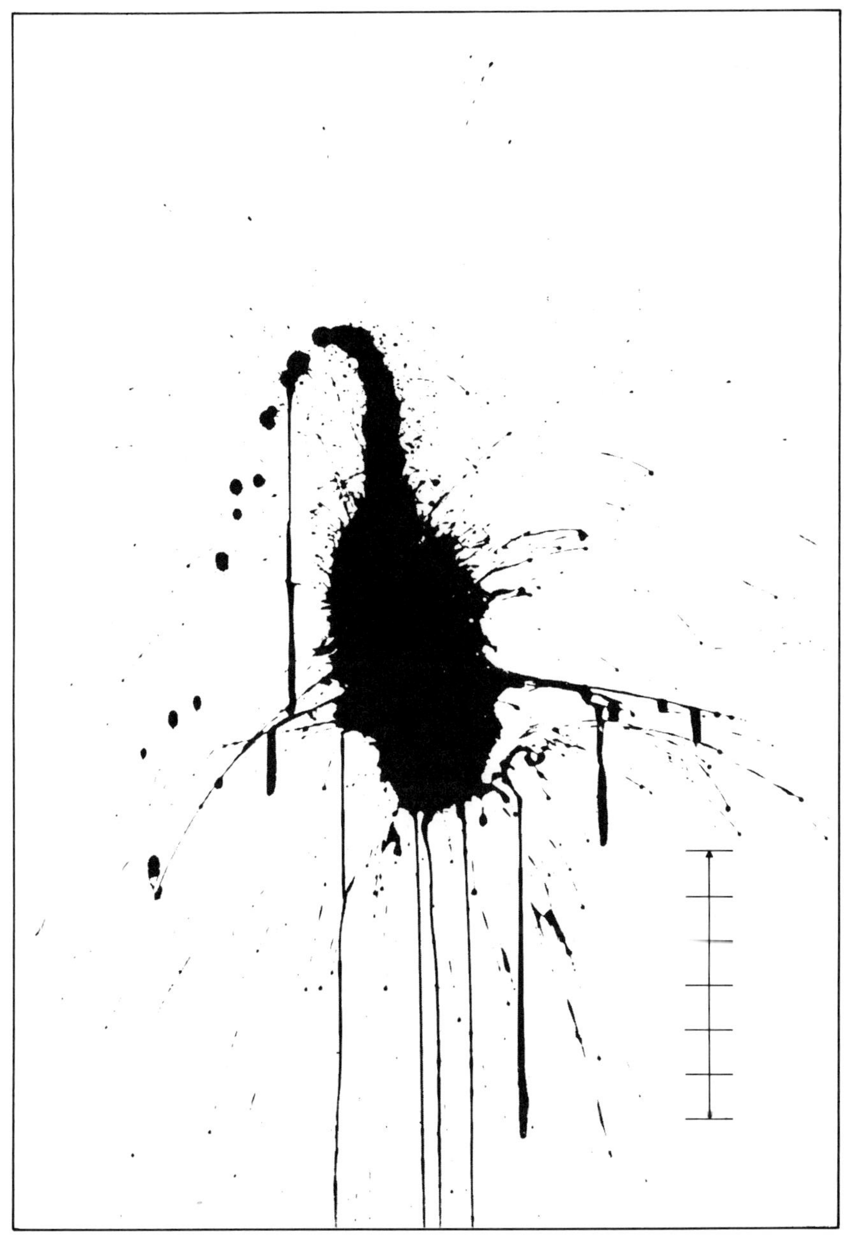

FIG. 5.14 Large bloodstain pattern produced when 10 ml of human blood were thrown slightly upward onto a vertical hard, smooth piece of cardboard (6" ruler).

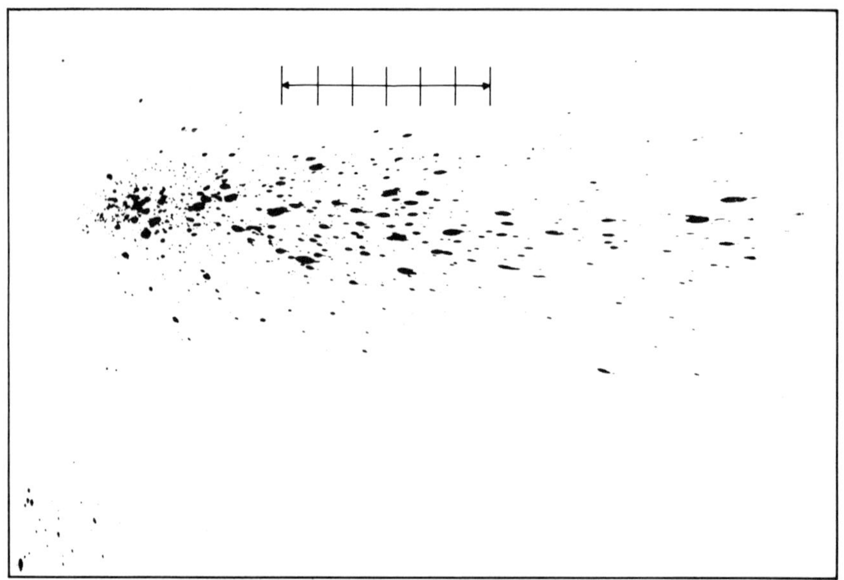

FIG. 5.15 Overall stain pattern produced by a 25-feet-per-second impact to human blood. Impact was from the left slightly above this horizontal target (6" ruler).

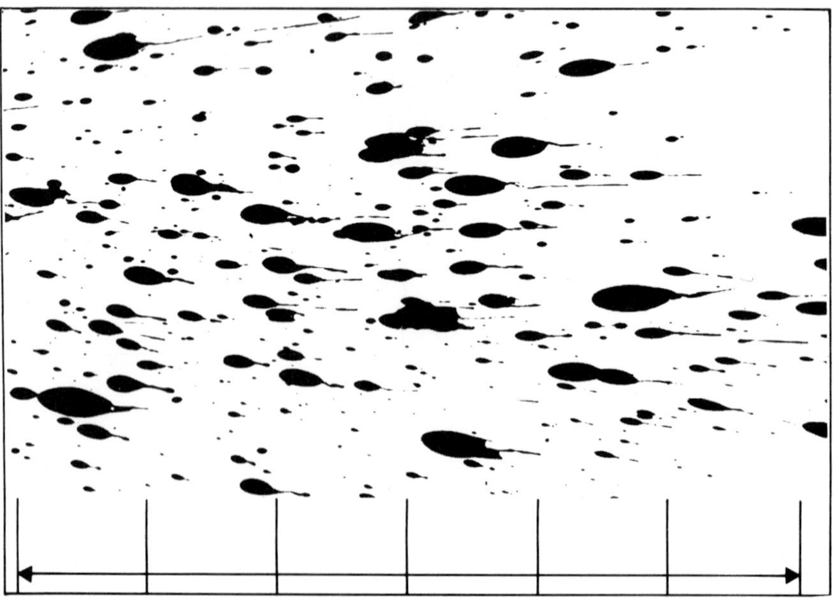

FIG. 5.16 Close-up detail of the central area of Fig. 5.15 (6" ruler).

Semen. Examinations will generally be conducted in sex crimes, or whenever it is possible that a sexual assault has taken place. Handling of the victim is discussed in a later chapter; however, the investigator should be aware that seminal fluid or traces are likely to be present at the scene on bedding, disposed undergarments, or other clothing. In order to prove the presence of spermatozoa, at least one cell (and preferably more) must be identified complete with head, neckpiece, and tail intact. For this reason it is imperative that material suspected of containing semen traces not be mishandled or improperly folded, for friction is likely to break up the cells. If a semen stain has "crusted," it should *not* be broken up.

The most effective way of determining the presence of semen is to use an ultraviolet lamp in a darkened room. Seminal stains will give off a bright white or bluish-white color under the lamp. However, any fluorescence or glow in an area where semen is suspected to be present should be examined, for the presence of other matter may be mixed with the semen, thereby causing a discoloration.

The presence of seminal cells may be used to prove *corpus delecti* (the fact that a crime has occurred) or, through examination of garments, that a suspect recently engaged in sexual activity. In some instances it may be possible to exclude a suspect through examination of semen, if the examination shows that it is dissimilar from that found on the victim or the scene. Semen may be grouped, just like blood, if the individual secreting the fluid is a *secretor,* a fact which is true of approximately 80 percent of the population. (A secretor is an individual of blood group A, B, or AB who secretes the antigens characteristic of the blood groups in bodily fluids, such as saliva and semen.)

If semen is present in liquid form, it may be collected with an eyedropper and placed in a test tube. In order to facilitate collection, distilled water should be added to moist stains. In most cases, the semen will be dried, and the investigator should deliver the stain, intact, to the crime laboratory. If it is necessary to fold the article, care should be taken not to fold over a stain; it is also advisable to place clean paper between the folds.

Stains. Those stains other than semen may also prove valuable in an investigation. Urine, perspiration, and saliva may yield certain pieces of information important in proving or disproving a theory. For example, saliva may be analyzed to determine blood type.

The collection of stains is similar to the method used to collect semen. Both urine and perspiration will fluoresce under ultraviolet light.

Fibers. These may be examined to determine their chemical properties and to discover any external trace evidence that may be present. This evidence might include blood, semen, alcohol, or any other substance that came in contact with the fiber. Prior to a chemical analysis, fibers are generally examined microscopically or by other means of instrumentation. If the article is somewhat large, a chalk or crayon mark may be drawn around the area to be examined. Small fibers should be recovered with a pair of tweezers and placed in an envelope or other suitable container. We will discuss the microscopic analysis of fibers in greater detail in a later section.

Paint. Paint exhibits certain physical qualities which enable the chemist to conduct a comparative analysis, or to identify a particular brand or type. Paint chips are particularly valuable in hit-and-run cases; laboratory analysis can provide valuable investigative leads toward the identification of the year, make, and color of the hit-and-run vehicle. If paint fragments are present at the scene of the crime, they should be collected and stored in an envelope or other suitable container.

Care must be taken in obtaining paint samples from a surface. A wooden tongue depressor (or a sharp steel knife, if use of the depressor is infeasible) should be used wherever possible. Paint should be chipped rather than scraped, since scraping may destroy the layers of the paint. If the paint is on an automobile, it is wise to have a laboratory technician remove it so as not to destroy the possibility of instrumentation analysis.

The comparison of paint samples can be used to link the suspect's auto or a tool to the scene. In searching the crime scene, the investigator should consider the probability of such evidence being present, and make an effort to ascertain its probable location. For example, in a hit-and-run case the victim may be thrown quite a distance from the point of impact, and this must be kept in mind by the investigator. In many cases, the crime scene is considered to be the immediate area surrounding the victim.

Paint traces are likely to appear on the clothing of a burglary suspect, and laboratory analysis may be used to link him to the crime scene. This may also hold true of a burglar's tools, which should be examined if at all possible. In many cases the suspect is apprehended some distance from the crime scene, and the strength of the case rests on linking him to the scene.

Trace Evidence. Any material that may have been imparted to the scene by the suspect or imparted to the suspect at the scene is considered trace evidence. This may include dust, dirt, powder, and the like, and can be an invaluable aid to the investigator. Chemical analysis of trace evidence is likely to provide information concerning its location (perhaps the type of soil in the area); or its chemical nature (which may be compared with material in the suspect's possession). This analysis may also link a suspect to the crime scene through residue traces on his clothing or body.

Poisons, Alcohol, and Narcotics. These may all be identified through chemical or other laboratory tests. In many cases the nature of the crime may be evident, thus aiding the investigator in his examination. However, upon initial examination some deaths appear to be the result of natural causes (especially in poisoning cases) and the investigator should take this into account.

Overdose cases have become quite common, and the investigator should be aware that criminal liability may be involved, especially if a minor is concerned. An examination of the body may reveal telltale needle marks, and a thorough search may result in the discovery of narcotic traces or implements.

DOCUMENTS

In an age where forgery and alteration are not uncommon, the examination of documents has become a highly sophisticated specialty in police work and an invaluable aid to the investigator. The types of examination a document examiner may conduct are:

1. Examination of writing materials, such as pen, ink, pencil, typewriter.
2. Examination of document or article.
3. Discovery of alterations, erasures, and obliterations.
4. The "age" of writing or impression.
5. The "order" in which the writing was entered.
6. Identification of the author, or instrument used.

Generally, document examination is conducted visually, microscopically, or chemically. Because handwriting and document analysis do not offer the specificity that other areas of forensic science do, there are a number of problems of which the investigator should be aware. To begin with, handwriting analysis is not an exact science, and success in this area depends largely on the examiner. However, this should not preclude use of the examiner's services, for his testimony is acceptable in court, and he is likely to provide other information which can be of immense value. In the case of mechanical impressions, such as those made by typewriter or printing press, virtual certainty of origin can be established. Also, the document examiner may be able to link paper, ink, or other material to the suspect, because these materials generally exhibit certain characteristics capable of identification.

An examination of the scene in apparent suicides is likely to result in the discovery of notes. These should be collected and an attempt made to gather other samples of the deceased's handwriting for comparison. Keep in mind that samples should be numerous; one or two items may not be sufficient. If a typewriter has been used, it may be advisable to forward samples of the typeface to the laboratory. (See Fig. 5.17.)

In collecting physical evidence of this nature, the investigator should place his initials on the back of the material in a location that will not obstruct analysis of its content. If possible, the paper should be kept in its original state, with no additional folds made.

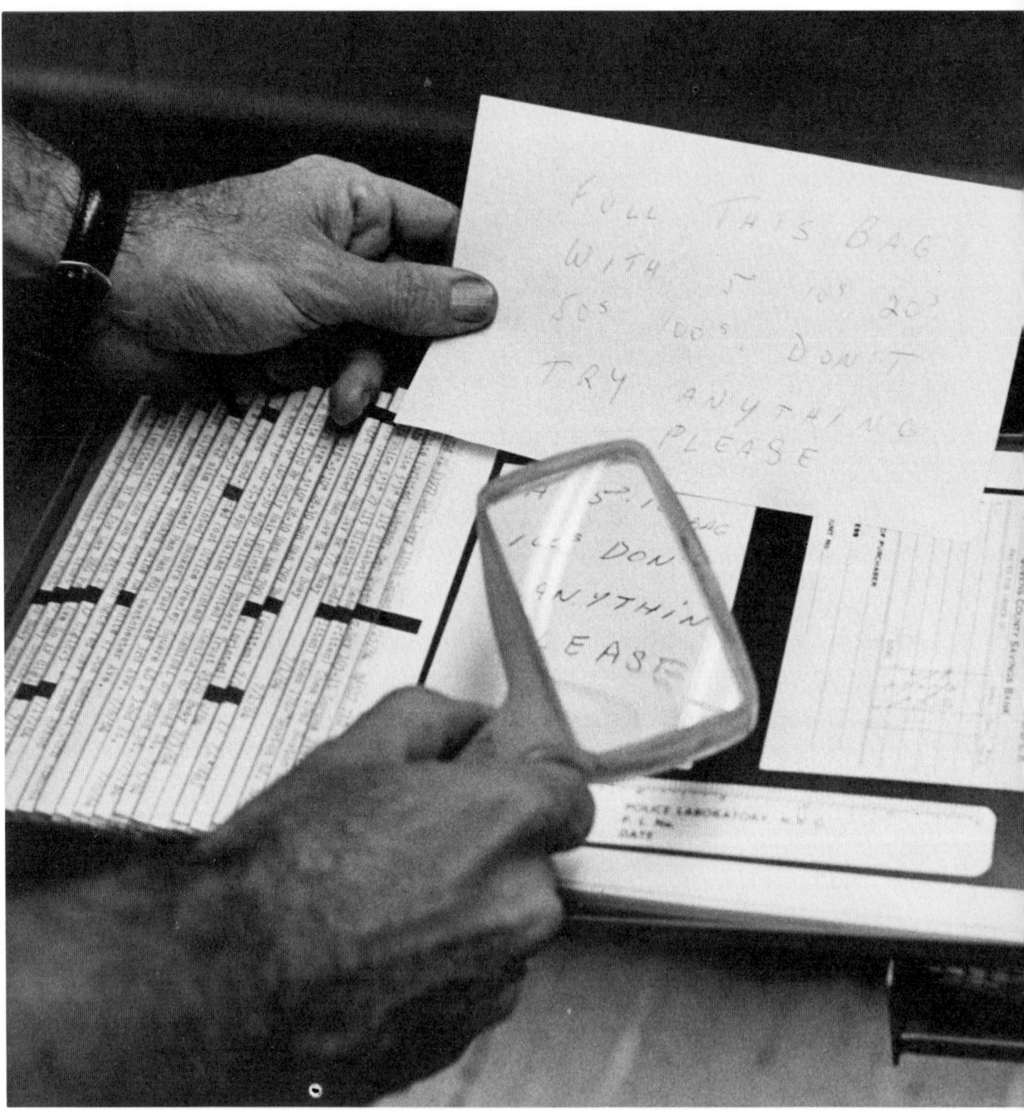

FIG. 5.17 Most laboratories keep a file of notes and samples of letters in kidnapping and threat cases. These can be used for purposes of comparison, and may result in the identification of a suspect. (Courtesy of SPRING 3100, New York City Police Department.)

At all times the investigator should keep in mind that this form of evidence can be exceptionally useful. Torn paper may be matched with its companion pieces; latent prints may be available; residue particles may exhibit information concerning the original location of the material; and in some instances, the emotional state of the writer may be theorized.

In handling a written document the investigator must be alert to the presence of alterations or erasures, attempts at patching, uncertainty of signature, the use of different inks, additions, deletions or crowding, and apparent differences in writing.

In cases involving fraud or forgery, these factors may not appear obvious. Nevertheless, the surrounding circumstances may indicate a need for further examination by the crime laboratory.

FINGERPRINTS

Fingerprints, palmprints, and footprints are the most accepted form of physical identification. Essentially, the unique characteristics of a print have been accepted by the courts in establishing identity. This acceptance is based on a probability factor, as in fact are all forms of identity evidence. However, science has shown that the probability of two persons having exactly the same fingerprints is so minute as to be conclusive. Since palm and footprints are of similar value in terms of identification (although they are different in classification than fingerprints), discussion here shall be limited to fingerprints.

Latent fingerprints are formed by the formation of perspiration and oils on the friction ridges of the fingertips. Often invisible to the naked eye, they may be found on any smooth nonporous surface. The usual technique in searching for fingerprints is to use fingerprint powder, "dusting" suspected surfaces. In some instances special laboratory techniques may be used to develop them; the presence of fingerprint impressions in soft substances such as clay or tar requires special handling.

In no case should an attempt be made to lift fingerprints before they have been properly processed and photographed. This practice records the evidence in case it is destroyed while being removed.

Dusting techniques to discover latent fingerprints will depend on the particular area under examination. If grease, blood, or some other sticky substance is present, it may not be advisable to dust. Keep in mind that dusting is used to bring out the print for identification, and this may not be necessary if the latent print exhibits ridge patterns clearly.

Dusting for Fingerprints. Fingerprint powders are available in various colors; on light surfaces a grey or black powder should be used. The powder is usually applied with a brush or "feather duster." A small amount of powder is *lightly* brushed over the suspected area. Care should be taken not to destroy or mar the fingerprint with excessive pressure. This is likely to occur on firm surfaces, such as glass or formica. (See Figs. 5.18 and 5.19.)

FIG. 5.18 When dusting for fingerprints on glass or other transparent surface, it is advisable to hold a piece of paper or cardboard behind the suspect area. This approach makes the latent prints more visible and reduces the chances of brushing away the prints. (Courtesy of SPRING 3100, New York City Police Department.)

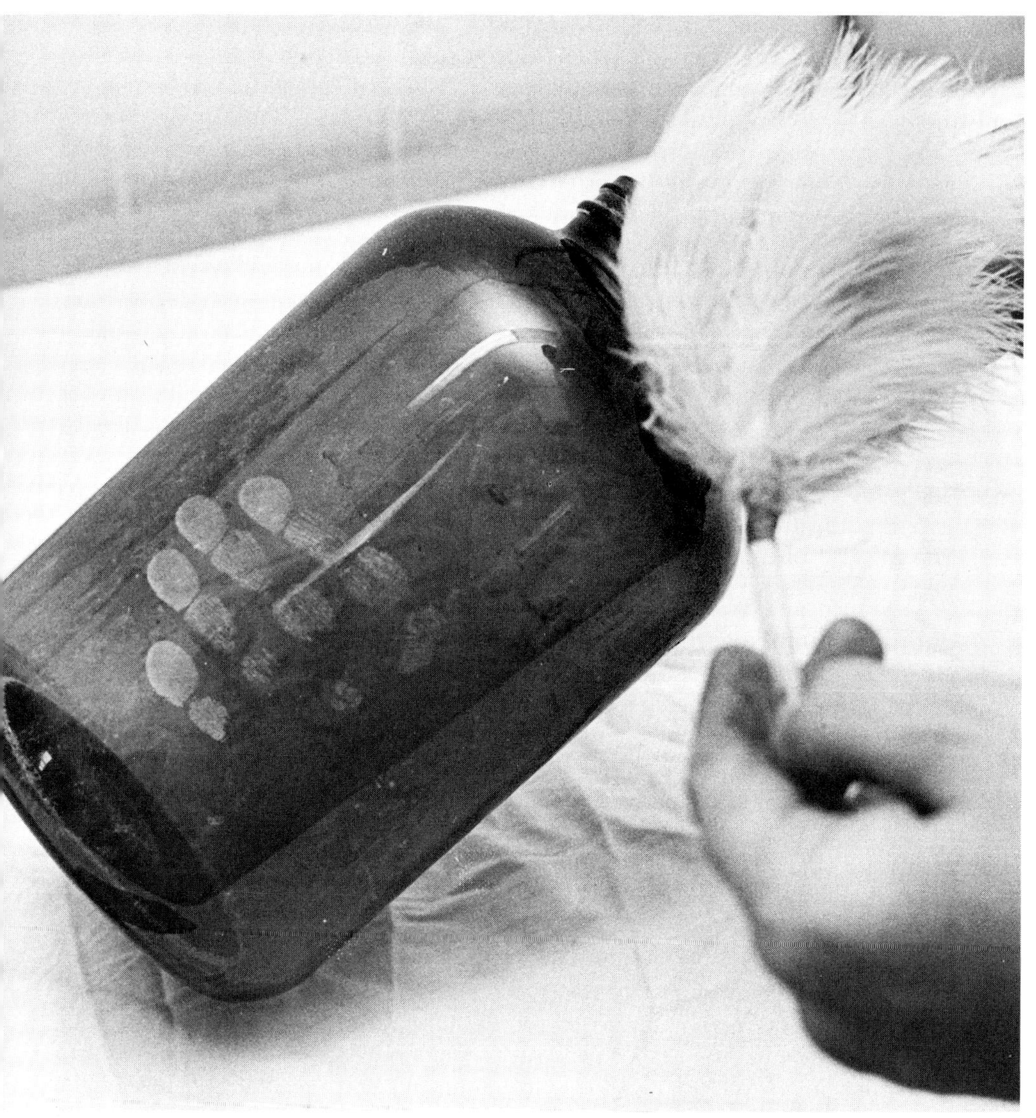

FIG. 5.19 When dusting for fingerprints on glass, a soft feather brush should generally be used. This reduces the chances of obliterating the print. (Courtesy of SPRING 3100, New York City Police Department.)

In all cases care must be taken not to use too little or too much powder. The goal is to develop a print which can be identified. Too little powder may result in inadequate detail, and too much powder might cause a "pointing" or "joining" of the ridge lines. It is always better to use a small amount of powder at first, for this can be corrected easily, whereas too much powder is likely to destroy the print entirely. If more than one fingerprint is available, care should be taken not to destroy an adjoining print while processing.

Special Techniques. If the suspect material is paper, unfinished wood, cloth, or a similar substance, the iodine fuming technique is likely to generate more favorable results than dusting. This method may also be used on firm surfaces, although it has certain disadvantages. Essentially, iodine fuming involves using an iodine vapor to bring out the latent print. While this technique is not especially difficult, it is generally advisable to have it performed by a laboratory technician who is familiar with the method.

In addition to iodine fuming, a number of other special techniques may be employed, including silver chloride development and the use of osmium chloride. The method of using nin-hydrin (which is a liquid spray), is popular for use on paper. However, these techniques should be used by a trained technician.

Photographing Fingerprints. Because of their peculiar nature, some mention should be made of the photography of fingerprints. The use of a special fingerprint camera is essential for the fine detail which is required cannot usually be obtained with the average camera. The goal in this type of photography is to produce a picture in which the ridge lines are clear enough for identification.

Since the light or glare from the surface will complicate photography quite often, the photographer must experiment with the illumination until favorable results are obtained. If the print is impressed in a soft material, indirect lighting may be advisable to produce shadows and facilitate ridge differentiation.

If the fingerprint is on glass or some other transparent material, it may be advisable to hold a white piece of paper behind the image, thus bringing out the image. If the fingerprint is on a bottle, the inside may be blackened by burning a strip of magnesium oxide within the bottle. Of course, white powder should be used for dusting in this instance. Another technique would be to fill the bottle with a colored liquid to bring out the print. Keep in mind that the contents of the container should be examined before using either of the above methods.

Fingerprints on colored surfaces may result in photographic problems, but these can usually be corrected by using filters.

Lifting Latent Fingerprints. Upon completion of dusting and photographing, the fingerprint should be preserved. If it appears on a movable object such as a bottle or weapon, it may be advisable to leave the print in place and protect it by covering it with transparent tape. Care should be taken in applying the tape so as not to destroy the image.

If the fingerprint appears on an immovable object such as a wall, or if its preservation in place is infeasible, it can be lifted and stored. The fingerprint kit should contain a role of transparent tape and various "backing papers" of different colors designed for this purpose. If black powder has been used, a white backing paper will be needed, and the reverse is true (see Fig. 5.20).

FIG. 5.20 On dark surfaces a white fingerprint powder should be employed, and black fingerprint tape used for removal of the print. (Courtesy of SPRING 3100, New York City Police Department.)

In applying the tape, the end is placed close to the print, but not covering it. The tape is carefully smoothed out over the image, taking care to press out any air bubbles as they emerge (Fig. 5.21), and then carefully removed and placed on the backing paper. The paper should be marked with the location, case number, time and date of removal, and the name of the individual who removed it.

Some departments prefer to mount fingerprints on plates or clear backing. If this is the case, the same procedure is used. The advantage in using a mounted print lies in comparing the suspect print with other fingerprints.

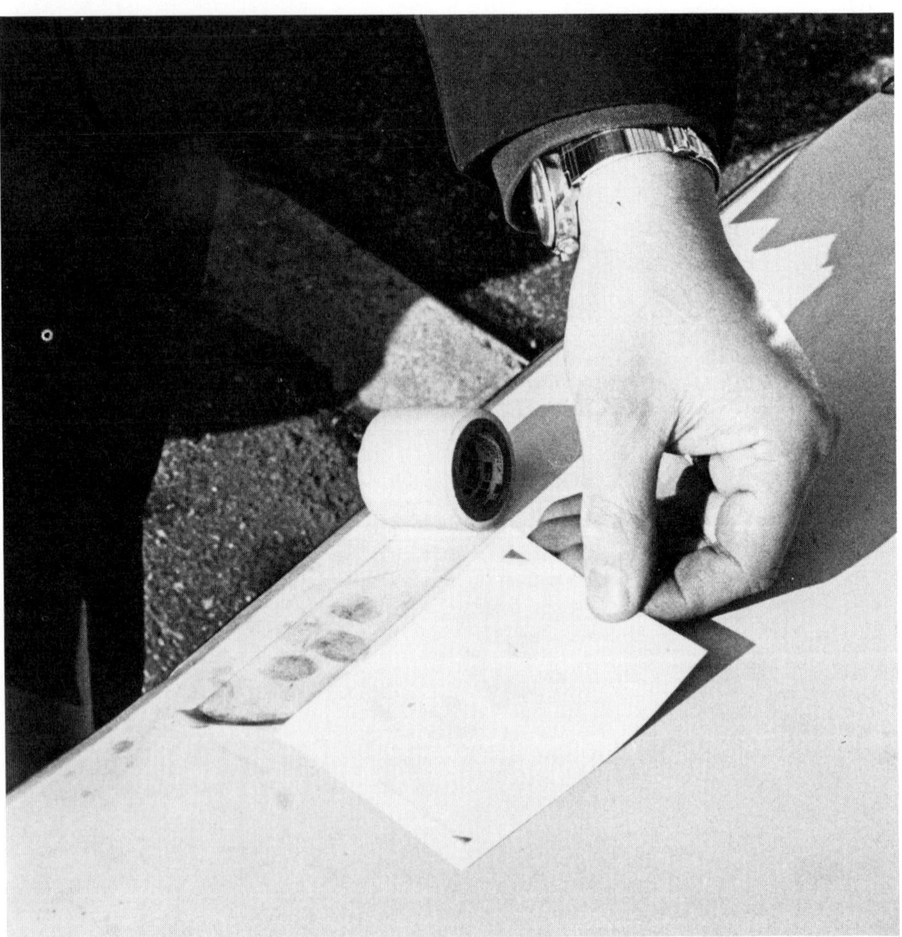

FIG. 5.21 Fingerprint tape should be applied carefully and smoothed out over the print, taking care to press out any air bubbles that might appear. (Courtesy of SPRING 3100, New York City Police Department.)

The Use of Fingerprints. Fingerprints offer a wealth of possibilities to the investigator. In addition to the identification factor involved in a particular crime, they may be used to identify suspects in other crimes, to eliminate suspects, and to conduct searches for suspects. Development of the computer has increased the identification capability greatly, and introduction of a computer-based single-digit classification system is near at hand. This in itself should revolutionize the field of criminal investigation.

In order to maximize the benefits of fingerprint identification, the investigator should be aware of a number of techniques. Among these are the use of elimination prints, the criteria for a usable print, and the search techniques involved in developing a list of suspects.

Each fingerprint kit should be equipped with an ample supply of standard fingerprint forms to be used at the crime scene to fingerprint anyone who had access to the area. Generally, police officers need not be included, but if a police officer arrived on the scene and gave first aid or touched property, it is advisable to take a set of elimination prints. Elimination prints are those used by the fingerprint technician to exclude the fingerprints of anyone who had legitimate access to the scene, and therefore is not suspect. The use of elimination prints greatly simplifies the technician's task and increases the probability of his being successful. Also, elimination prints may be used to determine the movements of individuals at the scene, which may help in checking statements. An example of this is where an individual denies being in a certain room or area, yet his fingerprints link him to the location. Elimination prints should also be secured of persons who may not have been present during the commission of the crime, but who had prior access to the scene (such as the occupants of an apartment in a burglary investigation).

Fingerprints are classified on the basis of ridge counts, which are formed by the papillary lines on the finger (Fig. 5.22). Each print is classified as either an arch, loop, or whorl, identification being made on the basis of individual characteristics in the pattern. The fingerprint expert must testify to various points of identification which exist in a comparison of fingerprints. Generally, the courts have held that twelve points of identification are necessary to establish an indisputable identification.[3]

While the investigator need not be familiar with the techniques involved in fingerprint classification, a basic understanding of the procedure will enable him to evaluate the worth of fingerprints at the scene.

Under present systems, fingerprints are classified according to a ten-digit system; fingerprints of all ten fingers are necessary to conduct a records search. However, a number of police departments have been somewhat successful in using a modified five-digit system, and in some circumstances individuals have been identified with a single latent impression. The expertise of some fingerprint experts is phenomenal; their capacity to recognize individual prints, as we might recognize the facial characteristics of an individual, enables them to identify suspects at a glance. Nevertheless, under the present system a fingerprint search can be a time-consuming activity, and the investigator should make every effort to provide the technician with as much evidence as possible. Do not assume that because one latent fingerprint has been discovered, the job is finished.

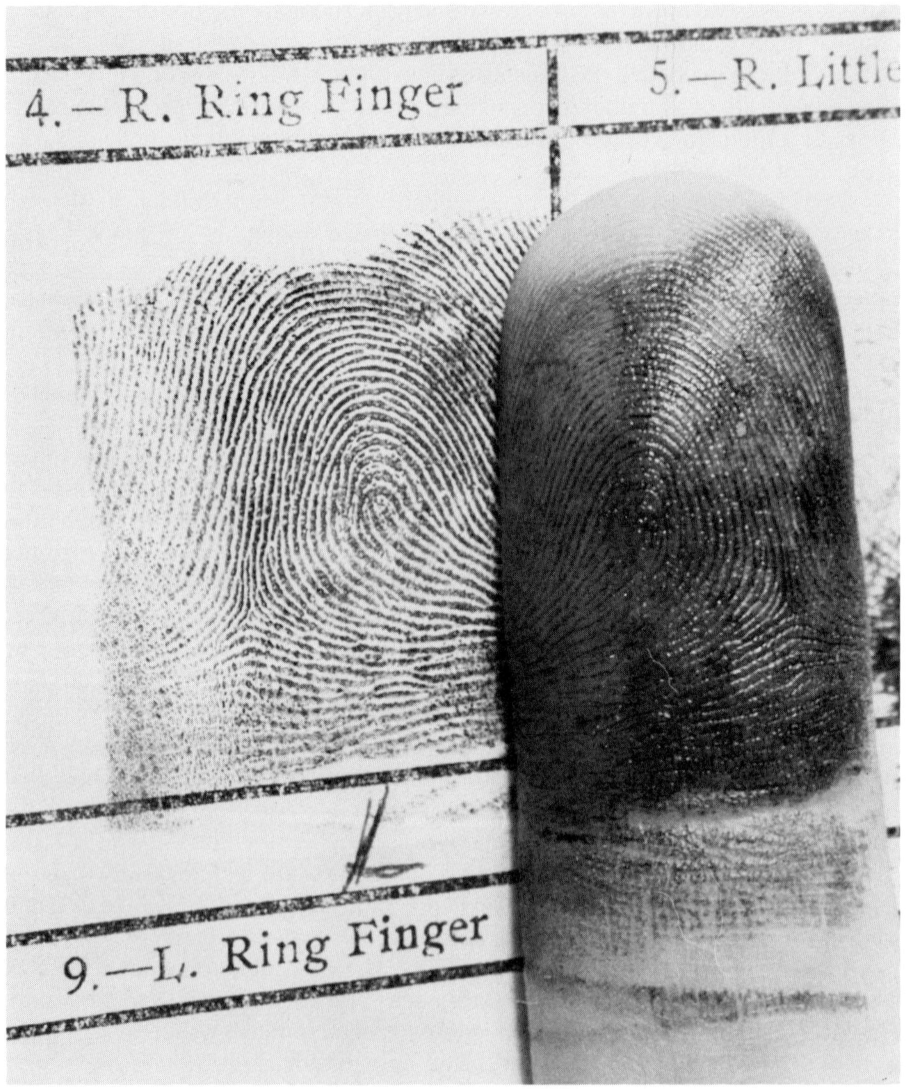

FIG. 5.22 Fingerprints are classified on the basis of ridge lines, which are formed by the papillary lines on the finger. (Courtesy of SPRING 3100, New York City Police Department.)

FIREARMS

The identification of firearms, bullets, and cartridge cases is an important aspect of many investigations. The term ballistics, which is generally used to identify examination of firearms, is something of a misnomer, for it refers to the science of the motion of projectiles. However, the term has come to be accepted in the rubric of police work and thus will be used here. In this sense ballistics refers to the examination and identification of firearms, bullets, cartridge cases, and other shells. Interior ballistics involves the examination of the functioning and internal aspects of the weapon itself.

Through examination of the bore of a rifle or pistol, an expert may be able to link a bullet to the firearm from which it was discharged. By examining the chamber, the breech (or base where the firing pin is located), the firing pin, or the extractor and ejector, an expert can usually link a cartridge to the weapon. This is extremely important in those cases in which a shotgun or smooth bore weapon is used.

Bullet identification is made by comparing the striations in the barrel, which are unique in all weapons. In addition, the calibre weapon employed and, in some instances, the model of firearm may be identified through ballistics examination.

Examination of bullet patterns and points of entry provide a rich source of information. Investigation may reveal the approximate distance from the weapon to the point of impact; the relationship of bullet holes may be useful in determining the action of the crime; and the location from which the shot was fired may be ascertained by tracing the trajectory of the bullet from the point of entry, or impact. If a bullet has passed through an object such as wood or glass, it is possible to determine the side from which it was fired.

Types of Firearms. As a general rule, firearms may be classified in one of four categories for identification: (1) pistols, (2) revolvers, (3) rifles, and (4) shotguns.

A pistol is a short-barrel hand weapon, and is usually of the automatic clip or magazine-fed type, or the breach "break" type, where the chamber is exposed by means of a hinged barrel. The most common types of pistols encountered in crimes are the .45 calibre automatic (which is used by the Armed Forces), and .22 and .25 calibre automatics, which have become extremely popular handguns in the United States.

Revolvers are the most common firearm used in crime because they are readily available and inexpensive. The types and makes of revolvers in use today are too numerous to mention, and range from the inexpensive "Saturday night special" (which is usually a poorly made .25 calibre weapon) to the costly weapons used in competition. The revolver is identified by a revolving cylinder, in which the chambers rotate into alignment with the barrel. The cylinder may be loaded either by rotating it outward (which is the more common form), by the breach break method, or by rotating the cylinder in the weapon and loading one shell at a time.

A rifle is defined simply as a long-barreled weapon having a series of "lands and grooves" in the barrel. Rifles may be single-shot, multiple, or automatic, simple or complex. Automatic weapons, such as submachine guns, fall into this category. The use of the rifle in crime is decreasing; it is too large a weapon. However, the use of a "sawed-off" weapon is not uncommon, and in recent years sniper attacks and assaults on policemen involving rifles have been increasing.

Shotguns are classified on the basis of their barrels, which are smooth and lack the "lands and grooves" common to the rifle. They may be single-shot or of various types, including double-barreled or automatic weapons. A shotgun fires a variety of "loads," ranging anywhere from a single "ball" (slug) to multiple pellets (shot). It is virtually impossible to link the weapon to the material fired because of the smooth barrel and lack of identifying characteristics on fired ammunition, although in rare cases this identification has been accomplished. An examination of the shell casing, however, can usually result in a positive identification of the weapon from which it was fired.

Care must be taken in handling firearms, and all weapons should be considered loaded until they have been examined. Since a major problem at the crime scene is the interest in a recovered firearm, the investigator should keep in mind that the weapon is not a showpiece and unnecessary handling must be prevented. If a firearm has been discovered, it should be photographed in place.

The parts of interest to the crime laboratory in examining a firearm are the barrel and its interior mechanism, as well as the exterior areas where fingerprints are likely to appear. Thus, in recovering a firearm, care must be taken not to destroy such evidence. If the firearm must be unloaded, the "action" or moving parts of the weapon should be used only a minimum number of times to assure that it is safe to handle. In no case should an attempt be made to dismantle or handle the internal parts of the weapon. If the firearm is of the cylinder type, each cartridge, whether live or expended, should be removed individually and numbered correspondingly with its location in the cylinder (see Fig. 5.23). Before this the firearm should be dusted for fingerprints. However, if cartridges are in a magazine or clip, they should not be removed.

In picking up a firearm, nothing should be inserted in the barrel; in the case of a handgun it is advisable to pick it up on the serrated handle if one is present, or by the barrel with two fingers. Of course, care must be taken to keep it pointed in a safe direction. In handling rifles a similar procedure may be used; it may be picked up with two hands, generally at the base of the stock and by the barrel.

Firearms should be stored in a container or tied to some form of backing. The weapon should be recorded for identification, and the following information listed: manufacturer and model number, serial number, calibre or gauge, and any other markings present. The person collecting the evidence should scratch his initials on an area of the weapon that will not affect the laboratory examination.

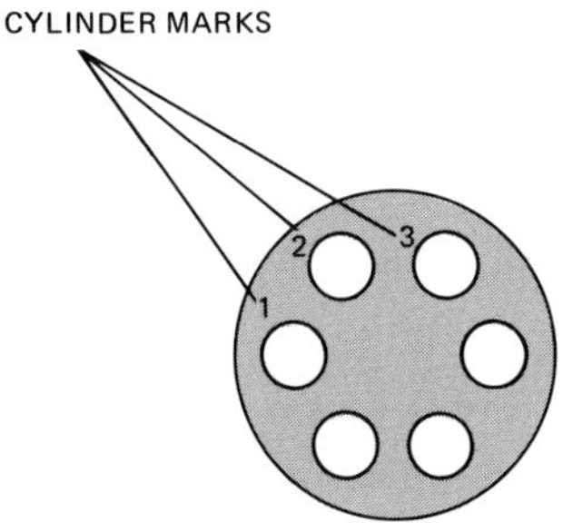

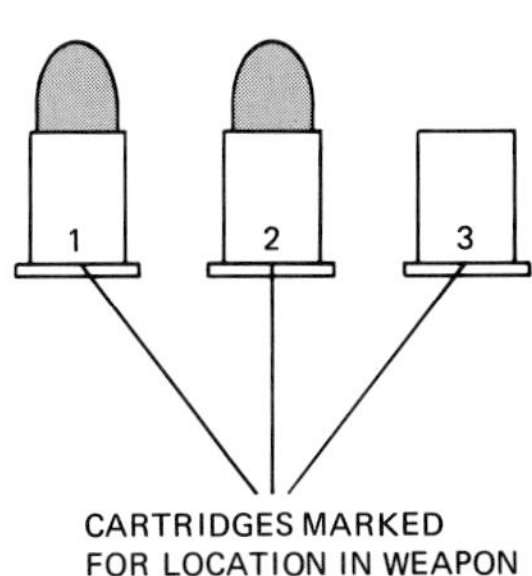

FIG. 5.23 Identification marking.

Cartridges and Shells. Cartridges, which are made up of a bullet, shell casing, and powder, and shotgun shells, which are made up of the "load," casing and powder, should be handled with care. To begin with, the location of expended shells or casings should be carefully recorded, for this information may be of value in determining the location of the weapon when it was fired. The location of shells or casings may indicate that either an automatic or semiautomatic weapon was used, or if a revolver were used, that it was reloaded. Because ejected cases may travel quite a distance, a careful search of the area may be necessary to uncover them.

The recovery of bullets is also of importance, and a thorough search of the scene may be necessary to discover their points of entry. If the victim has been struck by a bullet, the investigator should be sure to recover the bullet from the hospital or morgue. An investigator should be on hand during this removal in order to identify and record it. If a bullet is lodged in a wall or other location, care must be taken when removing it to avoid destroying distinguishing marks. A bullet should not be pried out with a knife or other object, but rather the area around the point of entry must carefully be removed until the bullet has been recovered.

Shell casings should generally be marked on the side, and bullets should be marked on the base. All that is necessary for identification are the initials of the person who recovered the item (see Fig. 5.24). Some departments do not mark bullets or casings, storing them instead in a marked envelope. Any additional bullets or cases recovered should be stored in separate containers. The investigator must remember at all times that lead is soft, and undue handling or friction can alter its shape.

Further Aspects of Firearms Investigation. In addition to firearm and cartridge examinations, the ballistics expert may be able to provide further information of interest to the investigation. A major consideration in many crimes is the distance from which the shot was fired. By conducting comparative tests the laboratory can assist the investigator in cases where suicide or a claim of self-defense is involved. In addition to determining distance by studying shotgun patterns, the ballistics expert can often conduct an analysis of powder patterns resulting from the discharge of rifled firearms. Generally, the further the weapon is from the target, the larger will be the pattern. A determination of distance can be considerably accurate, depending on certain circumstances. The most accurate predictions can be made if the same weapon, and ammunition from the same source as the suspect ammunition, are used. For this reason, the investigator should attempt to obtain any available unfired cartridges. If neither the original weapon nor the ammunition is available, tests may be conducted (although with less accurate results) with similar weapons and ammunition.

Powder patterns are likely to become imbedded in the cloth of the victim's wearing apparel, and they too can be developed chemically to determine distance. For this reason, clothing should be secured and marked as evidence.

If a suspect in a shooting has been apprehended shortly after the incident, a comparison of residue on the weapon may link it to him. In the case of handguns, thread, fibers, and other trace evidence are likely to be transferred from the sus-

EXPENDED CARTRIDGE MARKING

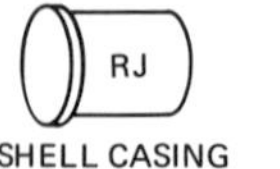

FIG. 5.24 Initials of the person who recovered them are marked on the side of a shell casing and on the base of a bullet.

pect's pocket or clothing to the weapon. Rifles and larger weapons coming into contact with clothing are likely to pick up trace evidence which can also be identified. In the event of such an occurrence, the investigator should attempt to secure the clothing the suspect was wearing at the time of the shooting, or any other apparel in which the weapon may have been carried. This is also important for any cases or objects in which the weapon may have been stored.

The paraffin or dermal nitrate test is sometimes used to determine whether or not an individual has recently fired a weapon. This test is based on the principle that firing a weapon results in the transfer of nitrates to the hand during discharge. It should be noted that this test has not been completely accepted by experts, there being some question as to its validity, and some crime laboratories have abandoned the use of powder tests. Neutron activation analysis and atomic absorption have also been used by some laboratories to test for firearm discharge residues.

If a bullet has passed through an object, visual scientific examination may be used to determine its direction of travel. In heavy substances this procedure is relatively simple, for the bullet generally expands while passing through an object and leaves a larger hole opposite the point of entry. If the bullet has passed through glass, an examination of the area will reveal striations originating at the point of impact (see Fig. 5.25). If more than one bullet hole appears in glass, a determination of the first hole can be made by examining the existing radial fractures. These fractures, which emanate from the point of impact, and the fractures from the second bullet will stop when they come into contact with radial or cross fractures from the first hole (see Fig. 5.26).

Reconstruction of the scene, in actuality or in the form of a model, will often provide the investigator with information that may not have been readily apparent. Diagrams and sketches might also prove valuable in establishing facts.

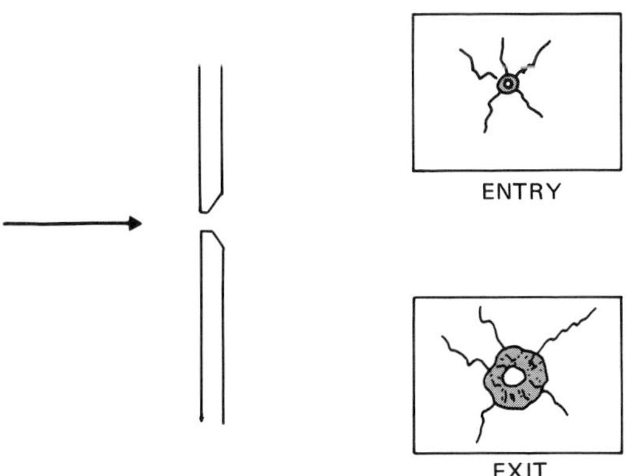

FIG. 5.25 Bullet holes in glass.

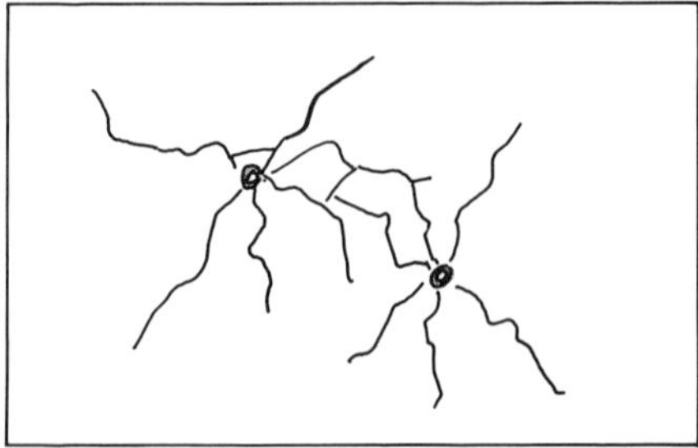

FIG. 5.26 Two bullet holes in glass. Radial fractures of the hole on the right stop when they strike fractures of the other hole, indicating that the hole on the left appeared first.

WEAPONS

The crime laboratory may be called on to examine various weapons used in a crime. In addition to revealing fingerprints, an examination of the weapon may show its relationship to the wound, produce physical trace evidence that may link the weapon to the victim or suspect, or provide facts of identification that will lead to the perpetrator.

As in all cases, this evidence should be handled and stored carefully. An accurate physical description of the weapon is necessary for identification; and if possible the evidence should be initialled by the person recovering it.

INSTRUMENTATION

Most well-equipped crime laboratories have a number of special instruments to aid the investigator. Some knowledge of the capabilities of these instruments enables the investigator to be more thorough in his examination of the crime scene, and to be aware of the value of certain types of physical evidence. The most common instruments found in the laboratory are listed below. However, keep in mind that this is not an exhaustive list; it would be wise for the investigator to be familiar with the instrumentation procedures in his own department's laboratory.

Spectrographs and Spectrophotometers. These may be used to examine metal, paint, soil, glass, and a variety of other materials to determine their physical composition and to make comparisons.

X-ray. The x-ray may be utilized to examine the internal aspects of an item without disturbing its physical condition. Its use is extremely valuable in determining the location of bullets in an object, or in studying suspected bombs.

Microscopes. The nature and range of microscopes in crime laboratories vary considerably. In addition to the comparison microscope, standard, medical, and photomicroscopes are also used to examine evidence.

Polygraph. While the polygraph, or lie detector as it is more commonly known, may not be an instrument used directly in the crime laboratory, it is one of the tools which the investigator may call on to assist in gathering evidence. Although the results of a polygraph examination are not admissible evidence in court, the test can be used in a number of ways throughout the investigative process.

PHOTOGRAPHIC

In addition to photographing the crime scene, the laboratory may be called on to assist the investigator in preparing exhibits, enlarging photographs, or examining pictures for detail. The crime laboratory also often photographs deceased persons or wounds. Quite often comparison photography is used to establish identity, or to prepare photographs for distribution to other police departments or specific persons in attempting to locate an individual or property. In some of the larger police departments the photographic unit may be separate from the crime laboratory, but a close working relationship should exist in all cases.

TOOL MARK COMPARISON

Quite often the crime laboratory is able to match a tool mark with the tool that inflicted it. Generally, tool marks may be divided into one of two categories: compression and sliding.

Compression marks are formed by a blow (such as that caused by a hammer), or by pressure exerted against an object. These do not usually provide as valuable information as sliding marks do.

Sliding marks are made by running a tool back and forth over a surface; because the edge of the tool is likely to be irregular, laboratory comparison is facilitated. Marks made by a saw, knife, or other such instrument may also result in detail which is capable of comparison.

The investigator can usually determine the value of a tool mark by observing it under a magnifying glass. Essentially, striations or indentations formed by the tool should be sought. If such evidence is discovered it should be photographed; a cast may also be made. If a tool is recovered it should never be placed in the mark to see if it fits. This task should be left to the crime laboratory.

PHYSICAL MATCHES

Throughout this chapter the subject of identification has been explored, for this is the primary task of the crime laboratory. The investigator should be aware that physical comparisons and matches cover a wide area, in addition to the subjects previously covered. If there is any doubt as to the value of a particular item, either as physical evidence or as a means of developing evidence, the investigator should not hesitate to call on the services of the crime laboratory. (See Fig. 5.27.)

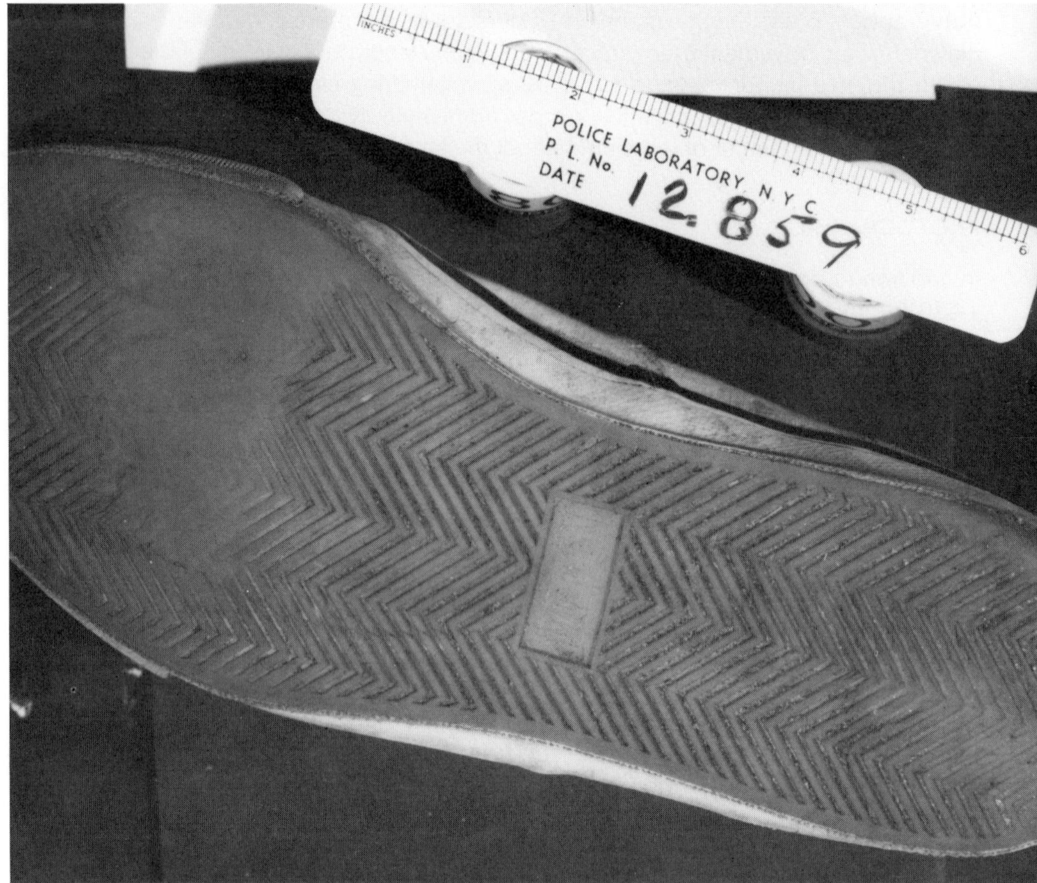

FIG. 5.27 The unique characteristics of an article or tool frequently make it possible to develop a physical match. The worn soles in the above figure made it possible to compare it with footprints left at the scene of a crime. (Courtesy of SPRING 3100, New York City Police Department.)

SUMMARY

In the preceding chapter, we discussed the various aspects of recovering and storing physical and scientific evidence, as well as some of the areas of the crime laboratory with which the investigator should be familiar. However although the role of the crime laboratory in processing physical evidence is a valuable part of the investigation, studies have shown that the laboratories are not used as frequently in criminal investigation as they might be.

Supreme Court decisions such as *Mapp* v. *Ohio, Escobedo* v. *Illinois,* and *Miranda* v. *Arizona* have placed greater emphasis on the crime laboratory and scientific evidence in criminal prosecutions. The investigator should keep in mind that his ultimate responsibility is to provide adequate evidence to allow the court to determine the guilt or innocence of the defendant. Ultimately only he knows whether or not he has carried out his function to the fullest, but the decision to cut corners, or the failure to process a case properly, will eventually catch up with him. The relationship between the investigator and the crime laboratory must be a strong one. An important aspect of criminal investigation that is often overlooked is the importance of giving credit where it is due. Thus, the investigator should strive to make a habit of crediting the crime laboratory and the individual technician concerned when they have aided him.

NOTES

1. Irving J. Klein, *Law of Evidence for Police.* St. Paul, Minn.: West Publishing Co., 1973, p. 11.

2. Burr W. Jones, *The Law of Evidence,* 5th ed., revised by Spencer A. Gard. San Francisco: Bancroft-Whitney Co., 1958, p. 1.

3. *State* v. *Viola,* (Ohio App 1947), 51OhioLAbs 577, 82 Ne(2nd) 306. Cited in James R. Richardson, *Scientific Evidence for Police.* Cincinnati, Ohio: W. H. Anderson Co., 1963, p. 296.

QUESTIONS FOR DISCUSSION

1. In what ways may physical evidence be used to aid the investigator? Discuss the types of physical evidence.

2. What is trace evidence? Discuss the various types of trace evidence and what may be determined from each.

3. So far as physical evidence is concerned, what are the various applications in which the crime laboratory may be involved? Discuss the relative importance of each as a form of identification.

EXERCISES

1. Each student should dust for and lift a fingerprint. What is the fingerprint pattern?

2. Conduct a comparative analysis of hair and fiber beneath a microscope. What are the noticeable differences?

3. Compare and identify a typewriter by studying various impressions.

4. Compare various forms of trace material, such as dirt, ashes, or soot, and identify their characteristics.

SUGGESTED READINGS

Allison, Harrison C., *Personal Identification.* Boston, Mass.: Holbrook Press, 1973.

Kirk, Paul L., *Crime Investigation: Physical Evidence and the Police Laboratory.* New York: Interscience Publishers, 1966.

MacDonnell, Herbert Leon, and Lorraine Fiske Bialousz, *Flight Characteristics and Stain Patterns of Human Blood.* Washington, D.C.: National Institute of Law Enforcement and Criminal Justice, 1971.

Moenssens, Andre A., *Fingerprint Techniques.* New York: Chilton Book Co., 1971.

O'Brien, Kevin P., and Robert C. Sullivan, *Criminalistics: Theory and Practice.* Boston, Mass.: Holbrook Press, 1972.

Parker, Brian, and Joseph Peterson, *Physical Evidence Utilization in the Administration of Criminal Justice.* National Institute of Law Enforcement and Criminal Justice. March, 1970.

Richardson, James R., *Scientific Evidence for Police Officers.* Cincinnati, Ohio: W. H. Anderson, 1963.

THE INVESTIGATIVE FUNCTION

part II

CHAPTER 6

interviewing and interrogation

Since the success of any investigation depends on information, the importance of good interviewing and interrogation techniques in criminal investigation cannot be overstated. While in the previous chapter we discussed the value of physical evidence in obtaining information, this chapter is devoted to securing information through verbal techniques. Quite often, the investigator fails to recognize the value of the spoken word, and is unaware that much can be learned in this area. More than diction or the ability to hold a conversation, verbal communication involves a basic understanding of human psychology, linguistics, and in some respects sociology. Often it is not what an investigator says, but how he says it, that proves to be the turning point in an interview or interrogation. A proper choice of words, selection of a setting, the impact of peer groups, and a recognition of individual perception all play an important role in the information process. No less important is the development of a logical approach to the case. The order in which persons are interviewed, the order in which questions are asked, and the decision whether or not to pursue a side point, rather than continue with the direct questioning, are all of crucial concern. The decision to question an inconsistent statement at the time, or let it pass, will often affect the ultimate outcome of the questioning.

Interviewing and interrogation should not be viewed as a simplistic process, but rather as a dynamic process affected by individuals, locations, and circumstances. In an earlier chapter it was noted that information can generally be defined as being of direct value, indirect value, or no value. The investigator, in evaluating the information he has collected, must determine which label applies. There is a difference between interviewing and interrogation, although at times the line between them may not be very clear. For example, it is not uncommon for an interview to turn into an interrogation as the case develops. The investigator should recognize that the difference is only in terms of his line of questioning or pursuit, and in conversing with an individual it is generally more advantageous to use the term "interview" rather than "interrogate," for it is not derogatory and generates less hostility.

INTERVIEWING

Simply stated, an interview may be defined as the questioning of a person or persons with a definite purpose in mind. It differs from a conversation in that the investigator is attempting to elicit certain information, and it differs from an interrogation in that the individual being interviewed is not generally a suspect and is cooperative.

The person being interviewed may be directly involved, such as a victim or witness, or indirectly involved, as one who may provide information relative to the case. And, of course, there is always the possibility that an individual being interviewed is the perpetrator of the crime.

Generally, it is the investigator's task to use the interviewing process in developing the facts of a crime. Essentially, this involves bringing all of the information together in such a manner as to present a logical conclusion. Thus interviewing may be used to corroborate or disprove other statements, to verify information developed by the crime laboratory, to eliminate suspects, to develop suspects, to recover evidence or property, and to locate other witnesses and the suspect.

Although the chief concern here is with verbal communication, it should be pointed out that a record of all interviews should be maintained. In a previous chapter the tape recorder was discussed as an effective tool for maintaining an accurate record. If one is unavailable, adequate notes should be kept. The investigator must be aware that all interviews should be recorded, even if they do not prove useful at the time.

The techniques employed in a successful interview will depend on the circumstances and the investigator. Nevertheless, an understanding of the basic principles involved in a good interview should enhance the investigator's capabilities. Essentially, the investigator should concern himself with five aspects of the interview: situation, setting, clientele, language, and method.

SITUATION

The situation refers to the particular event under investigation. As a rule, a homicide investigation will result in more questioning than the investigation of a larceny, but beyond this the attitude of those involved, either suspects or witnesses, is likely to be different. The number of persons to be interviewed, their identity, their relationship to the crime, and their order of importance for effective interviewing should be considered.

If many persons are involved the investigator must decide how much time he can spend with each, and whether or not he should have someone assist him with the interviews. Often this will depend on the crime. For the purpose of deciding on interviewing techniques, it is possible to loosely divide crime types into three categories: the unusual, the average, and the minor crime. In the first category are such crimes as homicide, bank robbery, kidnapping, or any crime that is likely to generate significant publicity. The average crime may be classified as those involving burglary, robbery, larceny, or the like and which are viewed as average by the department. In the third category are minor crimes, such as petty larceny, auto theft, and assault.

If an unusual crime occurs the investigator is likely to be given increased assistance, in the form of more manpower and technology. In the average crime he is usually expected to handle it himself, although he may call on the services of a specialized unit, such as the crime laboratory. If a minor crime occurs, the investigator will usually handle it himself, and quite often the investigation will be limited.

Interviewing of persons in the last two categories presents no problems unless the investigator is working with a partner. Although an investigator has assistance in the case of an unusual crime, he should consider conducting all the interviews himself. If this is infeasible because of the number of persons involved he should categorize individuals into "mental" groups, involving victim or victims, primary witnesses, and secondary witnesses. Primary witnesses are those who were closest to, or somehow involved in, the crime. This might include persons who were present during a robbery or who observed a shooting. Secondary witnesses are those who observed some particular aspect of the crime, but were not in close proximity to it. This group might include those who observed the perpetrator escape or who may have been present but were unaware that a crime was occurring.

The investigator should interview the victim and primary witnesses as a matter of course, permitting other witnesses to be interviewed by an assistant. If the investigator conducts all the interviewing he should use assistants to help take notes and keep persons separated.

The order in which witnesses are interviewed should be established beforehand, and an effort should be made to formulate the sequence of events during the crime, with a view toward maintaining this sequence in the interviews. Whenever possible, the victim or victims should be interviewed first. However, if the victim has been removed to a hospital for treatment and there is no apparent danger of death, the witnesses should be interviewed at the scene. All too often, the investigator proceeds to the hospital, where he has to wait while the victim is being treated. By the time he returns to the scene, many of the witnesses have either left or had second thoughts about providing information.

If the investigator is conducting a survey of the neighborhood, or is calling persons into the office to be interviewed, it is also necessary to give some consideration to the situation. For example, the investigator is likely to have some information at this point in the investigation; this also holds true for those he is planning to interview. Quite often, any number of rumors will have spread throughout the neighborhood, and persons are apt to respond on the basis of them. If an interview is being conducted in the office, an individual has probably had an opportunity to discuss the case with others, and may respond on the basis of this discussion.

If the investigator gives some thought to the total situation he is likely to increase the probability of a favorable interview. To rush headlong into an interview without adequate planning is a major sign of inexperience. This planning need not be lengthy, or in minute detail, but it should take the various factors involved into consideration. When the investigator has satisfied himself with respect to the situation, he should then consider the setting.

SETTING

Because not all interviews are apt to take place at the same location, or under similar conditions, some consideration must be given to the setting, i.e., the place where the interview is conducted. It may be in the investigator's office, at the scene of the crime, at a business, or any number of places.

Under ideal conditions, an interview should be conducted in a private room, preferably one with which the investigator is familiar. The room should be well lighted, with a minimum of distraction and a pleasant atmosphere. Thus, a stark room with merely a table and chairs and no decoration is not recommended for the interview.

If a window is present, the investigator should decide whether he is going to sit with his back to it, or adjacent to it. The presence of background light may be psychologically threatening to some individuals; however it is not advisable to seat the interviewee with his back to the window, for it places him in the dominant position. Overhead lighting is preferable for an interview.

It is not generally advisable to provide soft-cushioned chairs or couches; straight-backed chairs are preferable. In some instances, especially in follow-up interviews where an attempt is being made to relax or lull the interviewee, comfortable chairs may be advisable. Too much comfort, however, is likely to hamper the interview.

In many instances the interview must be conducted at a location other than the office of the investigator. If this is the case privacy is the major consideration. Indoors the investigator should conduct a quick survey to determine which room provides the best location in terms of the factors previously discussed. Keep in mind that the room should not be too large, or too distracting. In a house or an apartment, the kitchen is generally a good place to conduct an interview if it offers privacy.

Interviews outdoors create special problems, and once again privacy must be the prime consideration. The investigator must keep in mind that there are greater distractions present outdoors than indoors. Questioning in such instances should generally be limited to developing necessary information, and long drawn-out interviews should be avoided if possible. Conditions may require that an automobile be used for interviewing, but this should be avoided if possible, for the confining space and "fishbowl" atmosphere are not conducive to concentration.

In most cases a little imagination, and perhaps the movement of a few chairs, will provide an adequate setting. Unfortunately, too few investigators take time to consider the importance of the setting, and this failure is likely to detract from their results.

Once the setting and situation have been decided on consideration should be given to the clientele.

CLIENTELE

The persons to be interviewed are defined as the clientele. There are a number of groupings in which an individual may be placed, and each of these groups is likely to exhibit certain traits which will aid the interviewer. Most important, however, is the recognition that each individual is unique and should be treated as such.

To begin with, individuals may be grouped according to age and sex. In addition to males and females, persons may be classified as children, youngsters or teenagers, young adults, middle-aged, and elderly. The reader is, no doubt, aware of the need for various approaches in handling, for example, different age groups. But he should be aware also of differences between subgroups, and any commonality that each group may share.

Children. Young children are usually imaginative; thus they are likely to see things that did not actually occur. When interviewing children it is wise to have a parent present if possible, and often a discussion with them will assist the investigator in formulating questions. While it would be difficult to say at what age children begin to change, their perception of the real world becoming more acute, the investigator should be aware that a change of this nature does occur. Older children generally make good witnesses, because they often observe things of which adults are unaware. If it is made clear that there is no threat to them and that they will not profit by making up a story, they are generally very truthful. Their perception of the world is not as complex as that of the older person's; they usually see things as being only right or wrong. Quite often it is preferable to let a child tell his or her story, directing the interview where necessary but taking care not to interrupt frequently.

Youngsters or Teenagers. As youth approach the preteen and teenage years, they tend to lose interest in their exterior surroundings, focusing more on those things that directly affect them. For this reason they may be poor witnesses in certain cases. On the other hand, they are likely to be altruistic, interested in what is going on; thus they should not be dismissed until they have been heard.

A recent trend in the United States has been a growing alienation between the police and youth, which may have a bearing on the individual interview. If hostility exists, it may be important for the investigator to expose its existence before questioning the witness. Otherwise he may be receiving false information. A strong code of silence exists among young people, and this may also act as a barrier to communication. The worst thing the investigator can do is lose his temper or use threats.

Young Adults. In some instances young adults, especially those who are newly married and recent residents, can provide certain information that might go unnoticed by others. Generally this group is "self-centered," but they are also making new observations, often from a different viewpoint. Their perception of a scene will not generally be as acute as that of an older person. Nevertheless, they may be aware of "unique" things. Young housewives, for example, are just beginning to develop their life "patterns," and may observe things in more detail than the older woman. Young men who are new on a job are likely to observe certain characteristics or traits that others long ago came to take for granted.

The Middle-aged. Middle-aged persons are generally good witnesses, for they have certain perceptions based on experience that enable them to see things more clearly. The wide variance of individuals makes it difficult to stereotype, for any number of factors will come into play in making up a person's character. Nevertheless, the investigator will be able to recognize those individuals who exude a sense of confidence and who are interested in their surroundings. These persons are usually mature, and have a certain facility for observing their surroundings.

For the most part, the middle-aged are willing to cooperate, and can be of enormous assistance if handled properly.

The Elderly. Older persons are often good witnesses, although the investigator should ascertain whether or not an individual has any infirmities. Failing eyesight, senility, and an obsession with their own lives may be apparent, and will affect the interview situation, making them poor witnesses.

Nevertheless, patience in conducting interviews with the elderly may prove beneficial. The investigator must often listen to much extraneous detail in attempting to secure information. In more than one instance an elderly person has had information that an eager investigator overlooked in his haste to complete the interview.

In addition to the age classifications discussed above, individuals may be grouped into other categories that can be of aid in conducting the interview. Here the interview may be geared to the level of intelligence, cooperativeness, honesty, and exaggeration. All these qualities can be determined by the investigator, either during or prior to the interview.

In a sense, the investigator must "size the individual up." This is not difficult, or does not seem to be, for we all attempt this in our everyday lives; but the probability of error based on inadequate information is high. One need only think of the first time they met a certain individual, and compare one's feelings about him then and now.

If an individual displays certain tendencies, the investigator may choose to alter his approach and attempt to develop communication through the use of psychological techniques. Studies of human behavior indicate that while we are all unique, certain things have meaning or value to us and certain things do not; as individuals we tend to form opinions and attitudes about the world based on our perception of it; this is not always accomplished in a rational or objective manner. In a sense, we attempt to involve ourselves in those activities we are interested in or support, and shy away from those we do not like or do not understand.

A primary task of the investigator is to develop a rapport with the person being interviewed. One of the best ways to accomplish this is to listen when the individual has something to say, especially at the beginning of the interview. At this point the investigator can usually form a mental picture of the individual, his likes, dislikes, level of involvement (in the interview), and cooperativeness. In some measure, an understanding of these factors will enhance the interview, for the investigator should be able to adjust his approach to the situation.

While the individual techniques involved in perfecting interviews are perhaps best learned through practice and experience, a number of pointers may be of assistance.

Intelligence. To begin with, never assume that you are smarter than the individual you are interviewing; recognize instead that he is likely to have more information on the subject than you do. Gear the interview to the level of the interviewee. In other words, do not use abstract or complicated questions if it is evident that the person does not understand them. Also, if you do not understand his answers, ask him to clarify his statements. A major criticism of many investigative interviews is the tendency of the investigator to talk down or be too authoritarian; the investigator must learn to control this aspect of his demeanor.

Cooperativeness. In many cases the investigator will encounter persons who are uncooperative. Although their reasons for being uncooperative are varied, the first thing the investigator should do is try to find out why this feeling exists. Often the individual merely needs some form of reassurance. Generally, the interview should begin with a discussion of this problem. If the interviewee continues to be uncooperative, the investigator must make a decision as to the approach he will take. He may decide to appeal to the individual's civic sense, or some other trait that is apparent, or he may "escalate" the authority aspect of the interview. This approach involves slowly applying pressure by reminding the individual of the possible consequences he may face by refusing to cooperate, and ultimately threatening him with some form of official action. The "escalating authority" approach should be used with care; and it is not advisable to make threats you are not willing to, or incapable of, carrying out. Thus, if you state that you will take some legal action unless the individual cooperates, you must be prepared to do so. Of course, in some cases it may be possible to bluff; but this can be a self-defeating practice, for if the individual discovers you are bluffing, he is even less likely to cooperate.

In many instances the person's refusal to cooperate is based on fear, either real or imagined. In this case you must attempt to reassure the individual, and point out the reasons why it is imperative that they cooperate. Threats or cajoling may be useless, for the fear of retaliation may be greater than the fear of some threatened punishment.

The uncooperative witness is one of the more challenging individuals in an interview situation, and the investigator must be prepared to use his wits, guile, and powers of persuasion to be successful.

Honesty. The determination of whether or not an individual is telling the truth must be everpresent in the investigator's mind. Naturally, he should not take every statement at face value, nor should he be too quick to question a statement's truthfulness, for this may hinder the interview. If it appears that an interviewee is not telling the truth, you should attempt to ascertain if this is deliberate or merely the result of error. The person should not be accused of lying until all other alternatives have been explored, and then only when you are virtually positive.

In most cases it is possible to ask questions to which you know the answer as a means of checking the interviewee's truthfulness. If it appears that he is lying, you should rephrase the question to assure yourself that he has not misunderstood it. A common rebuttal to the accusation of a lie is that the question was misunderstood.

When a person is lying, it is because he has something to hide or does not wish to provide certain information. It does not necessarily mean he is guilty, nor does it mean that he knows the identity of the guilty person. Often he is merely trying to hide some aspect of his own life. This is a common occurrence when a sex crime is under investigation.

A person's actions may indicate that he is lying. Extreme nervousness, excessive perspiration, and a tendency to avoid answering direct questions may be revealing, and you should develop the capacity to observe these reactions. Finally, you should keep in mind the fact that a lie is still a statement, and can often be invaluable as the investigation proceeds.

Exaggeration. Some people have a tendency to see things that are not actually there. This ability to fantasize or exaggerate can be extremely detrimental to an investigation if the fact is not discovered. In this instance the individual is not purposely lying; he actually believes what he is saying. He may play up his part, or play down the part of a rival. Careful questioning can usually elicit the truth, but you should keep in mind that this individual is a poor witness, and is likely to destroy a case when it is brought to trial, unless adequate records are kept and he is apprised of his tendency to exaggerate.

LANGUAGE

Most people take words for granted. One of the world's foremost semanticists, S. I. Hayakawa, in his classic work *Language in Thought and Action,* stresses the importance of words in relation to communication. Too often, the investigator fails to recognize the importance of words in the interview situation. Yet his choice of them is often crucial to the success of an interview.

Words, of course, are symbols, and language a highly developed form of symbolism. Most people give little thought to their individual choice of words, their selection often being a subconscious one. Thus, we all know that it is possible to say "the wrong thing," at least in everyday conversation. For some reason, many investigators fail to remember this possibility during the interview. As an example, consider the following statements: "I'm conducting an investigation, and I'd like to ask you some questions." "I'm a detective and I want some answers to a few questions." How would you respond to these two approaches? Is the second statement more likely to generate hostility than the first?

No doubt there are a number of key words in each statement toward which an individual is likely to react, either positively or negatively. Most people recognize that a request is more likely to produce *willing* cooperation than an order. In the second statement, the words "I am a detective" are also likely to produce some hostility, for this may be considered a sign of boasting or pressure. Would it not be better to say, "My name is Detective Smith"?

When one considers the implications of such a simple sentence, the enormity of meaning in words becomes staggering, and it would certainly be impossible for an investigator to measure or evaluate each word during the interview. Nevertheless, he can train himself to use those words which are more likely to create a favorable response.

Words have considerable power and impact; some are weak and some are strong. For example, can you rank the following words in order of their impact: death, kill, murder, homicide, expire? Which has the most negative connotation?

If you were interviewing a woman whose husband had just been murdered and you did not want to upset her any further, which of the previously mentioned words would you choose? These are some of the questions the interviewer should consider before beginning an interview and, indeed, during the course of his normal workday. Through experience, many investigators develop this ability to choose their words carefully or perhaps some have a "sixth sense" enabling them to determine the right question to ask.

METHOD

All the various techniques of interviewing are brought together to develop an approach or method in handling the interview. To these are added the techniques of demeanor and attitude. The method chosen to conduct the interview will depend on the circumstances or situation, setting, and clientele. Language, of course, is also an integral part of the method.

The approach an investigator takes depends on the interviewee's relationship to the case. Thus, the complainant or victim may be handled in a different manner from the suspect, informants differently than witnesses. The interrogation of suspects is covered in the following section, and informants are discussed in a later chapter; thus this section will be concerned with the interviewing of victims, complainants, and witnesses.

The victim is one against whom a crime has been committed; he is generally the complainant (in some jurisdictions, when a child is involved, the parent or guardian may be the complainant). In some cases the complainant is not a victim, but rather one who is reporting a violation of law.

In either case the investigator should be sympathetic with the complainant, and during the initial interview should attempt to ascertain the facts of the allegation. If possible, any background information on the individual should be gathered before the interview. This should include a records search to determine whether the person has ever had any previous contact with the police, either as a complainant or as a suspect. If follow-up interviews are conducted the investigator should be sure to familiarize himself with the earlier interview.

The investigator must first discover whether or not a crime has in fact been committed. He should also determine whether there are any extenuating circumstances surrounding the allegation, such as a grudge or dispute between the parties involved. In some cases (e.g., arson, burglary, homicide), it may be necessary to determine whether or not the party had something to gain from the alleged crime (financial or otherwise) which may make him a suspect.

Witnesses to a crime should be permitted to talk freely, and if they are cooperative the investigator should merely attempt to maintain the dialogue, interrupting only to ask for specific information that may have been missed. The individual should be flattered, thanked, and generally given every courtesy. Handling uncooperative witnesses may require a different method; these techniques are discussed in the section on interrogation.

INTERROGATION

The primary difference between interviewing and interrogation is in the method used to question the individual. Generally, an interrogation may be defined as the questioning of a suspect, perpetrator, or individual who is reluctant, or refuses, to cooperate with the interviewer. In one sense, an interrogation is a stricter, more authoritarian approach to interviewing. As stated earlier, it is usually not advisable to tell an individual he is being interrogated, but rather that he is being interviewed.

An interrogation requires a greater level of skill than an interview, primarily because much of its success is dependent on the investigator. Information is not as easy to obtain, the individual often has something to conceal, and the probability of his lying is greater. Furthermore, the legal restrictions placed on the investigator in an interrogation are usually greater.

In a later chapter, legal aspects of criminal investigation are discussed. Nevertheless, the importance of the Supreme Court's decision in the case of *Miranda* v. *Arizona* requires that some mention of it be made here. The court held in this case that any person who is taken into custody, or deprived of his freedom in any significant way, must be advised of certain constitutional rights prior to any interrogation. He must be advised that he is not obligated to answer any questions; that, if he chooses to speak, anything he says may be used in court; that he is entitled to the assistance of counsel prior to and during the questioning; and that, if he wishes counsel and cannot afford one, counsel will be assigned.[1]

Volunteered statements do not fall within this ruling, but it is incumbent on the police to prove that a statement is voluntary. Thus, when an individual has become suspect, is placed in custody, or is deprived of his freedom, the Miranda rulings should be read to him.

The information drawn from an interrogation may be classified as either a confession, an admission, or a statement. A confession is an acknowledgement of guilt; an admission is an incriminating statement that indicates but does not acknowledge guilt; and a statement is a written or oral declaration regarding certain facts concerning the investigation.

Preparation for the interrogation involves similar steps to those taken in planning an interview, although certain details may differ somewhat.

SITUATION

The nature of the crime will have an impact on the interrogation, and in his preparation the investigator should review the information he has at hand. Generally, the investigator has specific information at this point, and is attempting to carry the investigation further through the interrogation. There may often be no way of telling which direction the interrogation will take, and the decision to halt it in order to check a detail will break the continuity and possibly ruin the chances for a successful outcome. Thus the investigator should familiarize himself in advance with all reports in the case, the results of interviews, the analysis reports on physical evidence, as well as the sketches and photographs of the crime scene. Also, in reviewing the situation it is often wise to make a note of those items that are of importance to the interrogation and should be covered in detail.

SETTING

An interrogation will usually take place at the investigator's convenience at a location designated by him. The impact of a psychological advantage by the investigator over the subject may be the difference between success and failure. For this reason, it is not advisable to interrogate an individual in his home or other familiar surroundings.

If possible, an interrogation room should be used; it should be somewhat different from the interview room in that there should be no undue distracting influences, such as pictures, excess furniture, or lamps. If available, a windowless room is preferable. Entrance should be through one door only, with some means provided through which the subject can be viewed from outside.

A straightbacked chair should be provided for the subject, and a desk or table and chair for the interrogator. The subject should be seated with his back to the door.

A major problem during an interrogation is often the presence of observers. This should be avoided, and anyone not participating in or necessary to the interrogation should be excluded from the room.

The ideal interrogation room is wired so that the interrogation can be recorded. If this is not possible a number of recording devices might be considered. In addition to recording equipment, a small microphone should be installed, which will permit outside observers to hear what is being said.

If it is necessary to conduct an investigation away from the office, an attempt must be made to secure a location that offers as many of the features previously mentioned as possible. Some method of recording should also be considered. Needless to say, interrogations should be limited to the investigator's office whenever possible.

One final word on recording the interrogation may be of value. As stated, a tape recording is an ideal approach. However if the investigator must take notes, it is wise to explain this to the subject; these notes should not interrupt the flow of conversation.

If this can be accomplished without the subject's awareness, the use of a sound movie camera or videotape to record the interrogation (perhaps through a two-way mirror) may prove beneficial. This film can be used later to observe the subject's reactions to particular questions, or to get the opinion of other investigators. Of course, it can prove extremely valuable in court.

In most cities, certain crimes require that a statement be taken from the suspect if he has confessed. Often used in court, this statement is a legal document, and it may be taken by a detective or the prosecutor, depending on the jurisdiction. Because the procedures for taking statements do vary, the investigator should familiarize himself with the method used in his city. Suffice it to say that this statement is a written record, usually in narrative form, to which the suspect affixes his signature.

CLIENTELE

The personalities of individuals being interrogated will, of course, vary according to many factors. The individual may be a professional or a novice, calm or nervous, innocent or guilty. The manner in which the investigator "reads" the subject sets the tone of the interrogation and affects the outcome.

Before the interrogation information concerning the subject's previous police history, reputation, traits and weaknesses, and associates should be gathered to provide a "picture" of the individual. If the subject has a police record it is wise to discuss the case with the police officers who handled him previously. Any specific pieces of information or story that are not common knowledge give the investigator an edge, making the subject think the investigator knows more about him than he really does.

Keep in mind that many individuals are quite familiar with police procedures, and they will be attempting to use their own brand of psychology. The more information available, the better off the investigator is. Much of the information discussed in the section on interviews will be of value in the interrogation process.

LANGUAGE

The importance of language in the interrogation should be apparent by now. Generally, the factors mentioned in the section on interviewing apply to interrogation as well. The effective investigator knows how to use language to work for him, rather than against him. He is able to pursue a point logically, recognize discrepancies, and move toward a specific goal. Too often the investigator fails to recognize that his vocabulary may be different, or have a different meaning from that of the subject. He must, in a sense, be on the same wavelength as the subject. He must formulate his questions carefully, and listen to the responses. How often is the interviewer unaware of the answer to a question because he is formulating another?

The good interrogator must be aware of the timing involved in getting the most information from an individual. In some instances an almost staccato-like series of questions may be used, whereas in others a long pause between each question and answer can be effective in building tension in the suspect. These techniques can be learned through observation and experience, but a basic understanding of the underlying psychology and linguistics of the successful interrogation can also be developed through education.

METHOD

Method is probably more important in the interrogation than in the interview, primarily because the investigator must choose from a greater variety of approaches. In the interrogation, an investigator may be called on to "be" a number of individuals, and in essence he must "act out" certain roles.

The number of methods used is only limited by the interrogator's imagination. In addition to the standard approaches, a number of variations of each are common. Generally, an interrogation should be conducted by one man. In some instances two investigators may work together, but it is not advisable for any more to be present. The methods used in an interrogation are classified as direct, emotional, authoritarian, and deceptive.

Direct. A direct approach is often the best and should be used first, unless there is information indicating that it will not work. In a straightforward manner the individual is told what he is there for and is asked to cooperate in telling the story and providing the details.

Emotional. This method involves playing on some aspect of the subject's emotions, in an attempt by the investigator to build emotional pressure. This might mean pointing out such things as jealousy, sympathy, pride, fears, suspicions. The investigator usually tries to appear a friend of the subject, agreeing with his plight, extending a sympathetic ear, or acting as an advisor. In many cases this method is extremely effective, for the individual does feel guilty about his actions. If this is the case, undue pressure or an antagonistic stance by the interrogator might stifle the person's willingness to cooperate. The investigator should keep in mind that he is not passing judgment on the suspect, and he should not display his feelings toward the subject or the crime, unless, of course, it is in keeping with the interrogation procedure.

Authoritarian. The authoritarian approach involves placing pressure on the individual to increase his anxiety. The individual may be threatened with imprisonment or other legal action, or reminded that there is a strong case against him as a suspect.

This approach is generally useful if the individual shows no emotion during the interrogation, or perhaps has some previous record. On the one hand you are appealing to the logical futility of his action, and on the other, applying psychological pressure in revealing certain information that you already have.

A number of variations of this approach are likely to produce results. The "good-guy, bad-guy" routine is used quite frequently. In this approach one investigator pretends to be highly sympathetic to the subject, while another investigator maintains that he is going to "get" the individual one way or another. The "friend" indicates that if the subject cooperates the "bad-guy" will be excluded from participation in the interrogation. This approach leads to some concern in the courts, since it is viewed as a form of coercion. However, some of the more subtle variations work just as well.

Deceptive. Using this approach, the investigator attempts to make the subject believe that he has more information or evidence than he actually does. This can be a dangerous method, since the subject might become aware that the investigator is bluffing, thereby decreasing any chance of success. This approach is generally recommended for use only as a last resort when other techniques have failed. It should be pointed out, however, that some investigators have mastered the technique of deception rather well. Using false latent fingerprints or other scientific evidence, or playing one suspect off against another are common techniques that are often used effectively.

With this method the investigator is taking a calculated risk, and he must have a pretty good idea of the subject's intelligence and possible responses. For this reason, it is wise to proceed slowly, taking one step at a time and observing the subject's responses to each question.

SUMMARY

The importance of interviewing and interrogation has been stressed in this chapter. The investigator's role in this vital aspect of criminal investigation requires that he be familiar with the various techniques and aspects involved in this phase of the case.

In addition to a discussion of the five areas involved in interviewing and interrogation (situation, setting, clientele, language, and method), a number of specific techniques were reviewed. The utilization of information obtained through interviewing and interrogation is the subject of the following chapter.

NOTE

1. *Miranda* v. *Arizona,* 384 U.S. 436, 86 S.Ct. 1602 (1966).

QUESTIONS FOR DISCUSSION

1. What is the difference between interviewing and interrogation? Discuss the similarities between the two.

2. What are the five characteristics or areas involved in interviewing and interrogation? Discuss them in detail.

3. When must the Miranda warning be given? Discuss the problems this does or does not create for the investigator.

EXERCISES

1. Set up an interview situation based on some particular event that occurred recently, and interview three individuals who were present. Be sure to keep them separated.

2. Using the same situation, show how easy it is to develop inconsistencies in the individual accounts.

3. Have each person write up a report of one of the interviews. Compare these to note the different aspects reported by each individual.

SUGGESTED READINGS

Gerber, Samuel R., and Oliver Schroeder, *Criminal Investigation and Interrogation.* Cincinnati, Ohio: W. H. Anderson, 1962.

Inbau, Fred E., *Lie Detection and Criminal Interrogation.* Baltimore: Williams and Wilkins, 1948.

CHAPTER 7

informants and information

In large measure the use of informants in criminal investigation represents the difference between success and failure. Despite the problems inherent in this aspect of the investigative process, an investigator's effectiveness often depends on his "contacts." These individuals come from all walks of life, and their activities are as likely to be illegal as they are legal. This, in itself, often generates moral as well as ethical questions, and the line between an acceptable act and an unacceptable act is at times thin. For this reason the investigator must be familiar with the procedures for developing and using informants.

The subjects of obtaining and using information run throughout this book. In earlier chapters the use of scientific evidence, interviewing, and interrogation were discussed in terms of their importance as sources of information. In the following chapter this will be expanded to include other sources of information with which the investigator should be familiar. Perhaps the primary difference between the topics discussed earlier and those following is in terms of the availability of the information, and the role of the investigator in developing it. For the most part, information previously discussed in this book is directly related to the crime. The crime scene, evidence, victims, and witnesses are producers of information; they are obvious facets of any investigation. On the other hand, the process of the further development of information in a case may not be so obvious, and depends greatly on the investigator's ability to use abstract reasoning to secure information that may not be readily apparent. Furthermore, his ability to know where to look for information is crucial, and the search should not be regarded as a haphazard process.

INFORMANTS

An informant is defined here as an individual who, for a particular reason, provides information. While an informant may be a witness, or in some instances a party to the crime, he usually is not. His reasons for providing information are varied, and will be discussed in some detail later, but it should be noted that they often go beyond those of the average witness, who is more likely to be an individual who just happened to be present at the scene of the crime.

Informants may be categorized in one of three ways: the confidential informant, the "one-time" informant, and the involuntary informant. In one sense all three may be classified as confidential informants, because they generally do not want their identities exposed. However, for purposes of discussion a delineation between the three will be made.

THE CONFIDENTIAL INFORMANT

Most policemen are familiar with the concept of a confidential informant, although there is apt to be some misunderstanding concerning his importance as an investigative aid. Essentially, the confidential informant is an individual who provides the police with information, but does not wish to have his identity disclosed. More often than not his reasons for doing so are related to something he expects to receive for the information, in the form of money, special police consideration, or prestige.

Generally, there are three types of confidential informants. First is the individual who is paid for his services, either for a specific item of information, or on a salary basis. Second is the informant who provides information, asking in return that the police overlook an illegal act or operation. Third is one who provides information because he gains a certain amount of prestige for helping a particular policeman. There are also those informants who act solely out of jealousy or revenge in providing information.

It should be made clear that all three types, but especially the first two, have something to gain, and are capable of giving false information. Thus, all information from confidential informants must be suspect, and the investigator should make every attempt to verify it through other sources.

Perhaps as important is the responsibility the investigator has to maintain an informant's anonymity. If an investigator develops a reputation for revealing the names of his informants, he is not likely to be successful in recruiting new ones. If it is necessary to expose a confidential informant, it is wise to let him know in advance. In some instances the informant may be used as a witness for the prosecution, but careful consideration should be given in so doing, for his value as an informant in the future may be destroyed.

Several legal and ethical questions are apt to arise when confidential informants are employed. For example, the decision by a policeman to overlook a crime in return for information is not to be taken lightly, and future developments may place the investigator's position in jeopardy. One should keep in mind that no case is worth compromising principles or losing a job over; this has been known to happen through the ill-advised use of informants. As a general rule, the investigator must realize that an informant is working for the police department, and while he may "belong" to a particular investigator, his ultimate value is measured in terms of accomplishing the investigative goal. For this reason, there should be a departmental policy concerning the use of informants, and someone other than the investigator (preferably a superior officer), should be aware of the circumstances surrounding the use of each informant. If the department is not willing to overlook a particular crime for certain types of information, the investigator should not take the burden of doing so on his shoulders.

In order to protect the anonymity of an informant a number of devices may be employed. In all cases, the individual's identity should be on a "need-to-know" basis. The use of code names or numbers may facilitate the handling of informants, and the investigator who is the contact man should provide an index file listing specific areas, by either type of crime or geographic location, in which his informant may provide information. Thus other investigators can consult the file if they are interested in particular information. Figure 7.1 illustrates an example of such a card. The amount of information provided on the card should not be sufficient to identify the informant by implication.

BURGLARY (WESTLAKE AREA)

Code name "IRISH" No. 41

Contacts Det. Sullivan or Jones

Information: FAMILIAR WITH FACTORY BURGLARIES IN WESTLAKE AREA. MAY BE ABLE TO PROVIDE INFORMATION ON FOLLOWING SUBJECTS: PETER McCALL, B#471320; ROBERT (Sonny) TRAVERS, B#204389.

FIG. 7.1 Informant Index. The above card would be cross-indexed in a location file under "Westlake Area." A notation to "See informant #41" might also be made in the "Suspect File" for McCall and Travers. The B# refers to the criminal record number.

Informant contacts should be kept to a minimum, and it is preferable that two investigators be assigned to one individual. Unfortunately, professional jealousy is not unknown in most investigative operations, and too many investigators tend to keep information that they have developed to themselves. This is especially true where confidential informants are concerned; therefore, every effort must be made to maintain a spirit of cooperation in the department. Each investigator has a responsibility to share information, and when such information pays off, the individual responsible for providing it should be commended.

MANAGEMENT OF THE CONFIDENTIAL INFORMANT

In some measure, the confidential informant might be compared to the client of a salesman in the business world: It is important to keep him happy. In order to do so the investigator must remember a few rules and be prepared to recognize the individual relationship that exists. To begin with, it should be noted that this is a business relationship and, while the investigator is not expected to become the individual's friend, he must show him a measure of respect.

There is often a tendency in our society to look down on one who informs or gives information to the authorities. The investigator must take special care to see that he does not project this feeling. Thus, while he should question the reasons for which an individual gives information, he should keep his findings to himself. In evaluating the information, knowing the reason it was given will be of value to the investigator. For example, if an individual is paid for his services, the information is not likely to be as unbiased as that of one who provides information freely. In a sense, the paid individual is expected to produce. Quite often the confidential informant expects to get something in return for his help; this should always be taken into account by the investigator when reviewing the information.

The relationship between the confidential informant and the investigator is a special one. In order to gain the informant's trust, the investigator should keep any promises that he makes; he should not make any promise unless it can be fulfilled, or the informant is made aware that it is based on considerations outside the investigator's control.

The type of confidential informant used will have a bearing on the way he is handled. If information is volunteered, the investigator must often seek out the individual, and frequent contact should be maintained. This frequently involves paying "friendly" visits in some cases, since the individual should not be made to feel that he is only contacted when information is required. Such an individual is apt to get great personal satisfaction from knowing the investigator, regarding the relationship as a friendly one, rather than as an investigator–informant relationship.

Cultivating confidential informants should be given high priority by the investigator. In a sense this involves an understanding of personality, and the ability to recognize those who are in a position to be helpful, and who may be willing to cooperate. Two general approaches to developing a relationship with an informant should be considered. The first approach involves those whose activities are suspect and who may be susceptible to pressure, including those who may be used as paid informants. The second approach is directed toward responsible members of the community who, because of their occupation or friends, may have valuable information.

The first type of individual can often be handled directly. Paid informants are usually established through an arrest, or a similar situation where the individual is a suspect in another crime. These individuals will often agree to make a deal in return for not being prosecuted. If the information is extremely important, the investigator may decide to take the case to the prosecutor and attempt to work out a solution. Of course, much depends on the charge on which the suspect is being held. As stated earlier, it is not advisable for the investigator to make a decision without consulting a superior officer or the prosecutor, since his actions may be open to suspicion at a later time.

Many times it is possible to complete an arrest, and then ask for leniency in return for information. Once the individual has given information he becomes a prime candidate for continuance as an informant. The agreement worked out between the investigator and a confidential informant should be approved by a superior. Special care must be taken if an agreement involves overlooking a crime, such as gambling, and in most cases it is not advisable to do this. Nevertheless, there may be circumstances in which this is done. For example, an investigation into organized crime or narcotics often necessitates overlooking the lower operatives in an attempt to secure evidence against the leaders. In any event, if an agreement to overlook something has been made, all parties should know what its limits are.

Meetings with the informant should take place away from the investigator's office, and they should be tape-recorded. This serves to both review the information, and protect the investigator from allegations of misconduct. Tapes may also be used to check the veracity of the information, and to confront the informant if he is caught in a lie.

Relationships with citizen informants are more likely to be casual, and do not require as strict a control. Information is not as likely to be firsthand and is often based on observation. The investigator may ask the individual to observe certain activities, or he may question him about a specific incident. It should be kept in mind that the person is apt to make mistakes, and while his information should be verified, any error may be due to poor perception rather than a desire to lie.

If an informant is deemed unreliable, or is not to be used any longer, it is not wise to let him know the reason, or to do anything that may cause hostility. Despite his inadequacy at that time, his information may be of value again in the future.

THE "ONE-TIME" INFORMANT

Frequently an individual will decide, for one reason or another, to provide information about a specific crime or occurrence. In such a case it is extremely important that the investigator determine the reasons for the person's actions. In most cases, the individual is not known to the police, and information provided may be fabricated or distorted. Nevertheless, the information should be investigated, and an attempt made to verify it.

In cases receiving a great deal of publicity through the news media, the investigator is likely to be inundated with anonymous telephone calls. Many of these calls will be from cranks, but each one must be investigated and an effort made to identify the caller. The same holds true of letter writers. A perfect example of perseverance in this area involves a homicide case in New York, where investigators spent months tracking down an anonymous letter writer, who eventually proved to be a key witness against a woman in the death of her two children.

The one-time informant is often an integral part of the case, but is not identified. It is important to impress on this individual the value of his testimony and information. Such an individual is particularly valuable as a prosecution witness, and should be given every courtesy.

THE INVOLUNTARY INFORMANT

In some cases the investigator is likely to come across an individual who has information, but refuses to divulge it, either because it may implicate him or because he is afraid of retaliation. Often it is possible to put pressure on the individual through his friends or acquaintances. If it is suspected that he is engaged in an illegal operation, close observation of his activities may cause him to relent and provide information. In a sense this may be considered harassment, and should be avoided if possible. If an involuntary informant has been forced to cooperate, the information he provides should be carefully analyzed.

The primary difference between an involuntary witness and an involuntary informant is in terms of their relationship to the case. The witness has information which he observed at the scene, whereas the informant is more likely to provide ancillary information that will aid in the investigation. This may involve the whereabouts of a suspect at a particular time, information the witness may have overheard, or rumors relative to the crime.

VERIFICATION OF INFORMANT STATEMENTS

As a general rule, all information secured from informants should be verified whenever possible. If such information cannot be verified, a notation should be made in the investigator's report. In some instances it may be possible to verify certain aspects of the information, such as the time and location of an event, but not the complete statement. Nevertheless, this will aid the investigator in his ultimate evaluation.

Through experience the investigator usually develops the ability to analyze and classify information. However, this analysis is often haphazard and is conducted in an illogical manner in many instances. It should be recognized that the amount of information an individual can retain and analyze in his mind at one time is limited. For this reason, the investigator should not hesitate to use visual aids and other devices if there is a vast amount of information in a case. The simplest device, of course, is a blackboard. By writing information out and observing it, one is more likely to see relationships that were not evident before.

The use of index cards may also facilitate comparing information. Essentially, the investigator should divide his informant's statement into its integral parts, and determine what is verifiable and what is not verifiable. A mass of written data is often difficult to digest, especially if it is descriptive of an object or location. Thus, it may be wise to diagram the statement.

Finally, a system of evaluating the reliability of information can be developed. Information analysis is used successfully by intelligence services in the government as a means of making decisions, and can be applied in a simpler fashion to criminal investigation. Such an approach is discussed in a later section.

Insofar as informants are concerned, the investigator must keep uppermost in his mind that they are a valuable aid when used properly. However, he must be constantly aware of the dangers involved.

INFORMATION

Effective use of the various sources of information is dependent to a great degree on the investigator's initiative. We live in a society that is noted for collecting information, and from the time a person is born a vast amount of personal records is collected. By the time an individual grows up and takes a job he has acquired numerous files covering everything from his marital status to his credit rating. A rundown of some of the numbers we acquire is indicative of but a few of these sources of information. They include a social security number, a driver's license number, an insurance policy number, a telephone number, an address, credit card numbers, and in some cases a criminal record number. Along with other information these numbers are recorded in many places. Often it is the task of the investigator to locate an individual through informational sources.

The advent and development of the computer has created an even higher order of information collection throughout the United States, making the collation of various data, and a complete record on an individual, from birth to death, a distinct probability. The implications of such a system give great cause for concern, and it should be recognized that information for its own sake is not within the realm of a free country. Nevertheless, the computer does afford distinct advantages and the investigator should be familiar with them.

Generally, informational sources may be classified as being governmental (including local, state, and federal), private (e.g., business information), and public (information in the public domain). Much of the information relative to government and private organizations (such as directories) is in the public domain, but it shall be discussed here in terms of its origin.

GOVERNMENT SOURCES OF INFORMATION

Federal, state, and local agencies compile an enormous amount of data that may prove useful in an investigation. While some information may be confidential and unobtainable, such as that regarding income tax returns, a wealth of data is available.

Each investigator should maintain a reference notebook or card file of his own which lists various sources of information. A simple 3 x 5 card file can be used to keep information on contacts and their names, as well as information of a general nature. This should not be committed to memory as a general rule. Some investigators go so far as to maintain their own name and location file of complainants and witnesses. This often comes in handy when information concerning a particular person or location is needed, for the investigator can contact anyone he knows. If such a file is maintained, a short synopsis of individual details and background information on the contact should be entered. These might include personal characteristics, traits, associates, etc.

With respect to government and private sources, recording the name of an individual can be an extremely valuable asset, for personal contact usually produces a greater willingness to cooperate and assist in the investigation.

Federal. Each investigative squad should have a copy of the *United States Government Organization Manual,* which is published annually. This book is an indispensable reference tool, providing information concerning the various agencies, their functions and personnel to contact for assistance.

A listing of federal agencies which are directly involved in law enforcement or some related aspect should be maintained, including the name of the supervisor in charge of the agency. These agencies, upon request, will provide material describing their functions, with which the investigator should be familiar. The amount of information an agency provides may be limited, and often depends upon the nature of the investigation.

When one thinks of federal sources, the first agency which comes to mind is the Federal Bureau of Investigation, which can provide valuable information; however, the investigator should not overlook the many other available agencies. The Postal Inspector's Office can provide information on the names of persons living at a certain residence, their forwarding address, and in some cases particular information concerning a neighborhood or the occupants of a home. The mailman, for example, is likely to see things that are generally overlooked by other individuals.

Information on veterans can be obtained through the Veterans Administration, and various other federal offices, such as unemployment, immigration and naturalization, and the selective service.

State. Most state agencies provide some form of directory listing their functions and personnel to contact. The State Police agency and the Attorney General's Office are likely to have access to information that is not available on the local level.

In addition to the various law enforcement agencies on the state level, there are other offices maintaining records that may be of assistance. Welfare and unemployment offices keep detailed records on an individual's background, including his places of residence and unemployment. Motor vehicle bureaus can also be used effectively to obtain information. Voter registration lists are also maintained by the state, and are an invaluable source of information. In some measure, there may be an overlap between state and local agencies, depending on the locality and the responsibility delegated to the city.

Local. Despite the close proximity and wealth of information available at the local level, few investigators take full advantage of local sources. Indeed, it is more than apparent that the records of a police organization are not put to full use, except in an unusual investigation. In fact, many investigators are often unaware of the type or amount of information that the department is collecting, and in many instances it is so obvious it is overlooked. Summonses, sick or aided cases, traffic accident reports, and inspections of licensed premises are actually frequently ignored as sources of information. In one case with which the author is familiar, a homicide was solved by reviewing parking tickets, and it was found that the suspect's automobile had been ticketed near the crime scene a half hour before the crime occurred. The suspect maintained that he had been in another part of town—with his automobile.

The importance of the patrol force as a source of information is generally recognized, but frequently overlooked. The investigator must make every effort to establish good relations with the patrolman. This subject is discussed further in a later chapter.

Various local agencies, such as records offices, the courts (both civil and criminal), election offices, licensing and health inspection bureaus (such as fire, housing, and safety), and public and private schools are prime informational sources.

The criminal justice agencies at the state and local levels include corrections, probation and parole, courts, juvenile courts, and the state identification and investigation bureau, where one exists.

PRIVATE SOURCES OF INFORMATION

Sources of information in the private sector are virtually unlimited, and most businesses are willing to cooperate in an investigation. Prime sources are those businesses that provide a public service, such as the telephone company, gas and electric companies, and other utility services. In addition to providing information concerning customers, they may be able to offer descriptions of the physical layout of premises, any unusual discrepancies in services (such as long distance or excessive phone calls), or other data that may be required or useful in the investigation.

Each squad should maintain a complete set of local telephone books, as well as a street index directory published by the telephone company. The street index directory is an invaluable tool for determining the names of individuals who live in a particular area or building.

Another important source of information is the credit bureau. Credit bureaus maintain records on anyone who has ever applied for a loan, credit cards, insurance, or bonding. They may also supply information on an individual's background, or employment record. Because these agencies operate on a nationwide basis, they are extremely valuable in the investigation of transients or newly arrived suspects. Indeed, the amount of data these businesses are likely to have on hand is staggering.

In addition, local businesses that may serve the suspect, such as trade stores, banks, loan offices, insurance companies, and department stores, may be able to assist in the investigation. Businesses issuing credit cards should also be considered. Gasoline companies, for example, may be able to provide information regarding an individual's movements or hangouts, just by an examination of receipts.

Taxicab companies may be able to show a suspect's movements by the examination of trip tickets. Operators of public transportation may also be familiar with a particular individual.

Finally, there are any number of directories published by various firms, that may be used to locate or check an individual. In addition, they may be used to conduct a survey if specific information is being sought. Thus, listings of doctors, lawyers, and other professionals and tradesmen should be consulted.

The National Auto Theft Bureau, which has its headquarters in New York City, can be consulted in cases involving the identification of automobiles, as well as in tracing them from the factory to the point of sale. Individual manufacturers may also be able to provide specific information regarding a particular automobile.

If other products are concerned, the manufacturer may be able to trace, through serial numbers, the location at which the article was sold and ultimately the customer's name. Television sets, typewriters, adding machines, and power tools are a few examples.

Pawn shops should also be utilized to the fullest, and if a reporting and inspection system on property is not maintained by the police department, investigators should check the pawnshops frequently. In addition to checking merchandise, the investigator should conduct an examination of the names of individuals who continuously pawn items.

PUBLIC SOURCES OF INFORMATION

At times the investigator should consider the use of citizens to assist in the investigation. For example, employees of various businesses and organizations may be able to provide specific information about the habits and movements of suspects. Routemen, salesmen, clerks, and persons of similar occupations frequently unwittingly come across valuable information.

Friends, neighbors, and other acquaintances of the suspect should also be questioned. Never assume that an individual will refuse to cooperate by supplying answers to questions, or other information. In some instances, even the refusal to answer a question will provide information; by observing facial expressions or asking questions in a certain way the investigator may be successful in obtaining what he needs.

THE UTILIZATION OF INFORMATION

As the investigation proceeds, the amount and types of information collected can become voluminous. Information is of no value to the investigator unless he puts it to use, either to prove or disprove a theory. Up to this point we have generally been discussing the various ways in which information is collected. Let us now give some consideration to the ways in which it can be utilized. In the following chapter the subject of forming conclusions and theory building is taken up in detail. However, prior to this, some discussion of the ways in which information can be handled and evaluated should be of interest.

Our concern here is not with the obvious, such as physical evidence that links a suspect to the crime scene, or a suspect's confession, but rather with the more complex attempt to place a value on the information that has been collected. What value, for example, is a set of fingerprints on the murder weapon? This depends, of course, on whose fingerprints they are. If they can be matched to the suspect, they are highly valuable, but what if they belong to the first policeman on the scene, or the victim? Naturally, the fingerprints of the policeman tell us little, but those of the victim may have some value, for they indicate either that he touched the weapon or that it was placed in his hand.

Concerning verbal information, let us assume that the following statements were taken from different witnesses:

1. "He was five feet four and was wearing a blue coat and overalls."
2. "He was a male, white, about six feet tall, and had an automatic. He also had a scar on his right cheek."
3. "His nickname is 'Pancho,' and he used to live in this neighborhood."
4. "I think his name is Paul and he went to the local high school."

Of what value are these statements? No doubt, there are a number of items which must be considered. To begin with there is a discrepancy in the suspect's height. Does this negate the statement of one of the witnesses? Probably not, for further questioning should result in clarification. For example, the investigator might ask each person how tall they think he is; knowing this, he should then be able to determine the witnesses' error in perception. Thus, a fairly reliable description can be compiled.

However, of the above statements, which one is likely to be most beneficial? Statement four offers a greater probability of locating the suspect than do any of the others, although success may depend on statement three, because witness four was not sure of the individual's name.

Taken on their face value, then, the investigator should not have too much trouble identifying the suspect. On the other hand, he may find that witness four's statement was a case of mistaken identity. Does this make the statement valueless? Perhaps not, for there may be some resemblance in the individual mistakenly identified that can be used to compose a drawing. In some measure, though, the value of the statement has decreased, and the investigator would probably give more weight to the statement of the third witness. In addition to canvassing the neighborhood, he may turn to the "nickname file."

In a sense, every investigation involves analyzing information, assigning it some form of value, making attempts to correlate it, and then acting upon it. Earlier a system of evaluating the reliability of information was mentioned. A simple approach, which has been used effectively in both the armed services and in large businesses, is to apply some numerical or verbal value to the information, and then consider the options. Thus, if the four statements above were handled in this manner, they might be given numerical values of one through four. Such an approach makes voluminous information easier to use to best advantage.

This approach is not limited to verbal statements, but may also be used in evaluating physical or other types of evidence. Thus, the reliability of informant information may be categorized, the value of physical evidence can be determined, and the strength of victim and witness statements can be compared.

SUMMARY

The preceding chapter discussed the use of informants as an investigation aid, and sources of information with which the investigator should be familiar. Every investigation hinges on information, and the manner in which it is collected, analyzed, and utilized is what makes a good investigator.

Three types of informants were discussed: the confidential informant, the one-time informant, and the involuntary informant. As a general rule, each type is handled by the investigator in a different way.

Sources of information are many and varied. For purposes of discussion they have been identified as being either government, private, or public, and the investigator must recognize the distinct possibilities that are raised by their use. Each investigator should maintain his own information file, to which he can turn for assistance.

Finally, the utilization of information was briefly discussed, and methods of analyzing its reliability explored. In the following chapter, this is carried a step further in an examination of information analysis and theory building.

QUESTIONS FOR DISCUSSION

1. What are some of the problems involved in the use of confidential informants? Discuss their value as an investigative aid.

2. Explain the Informant Index. Discuss the ways in which this index can be used.

3. What are the three categories of information sources? Discuss the types of information with which an investigator may be concerned, such as criminal records and property, and how they might be obtained.

4. What is meant by evaluating the reliability of information? Discuss the ways in which this approach can be used.

EXERCISES

1. Prepare an Informant Index card on someone you know. The information to which he has access need not be criminal, but keep in mind that he should not be able to be identified through use of the card.

2. Compile a list of information sources at the local level of government that might aid in an unidentified DOA (dead on arrival) case.

3. Develop a system for evaluating the reliability of information and explain what criteria are involved in testing and analyzing data.

SUGGESTED READINGS

McCormick, Mona, *Who-What-When-Where-How-Why-Made Easy.* New York: The New York Times Co., 1971.

Whisenand, Paul M., and Tug T. Tamaru, *Automated Police Information Systems.* New York: John Wiley and Sons, 1970.

CHAPTER 8

information analysis and theory building

Some mention has been made in the preceding chapters of the analysis of data, as well as ways in which to examine its reliability. The investigative process, however, involves analyzing information on a higher, often abstract, level, before decisions can be made concerning a particular case. In an earlier chapter the subject of logic was briefly discussed. Logic, of course, is the science of correct reasoning. One need not go very far to find persons whose ability to reason correctly is sorely limited. Such a person in investigative work is not likely to be very effective.

A logical approach to a problem is generally based on the amount of information available to the investigator, but information is only as valuable as the ability of the investigator to determine its reliability. Faulty reasoning and misleading information lead to faulty conclusions. Thus, information analysis is an important aspect of the investigator's internal capabilities.

Closely related to information analysis is the concept of theory building. A theory is essentially an explanation of something that has not been verified—in the investigation of a crime, for instance, the possible reasons why a crime was committed, or the basis for belief that a particular individual is the perpetrator. In the pure sciences such as physics, a theory can usually be proved or disproved mathematically. The social sciences, on the other hand, must often depend on a more subjective measure, although statistical tests are available to examine relationships and probability. In a sense, the investigator is utilizing the probability approach when he arrests an individual for a particular crime, as in fact are the judge and jury when they decide on a person's guilt. (However, questions of law, which the judge decides, do not generally fall into this category.)

The more proof against an individual, the higher the probability of his having committed the crime. Nevertheless, the investigator must recognize that the possibility for error is always present, and he must work toward a solution with this in mind. Thus, theory building plays an integral part in the investigation.

Before discussing information analysis and theory building, some thought should be given to the ways in which ideas and theories are developed by the individual. W.I.B. Beveridge, in his work *The Art of Scientific Investigation,* discusses various applications used in biological and other scientific research. Much of this material is of interest to the criminal investigator.[1]

Among the various considerations of which the investigator should be aware in taking a scientific approach are the subjects of chance, imagination, intuition, reason, observation, and strategy. One or more of these factors are likely to come into play during the course of an investigation, and a familiarity with each will aid in the development of a case. How the investigator uses them is directly related to his internal capabilities, intelligence, experience, and knowledge of things, events, and people.

INTERNAL ASPECTS OF THE INVESTIGATION AS A SCIENCE

Science, in the sense in which it is used here, refers to the logical, rational, systematic approach to solving a problem or a crime. One should not conclude that techniques of investigation in the area of crime can afford to be any less rigorous than those used in the natural or social sciences. The importance of criminal investigation need not be justified here, but perhaps it should be recalled that the investigator is working in a "living laboratory," where a mistake may result, and sometimes has resulted, in an innocent person being wrongly accused of a crime, tried, and convicted.

To be schooled in the art of evidence collection, interviewing, and information sources is not enough, for just as the sociologist or psychologist must not only be aware of the tools in his profession, but also be capable of using them to test his theories, so too must the criminal investigator. The following factors are likely to be a part of any investigation.

CHANCE

Virtually every investigation has some element of chance in it; and many a discovery is made by accident. Although such discoveries are frequently attributed to luck, they are quite often the result of an individual's learning to see an event in a different way. Few people recognize the importance of chance, or thoroughly appreciate and understand its significance.[2] For this reason it is important that the investigator be aware that when something unexpected or unpredictable occurs, he should pursue it further. Everyone is familiar with optical illusions (see Fig. 8.1), but how many of us are familiar with mental illusions, or the ability to form various mental pictures in the mind?

In order to recognize opportunities, one must be aware of the following:

1. *Infrequency of opportunities.* "Opportunities, in the form of significant clues, do not come very often."[3] The investigator must be willing to try out new procedures, and expose himself to the unlikely aspects of a case.

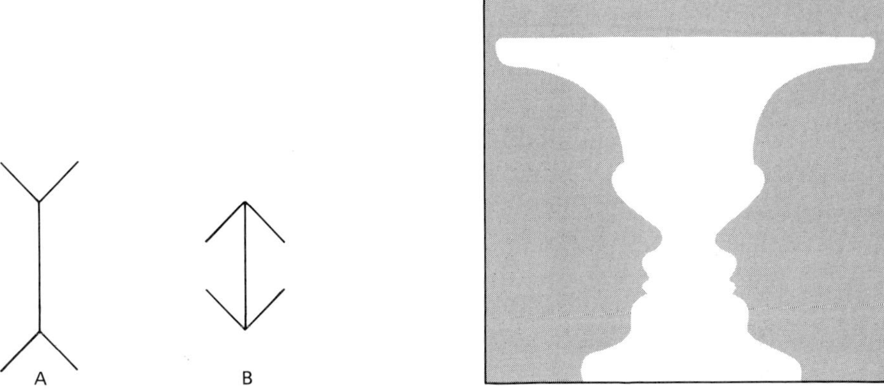

FIG. 8.1 Optical illusions. (Left) In observing both vertical lines, A looks longer than B, yet both lines are of the same length. (Right) Do you see two silhouettes or a vase?

2. *Noticing the clue.* "Acute powers of observation are often required to notice the clue, and especially the ability to remain alert and sensitive for the unexpected while watching for the expected."[4]

3. *Interpreting the clue.* To interpret the clue and grasp its possible significance is the most difficult phase of all and requires the "prepared mind."[5] Many cases have been solved when one investigator interpreted a clue differently from his colleague.

Utilizing chance means recognizing anything unusual or out of place. A piece of physical evidence that may provide more than the obvious, a retracted statement, or a slip of the tongue are but a few examples. Perhaps the most important thing to remember is that persons with fixed ideas or those who are positive about something are less likely to use chance to their advantage. The investigator must not be too quick to form an opinion concerning any piece of information.

IMAGINATION

Ideas originate in the mind, and a great many factors come into play in an individual's thought processes. One of these is imagination, the ability to formulate ideas or mental images. Dewey points out that conscious thinking, or the formulation of an idea, is not a voluntary act, but rather something that "just happens." The initial stage involves a recognition of a proposed solution, after which reason is employed to examine the idea; if it is rejected, the mind reverts back to the original problem and seeks another solution.[6] Generally, the process is a subconscious one.

Imagination may be seen as the ability to conceptualize things in different ways. The greater an individual's store of knowledge is, the greater the number of possibilities to arise. Quite often the ability to abandon the controlled aspect of thinking, and to daydream or allow one's mind to wander is more productive than tackling a problem in a systematic manner.[7]

In criminal investigation, the improbable is more often probable; that is, the criminal is likely to carry out the act in a manner which would be improbable to the investigator or other observers. We all tend to seek a state of order, or reasoned beliefs, but it should be noted that these states of order vary among individuals. Thus, the investigator who is able to imagine the various possibilities involved in a particular crime is apt to be more successful than one who bases his ideas only on his own limit of past experience, or on the accidental similarities between one crime and another. Why, for example, does an individual commit murder? The possibilities, in fact and of course, are endless—indeed, even the perpetrator may not be aware of the real reason for his having committed the crime.

Although imagination is an important consideration, one should realize that there are inherent dangers in its use. Quite often, an overactive imagination results in a person's projecting so much that reality is distorted significantly. For this reason, imagination must be balanced by "criticism and judgment."[8] The investigator must be aware that quite often an idea developed through imagination will be in error. He should never hesitate to question an idea, nor should he fall into the common trap of supporting the idea only because it is his.

Closely related to imagination is curiosity. In fact, curiosity is one of the fundamental ways in which one gains knowledge. Whereas the curiosity of the scientist is directed more toward why a particular thing occurs, the curiosity of the investigator is directed toward establishing who committed a particular crime. Their goals, however, are not mutually exclusive, for it is often necessary to establish *why* a person committed a crime (motivation), in order to establish *who* committed it. Closely related to this is the question of *how* a particular crime occurred. For example, the fact that an individual has been pulled from the ocean is not sufficient proof that he has drowned. Nor is a fire proof of arson, or the allegation of a sex crime proof of the victim's truthfulness. Often, it is the investigator's curiosity that results in establishing new facts. The ability to develop a sense of curiosity is of great importance in criminal investigation.

One of the methods by which curiosity and imagination can be expanded in the individual is through the use of what Beveridge terms "intellectual intercourse." A discussion of the problem or case with colleagues or other persons who may be able to assist, can prove beneficial in any number of ways. Among the benefits to be derived are the development of new ideas, an opportunity to discover errors based on false information or existing ideas, and the ability to escape from conditioned thinking.[9]

Conditioned thinking is a state in which a person is "locked in" by his habitual thought processes. It has been shown, from a psychological standpoint, that an individual can develop conditioned mental processes in the same way that he forms reflex actions. All learning represents some form of conditioning, and the individual must be constantly aware that his habitual thinking habits may distort any information that he is analyzing.

Of prime importance is the nature of the problem with which one is attempting to cope. It is not unusual for an individual to become so engrossed in his method of dealing with a problem that he is unable to see any alternative approach. As Beveridge points out, "once we have adopted an unprofitable line of thought, the oftener we pursue it, the harder it is for us to adopt the profitable line."[10] The tendency to fix an attitude toward a problem prematurely can be overcome by discussing the problem with others, and in some cases, by attacking it from the beginning in another direction. Perhaps the simple burglary case is not what it appears, for it may be an insurance fraud; or perhaps the outside robbery is actually a case of robbery by a dishonest or disgusted employee.

One must be aware that a fertile imagination is but the beginning of a sometimes lengthy process that is likely to prove an idea wrong. Nevertheless, this should not deter the investigator. Likewise, an individual must nurture his curiosity, or his mind is likely to become stagnant. One need not limit his curiosity to the subject of criminal investigation, but in fact should explore other areas of interest to him, as well as those in which he may think he has no interest. All mental experiences have the potential of bearing fruit for the investigation.

INTUITION

Somewhat related to imagination is intuition, which may be seen as the sudden onset of an idea or thought that usually arises spontaneously from the subconscious. Essentially, it is the formation of an idea that was not apparent when the information was first considered, and that is not obvious to all individuals.

Intuition plays an important role in criminal investigation, for quite often the progress of the case depends on the investigator's intuitive ability to conjure up various ideas. In everyday parlance this may be termed "to have a hunch," but there is usually much more than that to the process.

Research has shown that not all individuals have an intuitive capability.[11] Not all intuition is correct, and some individuals indicate that most of their intuitions are false. However, this does not negate the use of the process as an important aid, for many individuals do have the capacity to use intuition remarkably well.

Psychological research indicates that an intuition is more likely to occur after one has spent a period of intense work or prolonged thought about a problem, finally abandoning it to work on another problem.[12] It is believed that the subconscious mind continues to react to the problem and correlate ideas until it comes up with a possible solution.

In order to enhance the intuitive process, therefore, the investigator should allow for periods of relaxation and freedom, giving his attention to other problems; this will permit subconscious thought to surface. Quite often, ideas burst forth at the most unlikely time but they occur more frequently during a period in which the individual is not occupied with a particular problem.

Beveridge cites a technique process for seeking and "capturing" intuitions:

1. Prolonged contemplation of the problem and all of the available data until the mind is saturated with it. The more relevant the data, the greater the chance of success. An important coordinate aspect is the investigator's intense desire for a solution.
2. Freedom from other interests and problems which may compete for attention.
3. Freedom from interruptions, fear of interruptions, or diverting influences.
4. Temporary abandonment of problem, and idleness or involvement in such things as walking or similar pursuits.
5. Contact with others and discussion of the problem. Writing or reading may also act as stimuli.
6. Because ideas often appear and are gone quickly, it is often advisable to have paper and pencil near at hand to note ideas as they occur. One should keep these even on one's bed table. This is an extremely valuable approach when just awakened, since often an idea is forgotten by morning.[13]

The investigator should attempt to stimulate intuition in those investigations that are particularly important to him. In many instances they may not seem to be crucial cases to the department, but there is little doubt that quite frequently a case becomes of great personal importance to the investigator. While one should generally attempt to keep one's emotions from hampering his judgment, there are times when they can be used to advantage. One cannot deny that some subjectivity is involved in virtually every case. If it is recognized, it can be a valuable asset.

REASON

All too often the tendency to accept a conclusion because it has been reasoned out prevents the discovery of a correct solution. Generally, individuals see things as having some logical order that leads to the formation of facts, but it should be noted that this is not always the case. False reasoning is all too common, and one should not accept a statement simply because it *seems* logical.

In the development of an investigation it is usually necessary to use both inductive and deductive reasoning. Inductive reasoning involves the formulation of general principles from particular facts or theories. An example of this occurs in the typing of blood, where research has shown that there are various categories into which blood may be grouped. Deductive reasoning, on the other hand, involves applying a fact or a theory to a particular case. Blood tracings, then, can be analyzed on the basis of the previously mentioned research, and an individual may be "typed." Thus, inductive reasoning moves from the general to the specific.

The investigator develops a theory based on general information (induction), which permits him to deduce certain facts in a particular case (deduction). A major problem, though, may lie in the facts he uses to make an inference. For example, the discovery of a dead body with a pistol in hand is likely to lead to a conclusion of suicide. In this case there is a logical explanation, and taken at face value the reasoning appears sound. However, further examination may prove that a murder has been committed. Faulty logic or reasoning is more common than one might expect, and because it is often impossible to have all the facts of a case, the investigator should be wary of forming hasty conclusions.

In order to combat faulty reasoning, there are a number of techniques with which the investigator should be familiar. To begin with, he must carefully consider all the available information. If verbal or written statements have been taken, he should make every effort to clarify their meaning, and eliminate any ambiguities he might find. A distinction should be made between what is fact, what is probable fact, and what is questionable in terms of the information at hand.

Assumptions should be avoided whenever possible, and care must be taken in making an assumption. It may be said about any idea, "That's just common sense," but common sense has a notoriously bad track record for accuracy.

At every step in the reasoning process, the investigator should consider everything at hand, and assure himself that all possibilities have been taken into account. As the problem becomes more complex, the degree of error in reasoning increases. In discussing the possible suicide previously mentioned, it was pointed out that a logical explanation may be false. It is a fact that the individual is dead, but until an autopsy has been performed, the cause of death is merely a supposition. Thus, as the number of suppositions increase, it should be apparent that the probability of error is also magnified. Statistics can be of immense value in the reasoning process, for they reduce the factor of error. Statistics, for example, can be used to predict the probability of an event's occurrence.

The investigator should be aware that we are all prone to rationalizing, that is to say, developing a reasoned argument on the basis of preconceived opinions. If we think an individual is guilty, it is generally easier to find information, at least in one's own mind, which tends to implicate him.

In an earlier chapter the importance of language was discussed, and it should be clear that this aspect of the reasoning process is of great importance. The investigator must understand what his words mean, and one way of increasing competence in this area is by writing. He can learn to discipline himself to write in an orderly manner; this is but a reflection of the thinking process and, ultimately, of his reasoning capability. When writing up a case, the investigator should avoid words which are vague or likely to have double meanings. In some instances it is wise to write a case up by listing the events in chronological order, but it may be of as much value to consider the case in terms of its peculiar elements, such as scientific evidence, witness statements, or other information.

As a general rule, the investigator uses reason either to prove or to disprove a particular fact or finding. Rarely does he employ reason in proceeding from one idea to the next, because these ideas arise more from imagination, intuition, or, in many instances, observation.

OBSERVATION

There is little doubt that observation plays an important part in the investigative process, but it should be kept in mind that the difficulties in this area are many. The accuracy of observation depends on a number of factors, including the element of surprise, the amount of danger facing the observer, and the relationship of the observer to the participants. In many cases the investigator is working in a milieu which has all the above elements and these contribute to faulty observation.

Beveridge tells of an experiment performed at a psychologist's conference, where a man ran into the room chased by another who carried a revolver. After a scuffle, a shot was fired and the man ran out about 20 seconds after having entered. The incident had been planned, although the observers had no prior knowledge of it. Of 40 accounts, only one person had less than a 20 percent error about the principal facts, and 25 of the observers were in error on more than 40 percent of the facts.[14] This is a striking example of the possibility of error in observation, especially in view of the fact that the observers were trained in scientific observation.

Experiments in mass communication indicate that people tend to see what they want to. Edwin Schur points out that the news media tend to support existing outlooks; and by a process of "selective retention" people read and see things that reinforce their values.[15] In some measure, this holds true of observations one makes in his everyday life.

In a sense, an individual may, through observation, see something that is not there, or add to its detail. The investigator should be aware that he is as prone to such error as anyone—perhaps more so, since his work carries him into highly charged emotional situations more frequently than the average person.

The investigator's powers of observation must be keen, for he is expected to see the unusual as well as the usual; he should be able to recognize detail, and see things that are out of place in a setting or sequence of information. Thus, observation involves a mental operation that may lead to a spontaneous observation occurring unexpectedly, or an induced observation that the investigator is usually seeking.[16] In both instances the investigator should attempt to discern the *significant* aspects of that which is in his view. The trained investigator knows what to look for, even when he does not know what he is looking for specifically.

On the other hand, one must use caution about overlooking anything. This may be especially troublesome if the observation is part of a routine or common practice, as happens sometimes at the crime scene. The investigator *expects* to find certain things and thus may overlook the more important findings which he does not expect.

One can develop one's powers of observation, and the investigator should be constantly aware of this in his everyday work. He should practice describing various scenes, articles, locations, and persons, and then check his observations for reliability. As time passes this procedure will become almost automatic. In order to develop this technique further, the individual should constantly familiarize himself with the various things that are a part of his occupation.

The success of observation is measured by the ability to mentally record important information, as well as the capability to recognize the unusual and apply it to the problem.

STRATEGY

One area in which many investigators are deficient is planning. All too often the emotional atmosphere surrounding a case gives rise to hasty action, and consequently few results. Although some cases are almost accidentally solved in this manner, a methodically planned approach, with a developed strategy, is more likely to be successful. Furthermore, the strategy should be determined by the investigator assigned to the case, and *not* by a higher authority. Studies have shown that research is more apt to be fruitful if the individual conducting it has worked out his own tactics.[17] This is also true of the investigator; too much supervision or planning by his superiors can destroy his initiative.

In certain cases the investigator may be given assistance, and here, too, he should be permitted to devise his own strategy. A part of this strategy should involve consulting superiors and colleagues in determining a plan of action. Teamwork is essential, and the investigator should see that all those concerned are *involved*. In some instances, a specific investigator may be assigned to develop a particular aspect of the case, while in others each may be left free to choose his own course of action, within predetermined guidelines.

If the investigator is working on a case alone, he should still devise a plan of action. Usually this involves preparing a work sheet listing the goals he wants to accomplish. In some cases the plan may be more complex in determining the order in which the tasks should be carried out. If there are a number of alternatives that will have a bearing on the case (such as whether to interview a suspect, or leave him alone and observe him), the investigator must work out a solution. This aspect of the case is called developing tactics.

Tactics involve bringing together all the available information, as well as a list of the resources that may be used. In one sense, the investigator's approach could be likened to that of the field commander in the army who is faced with the problem of deciding which way to capture a hill. His success is often dependent on intelligence (information), equipment (resources), and manpower, and the way in which he chooses to use them. Quite often the unorthodox approach may be more successful than the traditional method.

Thus the investigator should realize that, while there are certain rules or guidelines to be followed, these rules are not rigid. He should be willing to be innovative where the situation calls for new ideas. The object of criminal investigation is to solve crimes, not to present a long list of the "right" procedures which have been followed. The only exception to this will occur if a law prohibits a particular action, in which case the investigator *must* abide by the rule. The professional investigator is always able to work within the law.

If a strategy has been worked out, it should be reviewed carefully, and the opinions of other experts should be considered. The investigator must keep in mind that he may often be biased against any criticism of his work. Finally, it should be noted that each investigator tends to develop his own style. If this style is successful there is little cause for concern, but careful and frequent review is mandatory. Success often leads to conditioned thinking and conditioned thinking to error.

DEVELOPING AND TESTING THEORIES

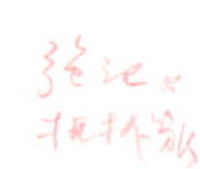

In attempting to solve a case the criminal investigator generally goes through a series of procedures, some by rote, others based on the unique nature of the case, and others determined by his particular orientation. In essence, he attempts to pool all available knowledge, apply degrees of value to it, and make a decision as to either who the suspect is, or how he will progress in attempting to identify the suspect. Thus he develops one or more theories. Theory may be defined as a reasoned set of propositions, which are supported by information that serves to explain a particular phenomenon. In this sense, it is more than a hunch or an idea, and should involve a careful, analytical approach to the problem at hand.

In many criminal cases a number of theories may be developed. This is generally not a problem, unless the investigator makes the mistake of mixing or confusing theories without carefully analyzing the component parts of each. For example, in any investigation there are likely to be a number of suspects. The investigator has certain information at hand which leads him to make particular decisions. In a homicide occurring in a residence, there is a strong possibility (at least, statistically) of some type of victim–suspect relationship. In developing a theory, however, the investigator must be aware that not all homicides evince this factor. Thus, he must recognize alternative factors based on other evidence. He should not discard evidence simply because it does not fit into his theory, nor should he attempt to fit evidence to the case. An example of this occurred in a celebrated murder case, where investigators discovered on the suspect a picture of what they thought was one of the dead girls. Subsequent investigation proved this to be false, but statements were made to the press that the suspect had a picture of one of the dead girls in his wallet.

All too often in the haste to solve a case, an investigator is likely to omit or overlook important information, or to misinterpret it. Once this occurs, the validity of the theory comes into question.

Once a theory has been developed the investigator must test it. From an objective and scientific standpoint, he should attempt to disprove the theory. In order for him to do so, the theory should be well developed.

THEORY BUILDING

One may compare theory building to the solution of a jigsaw puzzle: the investigator is attempting to put each of the pieces in its proper place. Unfortunately, in many instances a number of the pieces will be missing, and some will not even belong.

To begin with, the investigator should make every attempt to bring all his information together. This is usually done in the form of reports, although one often finds that a vital piece of information has been eliminated through carelessness, forgetfulness, or laziness. What may not appear important at the outset may later prove to be the key to the case. Thus, it is better to record something and later discard it than not to record it and forget it.

Once the information has been gathered the investigator must attempt to categorize it in some meaningful way. Thus, in addition to a general file in chronological order, he might also set up ancillary files in other categories, such as witnesses, physical evidence, rumors, etc. If this is not feasible, some form of cross-referencing may suffice.

Psychological testing has shown that an individual can only store and relate a minimal amount of information in his mind at any one time. Symbols are more readily adaptable to abstract analysis than are phrases, paragraphs, or words.

Once all available information has been collected and an attempt has been made to categorize it in some logical sequence, the investigator should attempt to place some value on the information. In most cases this can be done mentally, but in a complicated case it may be of value to develop a numerical or letter gradient. Thus, information of unquestioned value would receive a "1" or "A" and less reliable data, such as rumors, would be given lower classifications. While such an approach may seem too detailed or simplistic, the investigator should keep in mind that the more complicated a case is, the greater the likelihood for human error in interpretation. This is especially true if multiple cases, such as a series of robberies or burglaries, are concerned, and the investigator is attempting to develop patterns and other factors. Frequently, such an approach provides multiple clues which offer a solution when compared. The computer can be of immense value in accomplishing such correlations.

As information is recorded the investigator will generally come to some conclusions about the case: either that the case is not capable of solution given present information, or that there is a possibility of solution given further investigation, or that a suspect has been identified or is identifiable. We are concerned here with the latter two aspects of the decision-making process.* If the investigator decides to proceed he has generally formulated a number of reasons which lead him to believe that there is some possibility of success. These reasons may be seen as the initial development of a theory. Generally, the mental operation involved in formulating a theory is based on a logical interpretation of facts. Of course, it should be understood that one's interpretation of facts affects the accuracy and outcome of a particular problem.

Each theory developed is the result of decision making, a process of iteration, or cyclical operations, beginning with a hypothesis, the collection of information, the coordination of information, the development of alternatives, the decision, and ending with an action to implement the decision, resulting in either a solution of further information or the formulation of another set of hypotheses. (See Fig. 8.2). If a series of decisions supports a significant number of hypotheses, a theory is developed that brings these together as an integral aspect of the problem at hand. Figure 8.3 illustrates a theory building model, similar to the decision making model, with the exception that the theory is based on the results of information already collected and may be seen as a more advanced level of decision making. In this model the theory is tested for validity by the investigator. If information supports the theory significantly, there is a solution to the problem. If it does not, the investigator is faced with new information, i.e., that he has not coordinated the information properly, or that the information is false. Thus, he begins the process again.

In most instances this is all accomplished in a matter of seconds, and most people would not even be aware of the process at work. Nevertheless, each day we make thousands of individual decisions, and in many of our decisions we develop theories concerning the problems we encounter. Ultimately, we carry out these theories in the form of actions. For example, when buying a car each person has different ideas and perceptions that result in a number of minor decisions, and finally a theory as to which car suits his need and why. We know, of course, that in many instances, and for a variety of reasons, the ultimate decision may be the wrong one. This is also a problem in criminal investigation; there are numerous instances in which it appears that a theory has been proven, when in

*There is an assumption here that a decision to abandon a case is based on reliable decision making, and there is the recognition that in numerous cases such a decision is often hasty and generally ill-advised.

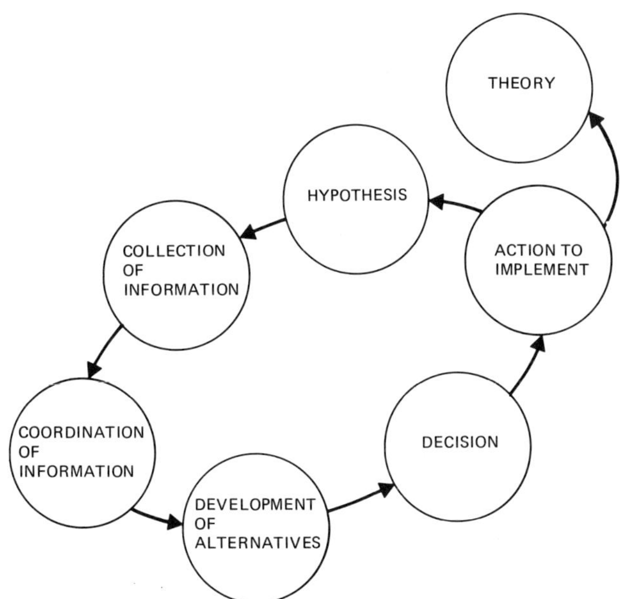

FIG. 8.2 Decision making.

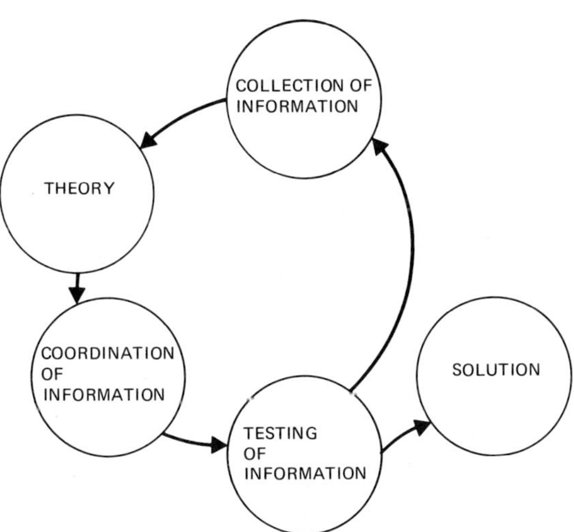

FIG. 8.3 Theory building.

fact it has not. Generally, this is the result of an error at some point in the decision making process. If we were to compare the process to a mathematical problem, it is similar to an error in computation or the use of irrelevant data.

The investigator should always keep in mind that he has his own biases, and it is virtually impossible for him to disregard them. Nevertheless, every attempt must be made to be objective in decision making and theory building. Thus, it often is valuable to consult with others in a difficult case. Care should be taken, however, just to present the facts, and not to prejudice the other person's decision with your conclusions.

The ability to make clear decisions and build sound theories is often overlooked insofar as qualities in investigators are concerned, yet it should be apparent by now that this is perhaps the most crucial aspect of the investigative process. Faulty reasoning leads to faulty conclusions, and faulty decisions lead to error.

SUMMARY

The importance of information, decisions, and theories was covered in detail in this chapter. Various approaches concerning the internal aspects of criminal investigation as a science have been discussed, including chance, imagination, intuition, reason, observation, and strategy. Additionally, the concept of developing and testing theories was raised, and a functional approach to decision making discussed. Too little attention has been paid to this area in the past; however, with the development of knowledge it will continue to grow in importance in years to come.

NOTES

1. W.I.B. Beveridge, *The Art of Scientific Investigation.* New York: Random House, 1957.
2. *Ibid.*, p. 43.
3. *Ibid.*, p. 47.
4. *Ibid.*, p. 47.
5. *Ibid.*, p. 47.
6. John Dewey, *How We Think.* Boston, Mass.: D. C. Heath, 1933. (Cited in Beveridge, *op. cit.*, pp. 72, 73.)
7. Beveridge, *op. cit.*, p. 75.
8. *Ibid.*, p. 78.
9. *Ibid.*, p. 85.
10. *Ibid.*, p. 87.
11. *Ibid.*, pp. 96, 97.
12. *Ibid.*, p. 97.
13. *Ibid.*, pp. 102–104.

14. *Ibid.*, p. 131.
15. Edwin M. Schur, *Our Criminal Society.* Englewood Cliffs, N.J.: Prentice-Hall, 1969, p. 142.
16. Beveridge, *op. cit.*, p. 136.
17. *Ibid.*, p. 163.

QUESTIONS FOR DISCUSSION

1. Why are information analysis, decision making, and theory building crucial to the investigator?
2. Discuss means by which an individual can improve his levels of perception.
3. Explain the various steps involved in decision making and theory building.

SUGGESTED READINGS

Austin, Robert, et al., *Police Crime Analysis Unit Handbook.* Washington, D.C.: National Institute of Law Enforcement and Criminal Justice, 1973.

Beveridge, W. I. B., *The Art of Scientific Investigation.* New York: Random House, 1957.

Brussel, James A., *Casebook of a Crime Psychiatrist.* New York: Bernard Beis, 1968.

Edwards, Ward, and Amos Tversky, *Decision Making.* Baltimore: Penguin Books, 1967.

Willmer, M. A. P., *Crime and Information Theory.* Edinburgh University Press, 1970.

CHAPTER 9

crimes and their patterns: crimes against the person

Like fingerprints, no two crimes are exactly the same. Nevertheless, experience and statistics have proven that certain types of crime are likely to exhibit similarities and that criminals generally tend to develop similar patterns of activity, as to both the types of crime they commit and the manner in which they commit them. A criminal pattern is known as the *modus operandi* (M.O.) or method of operation.

While there is insufficient data to indicate conclusively that criminals tend to commit similar crimes, studies in New York City support such a hypothesis.* If a criminal has been successful in his attempt to commit a crime, there is a strong likelihood that he will continue to commit the same type of crime, especially burglary or robbery. In conducting an investigation, crimes may generally be classified as those against the person and those against property. In this chapter and the following one, the focus will be on crimes in these two broad categories. In a later chapter the subject of victimless crimes and other special investigative crimes will be explored.

Although it would be impossible to delineate all the individual factors in any one crime category, much less the broad category of crimes against the person, there is a body of knowledge with which the investigator should be familiar, to aid him in handling the average case. As a working definition, a crime against the person is seen as a criminal act in which the perpetrator must *physically confront* his victim in order to carry out the crime. Thus, while robbery is often classified as a crime against property, it shall be discussed in this chapter as a crime against the person. In addition to robbery, the crimes of criminal homicide, rape, and assault fall into this category.

Each of these crime categories will be discussed separately. However, at the outset it should be noted that the legal definitions used in this discussion are of a

*A 1970 study showed that of 829 persons arrested for burglary, 314 had been arrested previously for the same charge. Of this group, 31 had been arrested five or more times, and 157 had been arrested two or more times. Over two-thirds, or 71 percent, of the 829 persons had at least one previous arrest. (See *New York Times,* "A Pattern in Crime," January 20, 1970.)

general nature; therefore, the reader should familiarize himself with the particular elements of each crime as delineated in the Penal Code of his state.

CRIMINAL HOMICIDE

Criminal homicide is defined as the death of a human being caused without justification or excuse by the unlawful act of another human being.[1] Within the category of criminal homicide are varying degrees of seriousness: murder being the most serious, with manslaughter and negligent homicide being considered crimes of a lesser degree. We will focus here on the category of murder.

Murder is defined as "the deliberate, premeditated killing of another human being."[2] Murder investigations vary considerably, but it is possible to differentiate between three general investigative categories: (1) premeditated murder in which the act is planned; (2) murder during the commission of a crime such as robbery or burglary; and (3) murder arising as the result of a physical assault, usually during a dispute.

While it is virtually impossible to determine which of these categories presents the greatest problem to the investigator, one can say that murders arising from an assault and premeditated murders *generally* provide the investigator with a list of suspects from which to work, whereas murders committed during the commission of another crime often leave the investigator with few initial leads, because there is no victim-suspect relationship. Naturally, there are exceptions to this rule, especially if unprovoked assaults and organized crime are concerned. The investigator is often faced with the problem of proving premeditation in assault cases.

PHYSICAL EVIDENCE AND CRIMINAL HOMICIDE

Although physical evidence is no more abundant in homicides than in other types of crime, the care, preservation, and collection of evidence at the scene of a homicide are usually recognized as being of greater importance in the investigation. In earlier chapters, the crime scene and physical evidence were discussed in detail; in this chapter the focus will be on their importance to the homicide investigation. Despite the numerous warnings received during hours of classroom instruction to preserve the scene of the crime, it is not unlikely that some physical evidence will be destroyed or overlooked by those investigating. Thus, it may be important that the investigator return to the scene at a later time to conduct a follow-up investigation.

The courts have begun to rely more and more on physical evidence as testimony, and the investigator must be aware that much of his function in this respect involves linking the pieces of evidence to form the thread leading to the perpetrator. Thus, although fingerprints represent a positive link to the crime scene or the murder weapon, other forms of physical evidence may provide circumstantial information which, when pulled together, offer a solution. With this in mind, the investigator should be aware of any evidence that is not obvious at the outset, such as cigarette butts, discarded or torn clothing, and other material or objects which might link the suspect to the crime or which might be of value in leading to a suspect. For example, a number of discarded cigarette butts may prove of no value after laboratory examination, but knowledge of the brand name may be of aid in reducing the list of suspects. The size of clothing may also be a valuable factor, although it is impossible to prove that it belonged to the suspect. The investigator must be aware that even if the laboratory cannot be of assistance, physical evidence has other values. In many instances such evidence may provide the only clue.

ESTABLISHING THE CASE

In the investigation of any crime, one must establish the *corpus delecti,* or elements of the crime. "At common law, murder is the unlawful killing of any human being with malice aforethought, either express or implied by law."[3] Thus, the investigator must prove that an *unlawful* homicide has taken place, and that it was accomplished with *malice aforethought.*

Under the felony murder rule, even if the original intent was not to commit murder, a murder committed during the commission of another felony such as burglary or robbery, establishes malice aforethought, and the perpetrator is liable to a charge of first degree murder.[4]

In conducting a homicide investigation, the investigator must take care to establish the elements of the case, and should be thoroughly familiar with the laws applicable in his jurisdiction. In certain instances the charge against an individual will be determined by the efforts expended by the investigator in preparing the case. Physical evidence, statements of the perpetrator and witnesses, as well as circumstantial evidence will all be of importance.

In all homicide cases the investigator must attempt to establish the motive and intent of the perpetrator. Motive is no more than the reason for which the crime was committed, and intent is viewed as proving that the act was purposeful and committed to inflict death or great bodily harm. In certain instances, reckless or dangerous behavior resulting in the death of another human being may be cause for a homicide charge.

The investigator should not hesitate to seek the advice of the District Attorney, and it is often wise to maintain continuous contact with him as the case develops. This approach allows for better communication and coordination, and is likely to reduce the possibility of error, both by the investigator in preparation of the case, and by the District Attorney at a later stage. Any number of cases have been lost because of poor communication between the police and the prosecutor, and in most instances it is too late to collect evidence as a case comes to trial.

There is nothing more frustrating than to believe that a case has been adequately prepared, only to find that it is lost on some technicality or oversight. The need for adequate record-keeping has been stressed repeatedly throughout this text, and its importance to case preparation cannot be overstated.

The investigator must never lose sight of the need for objectivity in the preparation of a case, and, as noted in the previous chapter, it is wise to make every attempt to follow up leads and prove the suspect innocent. This approach not only ensures that justice will be served, but also strengthens the case against a guilty suspect.

PREMEDITATED MURDER

A premeditated murder, as viewed here, occurs when some planning has been developed by one or more persons to take the life of another *identified* person. This is inconsistent with the legal definition of premeditation, which states that an individual may be charged with premeditated murder even though he did not know his victim, such as in the case of a sniping incident. This will be discussed at greater length in the section on murder arising as the result of an assault.

The investigative concept used here assumes that the suspect had some knowledge of who his victim was, and acted with the intent to kill that particular person. The differentiation, although it may appear to be a minor one, will have an effect on the direction that the investigation takes. For example, if there is an assumption made at the outset that the victim's death was purposely caused by another, the investigator will spend more time delving into the victim's background in an effort to turn up a lead. In a random sniping incident the investigator would generally turn away from the victim toward other ways in which the suspect can be identified, and an investigation into the victim's background is likely to be limited. Naturally, as the case progresses the approaches will begin to merge, until all avenues have been explored. But at the outset the investigator is often faced with a choice as to how he will utilize his time and that of support services.

Initially, it may be difficult to determine whether or not the murder was planned, since it is not uncommon for the perpetrator to attempt to conceal the act by creating the appearance of another crime, such as burglary. Thus, a careful examination of the crime scene is essential, and care must be taken not to make hasty assumptions. The author is familiar with one case in which the death of a young housewife led police to believe that she was murdered during a burglary attempt. Later investigation indicated that the husband was a probable suspect, but the time lapse between the event and this discovery enabled the husband to discard certain evidence, and better compose his story. The result was an inability to prosecute the case.

Since a careful examination of the scene may indicate that it has been staged, the investigator should give special thought to such things as the means of entry and exit, position of the weapon, placement of furniture, position of the victim, nature of the wound, and any other details that would indicate something other than what is apparent.

The nature of the wound may be misleading; thus, the investigator should not make a hasty decision as to the cause of death. An autopsy will provide a detailed examination, but care must be taken not to overlook anything that may be of value later, such as position of the body or its proximity to other objects. What may look like a suicide might turn out to be a murder.

Techniques of interviewing witnesses were discussed in an earlier chapter, and there is little need to go into further detail here. Nevertheless, it should be pointed out that the testimony of witnesses may provide the vital link that establishes a case. Extreme care must be taken to clarify statements so there is no misunderstanding as to what the witness is saying.

If there is some indication that the murder was premeditated, the investigator should attempt to compile a list of those persons who may have had some reason to wish the victim's death. Some of the reasons might include the following:

1. *Money or business interest.* Insurance beneficiaries, business partners, or trust fund recipients are often prime suspects.
2. *A dispute or feud.* If hostile relationships exist between the victim and others, there is the likelihood that one of his enemies is a suspect.
3. *Marriage and family relationships.* Statistics indicate that most homicides are committed by persons who know the deceased, and many are committed by a member of the immediate family. Investigation into the background of the spouse may reveal an illicit affair, or continuous disagreements between the victim and spouse.
4. *Acquaintances.* Because most homicides are committed by an acquaintance, it is wise to check the background of anyone who knew the victim.

If a homicide has been planned it is probable that someone had something to gain by the victim's death. The investigator should make every attempt to discover information that will lead to suspects. This often involves an extensive search of existing records, examination of the victim's personal effects, including memos and correspondence, and careful interviewing of persons who may not appear to have any knowledge of the case. Keep in mind that persons who knew the victim are often wary of giving any information that may be based on rumors, especially immediately after the crime has been committed. Therefore it is often wise to conduct follow-up interviews at a later date, and to be observant of any nuances and personal mannerisms when taking statements. Witnesses will often offer some clue, when they are actually speaking, that may indicate just the opposite of their implied statement. Be wary of such statements as, "He was a really great guy, not an enemy in the world, of course one never knows everything, does one?" In reality, the witness may have valuable information but is reluctant to divulge it without being pressed for it.

In some instances it is possible to link the statements of a number of people in order to determine a pattern, and then to return to those witnesses with your findings. Quite often they will be able then to provide further information.

Finally, the investigator must be aware that some external pressures may exist to prohibit the witness from providing information. The "Don't get involved" syndrome is not uncommon, and quite often the major problem will be in convincing the individual that his help is of primary importance to the investigation.

One of the major problems in the investigation of premeditated murders is in locating the various sources of information and then developing them. There are certain factors that give the investigator an advantage over the investigation of other types of homicide, one of them being that the homicide was committed for a particular purpose, and usually not in the commission of another crime. The investigator must develop this advantage to its fullest.

MURDER DURING THE COMMISSION OF A CRIME

This form of homicide will be discussed separately because it presents special problems to the investigator. The murder is generally committed as an ancillary act during an attempt to commit another crime, and in most instances it is accidental in that the perpetrator did not previously plan to kill his victim. Obviously, there are certain exceptions to this idea, but on the whole it is rare for a criminal to decide in advance to murder his victims. There appears to be a higher percentage of murders in the case of a sex crime, but even so, statistics bear out the fact that most sex crimes are committed without homicidal intent. This subject is covered in greater detail in a later section.

Probably the two most common forms of homicide in this category occur during the commission of a robbery or burglary. Unlike premeditated murder, there is usually no relationship between the victim and the suspect, and in this age of mobility it is not unlikely that the perpetrator is far gone from the crime scene by the time police arrive. On the other hand there is some indication that the perpetrators of robberies, and especially burglaries, are likely to live in relatively close proximity to the scene of the crime, and in a majority of cases in the city where the crime was committed.[5]

Once an examination of the scene, the collection of physical evidence, and the interviewing of witnesses have been completed, the investigator should turn to an examination and analysis of past crimes. It is often possible to determine whether or not the perpetrator was a professional, one who has committed a number of crimes and developed a *modus operandi* or style. If this is the case, there is likely to be a criminal file on the suspect.

If the investigator has exhausted all his primary leads, he must then turn to secondary leads. Frequently the perpetrator has committed a similar crime, and by examining previous cases it is often possible to recognize some that are similar to the crime under investigation. If similar crimes are discovered the investigator should conduct a follow-up examination. Keep in mind that earlier cases probably did not involve a homicide, and may not have received full investigative attention. Thus, the investigator should interview suspects and witnesses, recanvass the area, and examine any physical evidence that might have been collected or, in some cases, overlooked. If the department is equipped with a computer facility a records search is relatively simple, and also offers any number of approaches to the investigation.

If a pattern is established, it may be possible to develop a list of suspects based on M.O., physical descriptions, or other criteria. Given this information, the investigator must now attempt to link possible suspects to the crime.

Because much of the investigation at a robbery- or burglary-related homicide will be handled in similar fashion to a robbery or burglary case with no homicide, the reader should familiarize himself with the individual techniques discussed in these sections.

As a general rule, the investigator will have a greater degree of departmental support in the investigation of a homicide, and he should not hesitate to make use of it. In addition, the investigator may call on the services of the mass media by establishing a separate telephone number for information from the public. However, in homicide cases it is often wise to keep certain aspects of the investigation from the public in order to check the validity of callers' statements. Asking for a description of the weapon, physical characteristics of the scene, and the like may be used to eliminate crank telephone calls. Keep in mind, though, that *any* questionable information should be handled. A good rule of thumb is, "When in doubt, investigate!"

MURDER AS THE RESULT OF A PHYSICAL ASSAULT

It is obvious that almost all murders involve some form of assault. However, our concern here is with those homicides that occur as spur-of-the-moment actions or with no particular victim in mind, such as sniping incidents.

By far, most homicides are committed as the result of an argument, disagreement, or fight, and often in the heat of passion. Investigation of the case involves locating the perpetrator, if he has left the scene, establishing a sequence of events and obtaining witnesses, and preparing the case for court. Here again physical evidence is likely to play a crucial role, especially if self-defense or accidental death is claimed by the suspect.

The investigator should not assume that because at the outset he has a suspect who has made a statement the case is open and shut. His failure to satisfy procedural requirements may result in a dismissal. If the suspect's statement is dismissed, which is not unlikely under the Miranda and other recent decisions, the investigator must have more to his case than a victim and a suspect. The tendency in an assault-homicide of this nature is to view it as an open-and-shut case. However, one never knows what the defense will be, and it is often wise to anticipate probable defense options. Follow-up investigation into the backgrounds of both the victim and the suspect may reveal information that has a bearing on the case; the relationships of witnesses to both victim and suspect should also be checked out.

Assault-homicide cases are likely to be the result of arguments over property or a woman, or disagreements between married persons or lovers. Studies also indicate that in the vast majority of assault-homicides there is some relationship between the victim and suspect. In addition, most homicides are committed with a gun (approximately 50 percent), with knives and cutting instruments running a close second (approximately 40 percent).[6] Blacks are more likely to use a knife, whereas whites more frequently use a gun.[7]

A less common form of assault-homicide, but one that is increasing in numbers, is the random murder in which the perpetrator goes berserk killing anyone in sight, or the sniping incident where the perpetrator conceals himself for the purpose of assassination. In the latter form the sniper may attempt to kill a particular individual, such as a political candidate, someone in a particular occupational category, such as a policeman, or anyone in sight. The sniper presents a special problem to the investigator because he is usually unknown to the victim, is completely hidden, and is willing to lose his life. If the sniper escapes from the scene there is often little information other than physical evidence and, in some cases, witness statements, from which to proceed with the investigation. While there are no statistics available it would appear that most snipers or assassins do not have a previous criminal record for this type of assault, although they are likely to have come into contact with the law, especially in those cases involving police officers.

In all sniping incidents, the scene must be examined thoroughly in order to develop trace evidence that can be used to link the suspect to the scene. Fingerprints, footprints, fibers, shell casings, and the like may be the only linking factors. Care must be taken in canvassing the area, and anyone who might possibly have been in a position to observe the suspect must be located and interviewed. If there is an immediate follow-up investigation to the incident, it is often wise to have someone collect the license plate numbers of all cars parked within the immediate area; a registration check may produce the name of a suspect. If possible, it is also advisable to correspond with taxicab companies, which keep trip records, and interview the drivers of any cab that discharged or picked someone up in the immediate vicinity either shortly before or after the incident.

The success of such an investigation often depends on painstaking effort and a certain amount of luck. Nevertheless, the investigator should keep in mind that luck is often no more than making one's own breaks.

SUMMARY OF CRIMINAL HOMICIDE INVESTIGATIONS

In addition to the points previously discussed, the investigator should recognize that there are many forms of criminal homicide that have not been evaluated here. The author's intent was to provide a working knowledge of the homicide investigation. However, further reading will provide greater expertise in the intricate facets of homicide investigation, including the investigation of murders involving organized crime, hit-and-run cases, abortions, and poisonings, to name a few. The reader is encouraged to familiarize himself with the contents of the bibliography at the end of this chapter.

Homicide investigations present a unique challenge, and only through diligent study, observation, and perseverence will any degree of competence be realized.

ROBBERY

Robbery is one of the more serious felonies because of the risk to the victim. Hence, it is an important crime insofar as the investigator is concerned. Although robbery is viewed by many as being a crime against property, it is also a crime against the person, and is thus being discussed here as such. Robbery is defined as the unlawful taking of property from the person or presence of another by threat, violence, or fear.

A primary drawback in the investigation of a robbery is often a lack of physical evidence. Nevertheless, a careful examination of the scene should be undertaken, and anything the perpetrator may have touched should be dusted for latent fingerprints. The cash drawer, merchandise, and entrance are likely to provide clues in a business robbery. A discarded wallet or pocketbook may be of value in investigating a street robbery.

Because of the short time span usually involved in the commission of a robbery, witnesses may be unable to provide complete descriptions, and because of their emotional stress, may inaccurately perceive the course of events and actions. Thus, it is wise to separate witnesses immediately before taking statements. This initial statement may be crucial to the investigation, for over a period of time witnesses are likely to embellish or misconstrue the facts. Once a physical description has been obtained and broadcast, the investigator should have each witness draw a diagram of the perpetrator's actions, and list any statements he may have made.

The manner in which the crime is carried out may be crucial in developing suspects. If the robbery is a professional one, there is a greater likelihood that the perpetrator has a previous arrest record. It is also possible to develop an M.O. to aid in the discovery of previous crimes, or in follow-up investigation at a later date if the perpetrator is apprehended in the commission of another crime.

Some understanding of the types of robberies will aid the investigator in developing suspects. The following has been extracted from the New York City Police Department Robbery Manual.

BANK MESSENGERS

This type of crime is seldom attempted by amateurs, and is usually the work of experienced criminals, generally working in groups of from three to six. Sometimes they work in collusion with a dishonest employee who tips them off with information as to the movements of messengers, the procedure followed in making deposits and withdrawing funds, and the methods of transportation. The crime is planned in advance. Each criminal is drilled in the part he is to act. Cars are stolen days in advance, the number stolen depending upon the need for escape and transfer. License plates are removed from the stolen area and other plates which have been secured under a fictitious name and address are substituted for them. The cars are stored until the day of the crime. About one-half hour before the messenger leaves, the robbers drive to a spot adjacent to the bank; one remains at the wheel, while others act as lookouts to prevent interference with the holdup. The motor of the car is left running or, if stopped, is started up a few minutes before the messenger from the bank is expected. If he is riding, they force him to stop (usually under a ruse of arguing some traffic infraction or discourtesy in driving) and commit the robbery. Sometimes, they wait in a hallway near the place of delivery until he approaches.

BANKS

These are professional criminals who organize carefully, plan with ingenuity, attack boldly, and are equipped with adequate weapons such as machine guns, sawed-off shotguns, rifles, or possibly tear gas grenades. Sometimes they dress as a letter carrier, telegraph messenger, or even policemen, to gain entrance to the bank (if the door is locked) under this subterfuge, getting the watchman to open the door. After entering, the watchman is subdued and the front door is opened for confederates. The guard may be handcuffed in a back room while the arrival of other employees and bank officials is prepared for and then the crime is committed.

Another method is that of driving up to the bank and entering, leaving one confederate at the wheel with the motor running and another outside as lookout. At a given signal, guns are produced and employees are forced to move away from alarm devices.

Small banks are not amply protected and are often entered at night through an upper-floor window, or from an adjacent building by means of a rope. The guard and employees are then overpowered when they arrive in the morning.

ARMORED CARS

This crime is committed by thoroughly experienced criminals who go to the greatest pains in preparing plans for its commission. They have been known to use tow trucks or automobiles, speedboats, and even airplanes. Part of known strategy has even included a hearse, a pushcart, and other such business vehicles. They dress for the part (as peddler, undertaker, street cleaner, policeman, etc.). Equipped with machine guns, revolvers, shotguns, etc., they move with some degree of precision. Sometimes they operate through the tip of a dishonest employee.

PAYROLLS

The large payroll entrusted for transport to an officer or paymaster is taken by criminals numbering from four to six men. These bandits work similarly to that of the robbers of bank messengers. When they have definite information as to a large payroll protected by a guard who is not alert, they approach quickly, shoot the guard, cover others, take up the payroll, and flee.

The small payroll, entrusted to a girl cashier who draws it from the bank, is taken by a lone worker or criminals who operate in pairs. The bandit is usually a young and active man, not always professional. He observes a young girl going into a bank and drawing out two or three hundred dollars for the weekly payroll. Generally she carries this money in an envelope in the same hand with her pocketbook. The robber usually precedes her into the building and when she approaches, strikes her with his fist or a blunt instrument, takes the money, and escapes. He seldom has a gun, but has been known to use a piece of pipe wrapped in paper. He generally tries to lose himself in alleys and buildings, or among the pedestrian traffic in the street. He may also enter the office when the girl is making up the payroll and other employees are not present. He poses as a job-seeker or salesman, seizes the money at the right moment, and assaults her if she resists.

JEWELRY STORES

Experienced criminals, working in groups of from two to five robbers, usually engage in jewelry store robberies. The better-class stores are selected. The time chosen is just after opening or just before closing, when trays of jewelry are being put in or taken out of the window. Criminals usually use a stolen automobile which is provided with fictitious license plates. Again, a confederate remains at the wheel of the auto with the motor running; another acts as lookout while the others enter. Small leather bags or attaché cases are used to hold the jewelry. At the point of revolvers, the clerks and owner are held up while jewelry is removed from the trays and made safe, and the thieves escape after the issuance of a warning. If two automobiles are used for escape, the perpetrators ride a few blocks in the first to the point where they enter the second car which has a driver accomplice waiting. Sometimes, another confederate waits nearby and after they escape in a car, he enters another car and acts as an impediment in the event of pursuit. Those men are usually desperate and dangerous.

A second method used is that of the two thieves visiting the store ostensibly to make a purchase. A certain piece is selected and a payment by check is offered. The clerk refuses to cash it and one of the thieves leaves to get it cashed elsewhere. The other remains in conversation with the clerk. The thief who left to cash the check then telephones the store. As the clerk or owner answers the phone, the remaining robber covers him with a pistol. Then another accomplice enters the store and takes the available jewelry. If possible, they also have the safe opened and remove the contents. The clerk or owner is then tied and gagged, telephone wires are cut, and the escape is effected.

OUTSIDE JEWELRY SALESMEN

Professional criminals working in groups of two or three operate against the jeweler or salesman calling to show his line to a prospective customer. The criminal operation may occur anytime during business hours. Sometimes the thieves are tipped off by a member of the trade working in collusion. The criminals may hold him up while he is in a taxi or when he is in his hotel room. They will assault him if resisted, take the jewels, and direct him to walk up to the roof. They then escape after issuance of warning. If the jeweler or salesman is riding in a cab or automobile, he will be followed in another car. When traffic pauses, the criminals enter his car, cover him with a gun, direct him (or the taxi driver) to proceed to a given location, and abandon him after the robbery, using his vehicle (or the cab) for the getaway.

In buildings equipped with elevators, the elevator will be used as the place for the commission of the robbery. If the salesman is staying at a hotel for a few days, the criminals may engage an adjacent room, gain his confidence, and commit the robbery in his room. Members of the gang may even gain entry to the room by posing as a bellboy, Western Union messenger, etc.

CHAIN STORES AND SHOPS

All classes of criminals operate in this field. They select stores where there is a large turnover of money in a day, where there are only one or two clerks on duty, or where there is a large volume of business. Time of the robbery is generally just before closing time. It may be a Saturday night when banks are closed or when the money is held for pickup by a money collector on Monday. Several robberies may be committed in succession. The perpetrators drive up to a point near the premises, sometimes accompanied by a woman to avoid suspicion. A driver remains at the wheel of the auto (usually stolen) while the robbery is in progress. The motor is kept running. The criminals ask for a particular article. The clerk may turn around to get it and when he returns to the counter, the criminals will have him covered with a gun. He and other employees (and patrons) are usually ordered to the rear of the store and tied up or handcuffed back there while the robbery is in progress. Often the victims are made to undress to avoid pursuit. Pant legs are knotted in a further effort. While one (or more) of the perpetrators is in the rear of the store accomplishing this purpose, one (or more) may be outside posing as a salesman while rifling the cash registers. They may even wait on a customer during this time. At a favorable moment, the thieves will all return to the car and make their getaway.

RESTAURANTS AND LUNCHEONETTES

Criminals robbing small restaurants, lunch wagons, and coffee houses usually work alone or with one partner. The more experienced criminal mob select better, more expensive restaurants for the robbery. They usually operate late at night (around 11:00 P.M.). They will enter the store, order food, eat, and await an opportunity. They then hold up the cashier and may fire shots to effect their escape. The lone robber does not usually have a car with him and hails a cab to effect his escape, sometimes at gunpoint.

THEATERS AND MOTION PICTURE HOUSES

Many such robberies are committed by a lone bandit who forces his way into the cashier's booth. If there is more than one criminal, they usually commit the robbery in the manager's office, either preceding the cashier inside and awaiting his (or her) entry, or following the cashier into the office. These crimes are generally committed at closing time (before the crowds let out) or, at the better theaters, after curtain time.

GASOLINE STATIONS

Criminals operate against hose stations in groups of from two to four. At times, a female accomplice may be used or a male so disguised may assist. Stations in outlying areas are most prone, generally after 11:00 P.M.. The criminals will drive up in a car, order gas and oil, and produce a gun when the attendant comes to collect. Phony license plates are usually used. The attendant is usually locked in a washroom or tied up afterwards, while the robbers make their escape.

DRUGSTORES

The professional or amateur criminal may be found here. Sometimes a female accomplice will enter first and give the clerk or pharmacist an order. Her male companion will follow, produce a revolver, and commit the holdup. The clerk is usually left tied in a rear room. Besides emptying the cash register, narcotics may also be taken.

CLUBS AND PRIVATE HOMES

The hardened criminal element is involved in these types of crimes. Clubs or private homes, where gambling is the vogue, are very prone. The perpetrators in such instances wear masks to avoid being identified later.

GAMBLING GAMES

Professional criminals operate on crap games and other gambling locations such as lofts, garages, cellars, poolrooms, wire rooms, piers, and construction sites on payday if crap games are conducted on these premises. They usually arrive when the game is in full swing, having made a survey of the location in advance.

DEPARTMENT STORE DELIVERY TRUCKS

Robbery of trucks and delivery vehicles is usually the work of professionals. The gang consists of three or four in a stolen or hired car. The truck is followed to a quiet location and then forced to the curb. Guns are used. Sometimes the driver and/or helper are put into the thieves' car and abandoned at some distant point, while another member of the gang drives the truck to a safe location for unloading. Then the truck is driven to another location and abandoned.

TAXICABS

Amateur criminals are usually involved in this operation. M.O. patterns are often established, since the thief or thieves are narcotic addicts and tend to continue a successful pattern. Many times the same areas are used to commit the crimes. Drivers are directed to lonely areas where the robbery is committed. Often the cab is driven away and the driver left abandoned. A female perpetrator accompanying the male is not uncommon.

RAPID TRANSIT LINES

This type of robbery is usually the work of a lone perpetrator who is experienced. The times are usually during non-rush hours. At gunpoint, the agent is ordered to open the booth and the perpetrator enters and commits the crime. He may tie up the agent or knock him unconscious to effect the escape. An auto may be left upstairs at the entrance to the station to effect escape.

WAREHOUSES

This type of robbery is generally committed by gangs of experienced criminals operating in the early morning hours. One or more employees may be in collusion with the gang, or at times the robbery is planned based upon information obtained from an agent or a lieutenant of the fence or receiver. Warehouses which are used to store valuable merchandise, such as liquor or tobacco, have become favorite targets of this fruitful criminal activity. Careful planning goes into such robberies and the criminals are usually very heavily armed. Telephone wires may be cut. Goods are transported to the doors on hand trucks. The truck used by the criminals (the switch truck) now arrives at the premises and a lookout is strategically located during the loading. He will issue warning signals and all clear signals, for instance, by wiping his face with a handkerchief. There will usually be a lookout on the inside of the warehouse also stationed at a window. Such robberies usually occur in the early morning hours (5:00 or 6:00 A.M.). Since interstate and market trucks are in movement at these times, one truck does not attract much attention. After being taken to a prearranged drop, the merchandise has any identifying marks removed from it and is then taken to a fence.

PHYSICIANS AND DENTISTS

Thieves who specialize in this type of robbery are experienced criminals, usually operating alone. They pick a time when the office is empty of patients. Perpetrators are always armed, and sometimes gold and other items such as drugs are also taken, as well as cash.

PRIVATE CARS

During recent years, there has been an increase in the robberies of couples parked in lover's lanes and other such areas during seasonable weather. Mostly confronted by lone bandits, the couples have their cars stolen, as well as their valuables. A criminal assault may be committed on the female as well, especially if there is more than one perpetrator. Sometimes the perpetrator is picked up by the couple as he stands out on the road thumbing a ride.

ROBBERY INVESTIGATIONS

Successful robbery investigation often depends on perseverence. At the outset information is generally scarce and the investigator must utilize all the options available to him. If the police department employs an artist, it is often possible for him to develop an accurate sketch of the perpetrator. This can be extremely useful if the suspect displays a distinguishing facial mark or scar. The use of various identification kits has also been adopted in a number of departments. Generally this is a form of plastic overlay or composite with various facial characteristics. The advantage of this method is that investigators can develop a portrait of the suspect on the scene. Use of the crime laboratory and the distribution of photos and/or sketches of the suspect may also aid in identification.

In many instances the only means of developing a case will be through existing records; thus, an up-to-date records file should be maintained. Among the types of files that may be used are:

1. Robbery typology file.
2. Location index.
3. Nickname file.
4. First name file.
5. Physical descriptor and tattoo file.
6. Photo file.
7. Known offenders and parole file.
8. M.O. file.

Virtually all the above files are adaptable to computerization, and as departments move toward more sophisticated information systems, the investigator will have the advantage of quick retrieval and manipulation of data. In some cities it is now possible to ask the computer for possible suspects in a variety of ways. For example, a request may be worded in the following manner: Anyone arrested for robbery who is a male, white, between the ages of 30 and 35, between 5'6" and 6' tall, who lives within a specific geographic location, and who drives a blue car.

The computer is capable of searching its files and producing a list of possible suspects in a matter of seconds. If too many suspects are produced the number can be reduced by providing more specific information. If no suspects are produced, criteria may be removed, such as age or height data, and a new query initiated.

In many cases the investigator of a robbery will find himself at a dead end with no further leads to follow. Rather than closing the case immediately, it is often wise to maintain it as an active file and continue to check daily crime reports for similar crimes or arrests. Quite often a perpetrator is arrested by the patrol force, and the good investigator will be able to link him to past crimes and make an arrest.

Cooperation with the uniform force is extremely important and the investigator should make every effort to develop this source of aid. Quite often a patrolman will have the missing link to an investigation, but due to the hostility often existing between patrolmen and detectives, he is not anxious to offer it. By providing the uniform force with adequate information, and seeing that patrolmen are commended when they provide information, the investigator is enhancing the probability of successful investigations.

Informants are often valuable in the investigation of a robbery and the investigator should not hesitate to use those informants whose past performance has been favorable.

Perhaps the best key to successful robbery investigation is the ability to develop, link, and utilize information that leads to suspects. As technology is improved, the investigator will be equipped with newer and better tools to analyze information. Nevertheless, the manner in which the tools are used is what determines the success of any operation.

SEX CRIMES

While there are a variety of sex crimes with which the investigator must be familiar, discussion here will be limited to those crimes committed through the use of force or fear. Rape, sexual deviation by force or fear, and child molestation are three of the more common sex crimes with which an investigator will be faced.

One of the more difficult aspects of investigating sex crimes is the delicacy with which the case must be handled. In many instances the victim is reluctant to provide information out of fear or embarrassment, and if children are concerned, there is the added danger of the stigma which may result from victimization.

Secondly, suspects must be handled carefully, since the focusing of suspicion on an innocent person is likely to have grave ramifications. Care must be taken in the conduct of the investigation, and interviews should be as discrete and confidential as possible.

Information concerning the victim's identity should be kept from the media and others who do not have some specific involvement or interest in the case. Because serious physical injury and sometimes murder accompany this form of crime, it is one that can rapidly arouse public indignation and fear. The result may be pressure for a quick arrest, and any number of cases may be cited where an innocent person was arrested, or where a hasty arrest resulted in losing the case in court on a technicality.

RAPE

Rape is defined as sexual intercourse with a female to whom the subject is not married and in which the act was committed by force or fear, or where the victim was rendered helpless by preventing resistance. There are various categories or degrees of rape depending on the circumstances and age of the victim. If the victim is a juvenile (ages vary between 16 and 18 from state to state) and consented to the act, the suspect would be charged with statutory rape.

Generally, some corroboration other than the victim's statement is necessary to prove a rape case. This may be in the form of physical evidence, proof of opportunity or presence, or witness statements. In order to establish rape, it must be proven that some penetration did occur, a fact which makes it imperative that a physical examination of the victim be conducted at the earliest opportunity.

An interview with the victim should also be conducted as soon as possible, as this may be of value at a later time in establishing corroboration. The victim who fails to report the crime immediately is subject to close scrutiny by the defense concerning the truth of her allegation. In conducting the interview the investigator must attempt to develop specific statements pertaining to the crime; vague testimony will not suffice in court. A thorough description of those events leading up to and those immediately after the crime should be obtained. The degree of force necessary to establish a rape case is a subjective one, and an effort should be made to determine how force was applied or what threats were made.

At least one study indicates that the majority of rape victims knew their assailants; in less than ten percent of the cases, the perpetrator was unknown to his victim.[8] If there is a relationship between the victim and suspect, it is often difficult to establish a rape case.

If a suspect has been apprehended shortly after the crime he should be examined by a physician. His clothing should be turned over immediately to the crime laboratory, following the procedures outlined in Chapters 3, 4, and 5. In addition to proof of recent sexual activity, trace evidence linking the suspect to the victim (such as body hair, cosmetic traces, and other biological evidence) may be obtained.

In cases where the perpetrator is unknown to the victim, the investigator must often turn to the use of records in pursuance of the case. An investigation of this nature is somewhat similar to the investigation of a robbery although the known offender file is likely to be an effective source of information.

In some cases there may be more than one perpetrator, and an individual may be convicted of rape although he did not engage in sexual intercourse with the victim. In fact, in some cases women have been convicted for the crime of rape if they aided a male in carrying out the crime.

SEXUAL DEVIATION

Sexual deviation by force generally involves the crime of sodomy, although in some cases the victim may be forced to commit other sex acts, such as fellatio or cunnilingus. Investigations of these cases are similar to those involving rape.

In some instances the investigator may be faced with a case in which the victim was willing to have sexual intercourse, but was forced to commit other acts. Obviously, it is often difficult to establish such a case, and once again physical evidence is extremely important.

The range of sex offenses varies between states, and many have removed laws concerning the behavior of married persons. In addition, so-called sexual deviance among consenting adults is under review in many states and the investigator should familiarize himself with the laws of his jurisdiction.

CHILD MOLESTATION

The child molestor represents a specific problem to the investigator, for the young child makes a difficult witness. Prolonged questioning or graphic descriptive testimony is likely to have a lifelong impact on the child, and the investigator must proceed with caution in his interview. Nevertheless, the perpetrator of such a crime is a menace to society, and it is imperative that he be placed in a position where treatment is available and where he cannot commit similar crimes.

In certain instances the child is likely to be a willing participant, and reluctant to provide information. Here again, the manner in which the case is handled is crucial. The investigator should attempt to develop information slowly, beginning with indirect questions. He should refrain from moralizing or giving the appearance that the questioning is uncomfortable or abhorrent to him. In developing the case he should be careful not to confuse the witness; it is usually advisable to discuss events chronologically.

Naturally, the age of the youth and his experience will have a bearing on the questioning, and if a juvenile appears to be lying it is often wise to take a different tack and attempt to verify statements by asking the same questions in different ways. The procedures outlined in Chapter 6 will aid the investigator in developing the case.

If the suspect is unknown an attempt should be made to develop a pattern analysis based on location. Quite frequently such crimes will occur within specific geographic boundaries, and in some instances at a particular time of day or night.

Child molestation is viewed as a heinous crime by the public and is a difficult crime both to investigate and to prosecute. With this in mind the investigator must take extreme care in developing such a case.

SUMMARY

In this chapter crimes against the person were reviewed, with a particular emphasis on criminal homicide, robbery, and sex crimes. All these crimes are extremely serious because of the threat to human life, and public apprehension is probably at its highest where they are concerned. Because of their nature the investigator is often faced with the difficult task of developing information where virtually none exists, at least at the outset. Nevertheless, such crimes present a unique investigative challenge, and many of them are solved only through the relentless efforts of the investigator.

Unfortunately, too many crimes against the person go unsolved for lack of effort or a cynical attitude on the part of the investigator. There is no doubt that many investigators fail to utilize the external resources available to them, especially insofar as the crime laboratory and the records system are concerned.

Finally, there is often a tendency among investigators to prejudge a crime and make hasty decisions. It is wise to keep in mind that a thief can be robbed and a prostitute can be raped.

NOTES

1. Kerper, Hazel P., *Introduction to the Criminal Justice System.* St. Paul, Minn.: West Publishing Co., 1972, p. 107.

2. *Ibid.*

3. *Clark and Marshall, A Treatise on the Law of Crimes,* 7th ed., Marian Quinn Barnes, revising editor. Chicago: Callaghan and Co., 1967, p. 628.

4. The courts have held that if an individual is in the act of committing a felony, and as a result of this act commits a homicide, he may be charged with murder. See, for example, *The People* v. *Fallie Sutton,* 17 Cal. App.2d 561, 62 P. 2d 397 (1936). Cited in Kerper, *op. cit.*

5. A study conducted by the author in cooperation with Joseph Peterson and Richard Natoli in Richmond, California, indicated that of 293 felony arrests, 67 percent of those arrested lived in Richmond, and 15 percent lived in an adjoining county.

6. O'Hara, Charles E., *Fundamentals of Criminal Investigation,* 2nd ed. Springfield, Ill.: Charles C. Thomas, 1970, p. 524.

7. *Ibid.,* p. 524.

8. *Ibid.,* pp. 280–281.

QUESTIONS FOR DISCUSSION

1. Discuss the probability factors in crimes against the person: Who is more likely to commit a murder, what type of criminal is likely to be involved in a bank robbery, and what is the probability of a victim-suspect relationship in sex crimes?

2. What are the *corpus delecti* of murder, robbery, and rape?

3. How can information be used to develop a case, and what types of files should be available?

EXERCISES

1. Develop a chronological approach to the investigation of a robbery where there are no witnesses other than the victim. What steps should be taken to pursue the case?

2. Utilizing a role-playing situation, develop the interview of a juvenile who is the victim of a sex crime. Criticize the approach of the investigator concerning his technique and questions.

SUGGESTED READINGS

Conklin, John E., *Robbery and the Criminal Justice System.* New York: J. B. Lippincott, 1972.

Hunt, Morton, *The Mugging.* McClelland and Stewart Ltd., 1972.

Irwin, John, *The Felon.* Englewood Cliffs, N.J.: Prentice-Hall, 1970.

Misner, Gordon E., and William F. McDonald, *Reduction of Robberies and Assaults of Bus Drivers: Volume II: The Scope of the Crime Problem and its Resolution.* U.S. Department of Transportation Demonstration Project, 1970.

CHAPTER 10

crimes and their patterns: crimes against property

Burglary and larceny are the two most common crimes against property. Only *personal* property is subject to theft, and differs from *real* property in that *real* property consists of land and that which is affixed to it. *Personal* property is all other property. As a general rule, anything that may be removed, either by hand or through mechanical means, is considered personal property. As Hazel Kerper writes:

> If a house is taken off the land and put on a trailer for moving, it has been changed from real property to personal property. Oil still in the ground is real property; when it is pumped out of the ground and put in storage tanks, it is personal property. A lavatory is personal property as long as it is in the crate; when it is installed in a bathroom, it has become real property; when taken from the wall, it is personal property again.*

The types and number of larcenies and burglaries differ markedly, despite the commonality of terms. The investigator should be familiar with the various methods used to carry out these crimes.

LARCENY AND THEFT

The terms larceny and theft are usually synonymous, although there may be some slight differences in legal definition among states. In order to establish the crime of larceny or theft the investigator must show:

1. an unlawful taking of the personal property of another,
2. without consent and with intent to deprive the owner of its value,
3. and with intent to use the property to the benefit of the person taking it.

---

*Reproduced with permission from Hazel B. Kerper, *Introduction to the Criminal Justice System.* St. Paul, Minn.: West Publishing Co., copyright © 1972, p. 135.

The degree of the crime is generally based on the value of the property stolen, and in certain instances this may include property stolen over a period of time. In the latter case the investigator must establish that there was some common scheme and plan used to deprive the owner of his property, i.e., a construction site from which a worker removes a quantity of material each day. Although the amount of theft each day may not be sufficient to warrant a felony charge, the total of the property stolen over a period of time may justify such a charge. In any case the theft must be from a single owner.

Although the investigator must establish that the perpetrator took possession of the property, this possession need not be physical. For example, constructive possession may be shown in cases in which the perpetrator causes a removal of property for his own use, such as the transfer of stocks or bonds to his personal account, even though he did not actually touch the property. In addition, if a person borrows property and does not return it, he too may be subject to a larceny charge. This occurs frequently in the case of property rentals.

It is necessary to locate the owner of the property before a larceny charge can legally be established, and in many instances the investigator may be faced with the problem of determining ownership. Even if an individual states that he owns the property, he must be able to explain satisfactorily how he knows it is his. This is best accomplished by identifying a serial number, which can be matched with a bill of sale, but other identifying criteria, such as a physical mark or alteration, are also generally acceptable. Most items bear some physical characteristic which makes them unique, but it is sometimes difficult to find one of which the complainant is aware.

The value of the property must be established in order to determine the proper degree of the charge. In general, the market value of the property is used by the courts. In all cases the value is based on currency, and emotional or so-called personal loss is not a factor.

Motive and intent indicate the reasons for which the crime was committed. In most cases the motive is pecuniary, although kleptomania or a desire to harass the victim may also be factors. The intent in larceny must often be inferred from the perpetrator's action. The investigator must keep in mind that he must establish a desire for gain on the part of the suspect. If a person borrows property from another it is difficult to sustain a larceny charge unless it can be shown that the person either intended to keep the property or sold it to another. However, the perpetrator's statement that he intended to return the property is not sufficient to remove the onus of larceny.

In conducting the larceny investigation care must be taken to ensure that an accurate description of the property, including serial numbers or any other specific identifying characteristics, is recorded. When a suspect has been apprehended, the owner of the property must be able to testify as to ownership. For this reason, it is wise to ask the owner how he knows the property belongs to him. Scratches, marks, additions, and deletions may all be used to assist in identification.

Persons who had access to the property and the opportunity to remove it should be questioned. A background check on these individuals may reveal a prior criminal record, indebtedness, or some other circumstantial evidence which will assist in the development of a list of suspects. The location of the property is likely to indicate whether or not the theft was an "inside" job; thus, in the case of a business larceny, the investigator should familiarize himself with the routines of employees. If it appears that an employee is involved, it is not unlikely that one or more persons are either involved or at least aware of who the thief is.

Although physical evidence may be difficult to find on the scene, a careful examination should be conducted. Latent fingerprints and other trace evidence may reduce the possible number of suspects. If property has been recovered, latent prints may link a suspect to the crime. Naturally, the type of larceny dictates the manner in which it is to be investigated; thus, the following discussion centers on various categories of theft.

COMMERCIAL AND BUSINESS LARCENIES

While there are no accurate figures regarding the loss suffered by businesses from theft each year, the cost is monumental. When one includes the proceeds from other forms of white-collar crime, the dollar value runs easily into the millions. The subject of fraud is discussed in a later section; the focus here is on the theft of goods from businesses, warehouses, and factories.

In attempting to understand this form of larceny, the investigator should familiarize himself with the particular business that is being victimized. Thefts of this nature are usually committed by dishonest employees or professional thieves. The shoplifter is excluded from this discussion, as this particular form of criminal activity is generally handled by security forces working for a department store.

The initial investigation of a reported theft should include a careful examination of the scene to determine whether it would have been easy for an outsider to commit the theft. Quite often, loading docks or open supply areas are targets for the professional thief. In such a case it may be difficult to establish proof of ownership once the thief has left the scene. Bills of lading, serial numbers, or model numbers may be of value. In general, however, the amount of merchandise removed in this type of theft at any one time is minimal, and tracing is often difficult because the property is frequently sold on the street or in a bar. Finally, it may be some time before the property is discovered missing, a fact which also inhibits efficient investigation.

If there appear to be continuous thefts over a period of time there is a strong likelihood that an employee is responsible. Thus, the investigator should attempt to determine workers' routines and movements. This should assist in eliminating those employees who are probably not suspect. Discrete observation of suspected employees may provide further leads regarding their hangouts and acquaintances.

Perhaps the major problem in conducting an investigation of dishonest employees is the feeling of most people that what they are doing is not really criminal. Because the corporation is regarded as the victim, most employees are unwilling to provide information against co-workers. In order to overcome this, the investigator should attempt to show employees the seriousness of the crime and its impact on others.

In many instances the investigation begins after the property has been recovered, when an attempt must be made to trace the property backwards, i.e., through the persons who came into contact with it. In the case of a large-scale theft, the perpetrator generally sells the goods to a fence who in turn distributes it to one or more persons who will either dispose of it to individuals or to another business.

THEFT

In addition to committing thefts from businesses, a great number of thieves make their living by stealing from careless or unwary citizens. In urban areas the practice of breaking into automobiles to steal property is not uncommon. In addition, sneak thieves are likely to grab money from cash registers when the salesperson is away from the counter or otherwise distracted. It is not uncommon for sneak thieves to work in pairs, with one acting as a lookout. While a great many sneak thieves are not classified as professional criminals, drug addicts are frequently involved in this form of criminal behavior.

Investigation of these types of crime is difficult because there is little information on which to proceed, and if a thief has been apprehended with stolen merchandise, the complainant may be hard to locate. Close liaison with pawn shops and secondhand dealers is sometimes fruitful, although they are not likely to provide information unless carefully controlled. A file on stolen property should be maintained for a period of time, listing the property, complaint number, complainant, and location of theft. If property cannot be identified by a serial number, it may be advisable to keep a brand name or specificity file (which identifies unusual or recognizable items, such as a tool chest or jewelry). This file should be cleaned periodically (weekly or monthly) in order to make searches relatively simple. Quite often an item of property will turn up a week or two after the theft, and such a file facilitates identification.

Because thefts in this category do not involve large sums of money or property of significant value (although it may be difficult to explain to a complainant that his $30 camera is not of much concern in the total crime picture), police departments are not likely to expend much manpower on these investigations. Nevertheless, the investigator should familiarize himself with the persons involved in this form of theft, and make an attempt to apprehend the major perpetrators. While the thefts may appear to be of minimal significance, the author knows a number of persons who claim they can make in excess of $100 a day as petty thieves. When one assumes that they must steal anywhere from $500 to $1000 worth of property in order to make $100, the cost rises considerably.

Finally, the investigator should be aware that the complainant may be making a false complaint for any number of reasons, and he should conduct the interview with this in mind. Truckers are not averse to stealing property they are carrying, and citizens are not unlikely to report a normal loss as a theft for insurance purposes.

CREDIT CARD AND CHECK THIEVES

The credit card business has grown to monumental proportions over the past decade and all signs indicate continued growth in future years. The stolen credit card presents a relatively new problem to law enforcement, and techniques for investigation of such cases and apprehension of suspects have not advanced significantly.

Virtually all companies using credit cards have their own enforcement units, and the investigator should familiarize himself with their operations. In addition to the thief who may steal a pocketbook and use the credit cards for a short time, organized crime has become active in this area of theft, and the cost to the taxpayer each year runs well into the millions of dollars.

In most cases the investigator becomes involved in a credit card investigation when a suspect has been picked up for another crime and discovered with a card not belonging to him. Most major companies utilize a central number which may be called to check on credit cards. If the card has been reported stolen the investigator will be notified. However, the card may not have been reported stolen, and the investigator should conduct a follow-up search by contacting the owner of the card.

If a report of illegal credit card use occurs, the investigator should secure documentary evidence (usually the receipt), and turn it over to the laboratory for a latent fingerprint examination and handwriting analysis. If a suspect has been apprehended, specimens of his handwriting should be secured and forwarded to the laboratory. Because a signature is usually all that is required for a purchase, it may be difficult to secure a positive identification. For this reason the investigator should take care to develop other aspects of the case, including witness identifications and interrogations. A search of the perpetrator's belongings may produce a receipt or the property purchased. Establishing the perpetrator's presence at the scene may also be invaluable at a later time, and the investigator should take care in checking the suspect's alibi. Credit card companies often keep their own files on known offenders, and contacts here may be invaluable in establishing patterns or in making positive identifications.

The theft of checks from the mails is a federal offense, and has become a major problem in recent years. In many cases the reported theft is fabricated and the complainant is acting in collusion with another. A disclosure of welfare fraud in one large city in 1971 indicated that falsified reports of check thefts were not uncommon. While the investigator should keep this in mind, he should not make a hasty conclusion, and until proven otherwise he is obligated to take the complainant's word and conduct a thorough investigation.

In general, the investigator works with postal inspectors and investigators from the agency involved. Once the check has been cashed an attempt should be made to identify the suspect by interviewing the person who cashed the check. Here again, handwriting analysis and witness testimony may be the only solid evidence, and if a suspect has been identified, a thorough background investigation should be undertaken.

If it appears that the complainant may be making a false report, a handwriting specimen should be taken and compared with the endorsement on the check. In numerous cases the complainant has been found to have cashed the check himself and then reported it stolen.

COUNTERFEITING AND FORGERY

Counterfeiting and forgery, while not generally thought of as crimes against property, are discussed in this section because the ultimate goal of the perpetrator in such crimes is to realize illegally some material profit. The United States Secret Service is responsible for all crimes involving the counterfeiting of United States currency and other securities. In such cases the investigator should immediately contact the Secret Service.

Development of the offset printing press has resulted in a greater number of counterfeit bills being produced each year. Between 1965 and 1969, the passing of counterfeit notes increased 267 percent. Although much of the investigator's work in this area will be in cooperation with the Secret Service, he should be familiar with counterfeit notes and be able to detect them. Figures 10.1, 10.2, and 10.3 illustrate the quality of genuine and counterfeit currency. In addition, genuine currency exhibits what appear to be red and blue threads imbedded in the paper, and may often be distinguished by texture. The counterfeit note appears flat and lacks the three-dimensional quality of genuine notes. Note the squares in the background of Figs. 10.2 and 10.3. In the genuine currency the squares are distinguishable, while in the counterfeit bill they are often filled in or missing. If there is any doubt a comparison of the suspect bill with a genuine one should resolve it.

In addition to counterfeit currency, the Secret Service is also responsible for the investigation of forged government checks and bonds. Frequently these are stolen from the mails and the thief forges an endorsement.

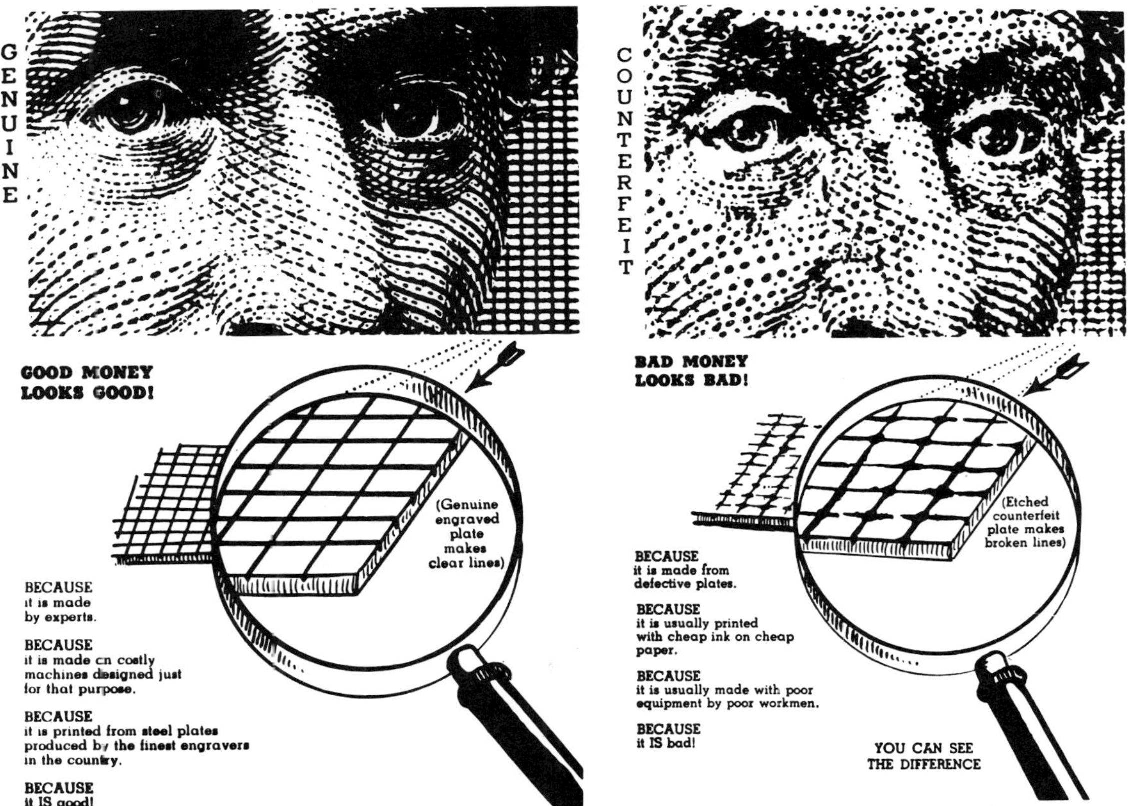

FIG. 10.1 Genuine vs. counterfeit currency. (This photograph and the following two figures courtesy of the United States Secret Service Visual Intelligence Branch.)

FIG. 10.2 The fine detail in the portrait of a genuine note stands out prominently when compared with the portrait of a counterfeit note.

FIG. 10.3 Note that the inferior workmanship of the counterfeit currency is easily detected.

Forgeries of personal checks, stocks and bonds, letters, and records may also be the subject of an investigation. In order to establish a forgery case, the investigator must prove that the perpetrator knowingly uttered a forged article with the intent to defraud another. Laboratory examination of the document will usually detect a forgery or alteration and may uncover latent prints. The investigator should take care to preserve all documentary evidence. Photographs should also be taken.

In cases of handwriting forgery, specimens should be obtained from suspects and forwarded to the laboratory. The methods employed by forgers vary, and some familiarization with various techniques should aid the investigator in his initial investigation. In no case, however, should he handle or mutilate the document in order to conduct a comparison. The freehand forger is adept at copying a signature or writing. However, microscopic examination will usually indicate whether the writing is stilted, or whether the forger paused in forming certain letters. The use of carbon or tracing paper to copy a signature is also generally apparent under a microscope. It should be noted that no two signatures are exactly alike. The use of an eraser or ink eradicator to alter a document will be evident due to fiber mutilation or chemical traces, which will appear under ultraviolet light.

Mechanical forgeries, such as those using a typewriter or stamp, are distinguishable and laboratory examination may be conducted to link the suspect document to its source. Finally, perforations and tears in the document may also be compared to determine source.

CONFIDENCE GAMES

Because of the uniqueness of this category of crime, it would be unwise, if not impossible, to attempt to discuss each of the confidence games in detail. Suffice it to say that the range and scope of confidence games encompasses virtually all levels of society, from the poor person who may be deceived of his or her life savings to the large company that may lose hundreds of thousands of dollars. One need not look far to find examples of the lengths to which individuals will go in perpetrating this type of fraud. The supreme example is probably the Clifford Irving–Howard Hughes case, in which Irving's claims to have written a factual biography of the famous recluse were later proven to be fraudulent.

Most confidence games, however, achieve little notoriety except to the victim and the investigators faced with the problem of solving them. A confidence game is classified legally as a fraud; therefore in order to establish a case the investigator must establish the elements of a larceny: that there was an unlawful taking of the personal property of another, without his consent, or *by false or fraudulent representation or pretense,* with the intent to deprive the owner of its value, and with the intent to use the property to the benefit of the person taking it.

The types of confidence game used vary somewhat, although there are a number of similar techniques. A brief description of some of the more popular con games will suffice to familiarize the investigator with methods used. Nevertheless, it should be recognized that con games are usually the work of a professional, and are generally handled in large cities by one or more specialized investigators. Cooperation and information concerning *modus operandi,* physical descriptions, and number of persons involved will often yield a list of suspects. Some of the more common con games are:

Pocketbook or Pigeon Drop. In this scheme two or more participants pretend to find a large amount of money that cannot be identified. The victim, who is a witness to this discovery, is asked to put up a sum of money to show "good faith." The victim is then told that all the money will be held by a third party for a few days, to see if the found money is claimed, and they all agree to meet at a specific location a few days later to divide the money. Of course, the perpetrators never show up.

Lemon Pool, Lemon Craps, or Three Card Monte. While these three techniques are similar, the result determines the name of the game. In this game the victim is told that if he accompanies the perpetrator to a house of prostitution he will not have to pay the fee. Once there the victim is told that the girls are unavailable at the moment, and he is invited to play pool, craps, or three card monte while waiting. The games are fixed and one of the perpetrators will pretend to work with the victim to cheat the other thief. Once sucked into the scheme the victim is taken for all his money.

The Murphy Game. The perpetrator pretends to be a pimp and entices the victim to a prostitute's apartment. Once outside the apartment the perpetrator tells the victim to give him his money so the girl does not steal it. He then tells the victim to wait outside or in a stairwell while he goes upstairs to see that the coast is clear. He disappears over the roof with the victim's money.

Handkerchief Switch, Tin Box, or Aspirin Switch. After gaining the victim's confidence the perpetrator tells him that he does not trust banks and bets that the victim cannot withdraw a large sum of money from the bank. When the money is withdrawn the perpetrator places it in a handkerchief or tin box for safekeeping. Once the switch has been made he absconds with the money. In the aspirin game the perpetrator feigns a headache and asks the victim to go for aspirin at which time he takes off with the money.

Diamond or Gold Switch. The victim believes he is buying diamonds or gold when he is actually buying glass or pieces of brass.

Marriage Swindle. The victim, believing he or she is going to marry the perpetrator, is asked to use his or her savings to help plan the wedding, because the perpetrator's savings are tied up in an investment.

Gypsy Blessing. The types of frauds perpetrated by gypsies are many and varied. One approach is to convince the victim that an illness will be cured. Another is to make the victim believe that his money will be doubled or that the gypsy can ward off evil spirits if he will put up his money.

Money-making Machine. The victim is convinced by the perpetrator that the machine makes money. Once his money is placed inside, the machine explodes and the money is supposedly destroyed in the explosion.

PICKPOCKETS

Fortunately, the skills necessary to be a successful pickpocket limit the number of persons actually engaged in this activity. Nevertheless, wherever large numbers of people congregate, the pickpocket is likely to be present. Investigative activity usually centers on apprehending the pickpocket in the act; follow-up investigations are difficult if not virtually impossible, for the thief is primarily interested in currency and is quick to rid himself of the victim's wallet or pocketbook. In some instances it may be possible to identify latent fingerprints or discarded items, which may have some value in identification or in court.

The Pocketbook Thief. This thief, as distinguished from the purse snatcher who grabs the bag and runs, is discussed in this section, since this activity has become more commonplace in recent years. He operates alone or with an accomplice, and when the victim is distracted will either open and remove her wallet or, in some cases, cut the pocketbook from its straps. It is not uncommon to find women involved in this activity, operating with an accomplice. A standard ploy is to create a disturbance, or jar the victim, while the partner works to remove property.

The Fob Worker. This thief usually steals from the jacket pockets or other accessible locations. Because few people carry their wallet or currency in an outside pocket, it is difficult to accomplish this type of theft. Persons involved in this activity are likely to be novices or older professionals who are not as adept at removing property from more inaccessible locations.

The Pants Pocket Operator. This man is a professional thief who has mastered the art of removing a victim's wallet from his trouser pocket. He is often assisted by one or more accomplices, one of whom may act to distract the victim, and the second of whom takes the wallet from the pickpocket once it has been retrieved. This precludes discovery in the event a victim discovers he is being robbed.

The Drunk or Lush Operator. He steals from victims who have passed out from drinking, or are sleeping in subways or other forms of mass transportation. He is held in low esteem by his colleagues. Juveniles are frequently involved in this form of criminal activity.

AUTO THEFT

The extent of automobile theft in the United States has reached an epidemic proportion, and while the majority of almost a million cars stolen annually are taken for the purpose of joyriding and are later returned to their owners, the professional auto thief is becoming more common. Most auto thieves are juveniles; this is a major problem to law enforcement officials, for investigation is often quite difficult in cases involving juveniles. If a stolen car is found abandoned, it should be dusted for latent prints and other trace evidence, and a canvass of the neighborhoods from which it was stolen and recovered should be undertaken. Because juveniles are not likely to have a fingerprint record, follow-up investigation may be stifled until a later date when and if the juvenile is apprehended in another crime.

A major problem for the investigator is the professional thief who steals automobiles for resale. This activity is usually conducted by a well-organized group, and has become increasingly popular in organized crime. Professional thieves are often equipped to repaint the car, provide false registration or title, and relocate it to another state or county for sale. The meticulous operation involved, and the relative ease with which it is often carried out, would astound the casual observer. The author is familiar with one group that had the capacity to steal an auto, repaint it, provide identification numbers and documents, and have it on its way out of the state within six hours from the time it was removed from the street. This ring employed juveniles to steal the cars, and processed as many as six autos in an evening. Often the cars were stolen on an order from the prospective customer; buyers ranged from the lower to the middle and upper class, and came from a variety of occupations and professions.

The *modus operandi* of professional auto thieves varies somewhat from state to state, often depending on registration laws. One common practice is to buy title to an auto of the same year and model number which has been junked as the result of an accident, and use the numbers from this auto on a stolen one. Another approach involves forging the registration and re-registering the car in another state. In most cases the door or window plate exhibiting the identification number is removed and replaced with a fraudulent one. In addition to this plate, each automobile has a hidden serial number as well as the number stamped on the engine block. Rarely are these numbers removed, and an investigator familiar with their location may be able to determine quickly whether or not the car is illegally possessed.

Professional thieves generally steal higher-priced cars, and apparently have little trouble in disposing of them to "honest" citizens. The investigator should be familiar with the operations of the National Auto Theft Bureau, which has its main offices in New York City, and which can often assist in tracing an automobile from the manufacturer, or in providing information as to where the car might have been stolen from. NATB issues an annual guide for the identification of autos by year, make, and model number, and each investigative unit should have a copy of this on file. In addition, the investigator should become familiar with the operations of the Motor Vehicle Bureau of his state, and verse himself in the types of information that can be retrieved from this system. Most states have now computerized this operation, which makes it possible to conduct various inquiries in a short period of time.

If a person has been apprehended operating a stolen auto which has been re-registered, it is often possible to elicit information from him that will result in developing a major investigation. If this is the case, care must be taken not to tip the thieves; this is likely to happen once the suspect has been released or permitted to consult with his family. The investigator should attempt to place the suspect in a position where his cooperation will be beneficial. This should always be accomplished in cooperation with the District Attorney; the investigator should not attempt to develop such a case on his own. Keep in mind that persons involved in this type of crime are likely to be well organized, have numerous contacts, and may be backed by organized crime.

In addition to being taken for joyriding and resale, stolen autos are often used in the commission of other crimes, such as robbery and burglary. If this may be the case, care should be taken to see that a thorough examination of the car for physical evidence is undertaken. In addition to the more obvious locations, latent prints may be found behind the rearview or sideview mirrors, inside the trunk, and on the seat adjustment knob.

Finally, it is not uncommon for the owner of an auto to report his car stolen in order to collect on his insurance, or to cover up an accident. If the car is found burned or otherwise totally destroyed, there is the possibility that the owner is attempting to collect insurance. A background investigation, as well as an interview of witnesses in the vicinity where the car was found, may prove fruitful. If the car has been involved in an accident, an attempt should be made to determine the time of the accident and the time the car was reported stolen. This will aid in establishing the validity of the complainant's statement. The investigator should take care, during the initial interview, to clarify any discrepancies that might arise in the complainant's statement. An effort should be made to interview him as soon as possible after the accident or reported theft, since he is likely to be in a highly emotional state, not having had time to formulate a story if he is not telling the truth.

OTHER FORMS OF LARCENY

In addition to the crimes discussed above the investigator is likely to be faced with cases involving criminal receiving and embezzlement. The major obstacle to the investigation of crimes involving stolen goods is in the identification of the property. Most state laws regarding criminal receiving are weak, and the investigator must prove that the suspect had knowledge that the property was stolen, or that there are reasonable grounds to lead one to believe that the property was stolen. Thus, if a person buys a color television set from a man on the street for $25, he might be arrested for criminal possession if the set can be identified, but unless he has a previous conviction for criminal receiving it may be difficult for the investigator to gain a conviction. Generally, if the person is a dealer and if it can be shown that he possesses the property of two or more persons which was stolen on separate occasions, or that he has purchased the property at an unreasonably low price, a case for criminal possession can be established.

In such cases the investigator should ensure positive identification of the property, and thoroughly interrogate the suspect, with a view toward eliciting information that may show he is lying. If an individual is suspected of buying stolen property it is often wise to maintain surveillance for a period of time before making an arrest. In addition to an eventual charge of criminal receiving it may be possible through such surveillance to identify known or suspected burglars.

Embezzlement is the fraudulent appropriation of property by a person to whom it has been entrusted. This crime presents numerous technical problems to law enforcement officials, and such cases should generally be handled by an experienced investigator. Quite frequently it will be necessary to utilize the services of expert witnesses, such as accountants, in order to develop a case. Embezzlers are often adept at concealing their operations and the thefts may occur over an extended period of time. In order to establish a case, documentary proof, usually in the form of records and receipts, must be obtained, and it must be proven that the suspect had both the knowledge of and the opportunity to commit the crime. Circumstantial evidence, which may prove that the suspect possesses or has spent large sums of money with no reasonable explanation for its source, is likely to be important. Thus, the investigator should conduct a thorough background investigation into the suspect's life. Because of the complications involved in this form of criminal activity, it is wise to contact the prosecuting attorney at an early point in the case.

BURGLARY

Burglary is one of the more common crimes against property, accounting for significantly greater financial losses than robbery or any of the other Part I crimes.[1] Although the motive of the burglar is financial gain, danger to the public is a primary concern, and while the actual number of assaults committed during the commission of burglaries is small, the perceived fear of the populace places great pressure on law enforcement for prevention of burglary and apprehension of suspects.

The Model Penal Code offers the following definition of burglary:

> A person is guilty of burglary if he enters a building or occupied structure, or separately secured or occupied portion thereof, with purpose to commit a crime therein, unless the premises are at the time open to the public or the actor is licensed or privileged to enter. It is an affirmative defense to prosecution for burglary that the building or structure was abandoned.

Closely related to burglary is the crime of criminal trespass, a lesser crime usually charged if the elements of burglary are not all present in the case. Keep in mind that the *intent* to commit *any* crime usually constitutes burglary, if the other elements are present. Thus, a rapist may also be charged with burglary.

Nevertheless, the primary motive of the average burglar is to remove personal property. The type of burglary, the time of day, and whether or not the perpetrator is armed may all have an impact on the severity of the charge. The burglary of a residence at night, while the criminal is armed, will generally result in a higher degree or charge than the burglary of a factory during daylight hours. In addition to the charge of burglary, a suspect may be charged with one or more additional crimes, such as larceny or assault, depending on circumstances.

Because there are usually no witnesses to a burglary, the investigator must often depend on physical evidence to establish a case. Although studies have shown that there is likely to be discoverable physical evidence present at the burglary scene, they also indicate that its collection and use in the criminal justice process is relatively rare. In some measure this may be attributed to a lackadaisical or cynical attitude on the part of the investigator or evidence technician. The investigator must realize that burglaries can be solved through diligent effort; he should not become discouraged at the outset when evidence appears scarce.

In addition to physical evidence, the type of burglary, *modus operandi,* property identification and recovery, pattern analysis, and primary and secondary witness information are of importance in burglary investigation. Each of these factors will be discussed separately.

BURGLARY TYPES

Burglary typology differs from M.O. in that a general category can be used to reduce the range of burglary types in order to deal more effectively with the specifics of *modus operandi.* Some understanding of burglary typology, for example, will assist the investigator in formulating hypotheses concerning possible suspects. For example, the burglary of a school is likely to be committed by juveniles; this fact places some limits on the number of records available, or the possibility of fingerprints being on file.

The two general categories of burglary are residence and nonresidence. Within these categories a further division may be delineated. Included in the residence burglary category are the following.

Private Homes. One of the more common types of burglary, the robbery of a private home may be perpetrated by juveniles or professionals. Theft may be of jewelry, appliances, or other property; the thief will not usually find large amounts of cash left on hand. Entry is usually made through a rear or side window or through the use of a key discovered in a milkbox or above a door.

Apartments. The apartment burglar is more likely to be a professional, although juveniles are apt to be involved in lower socioeconomic neighborhoods. Entry is accomplished either by "slipping" the lock with a piece of acetate, picking the lock (less common), or forcing the door. In some instances, the burglar may effect entry through a fire escape window. The property stolen is likely to be easily concealable in order to escape detection. The apartment house thief generally works on the upper floors, where the traffic is lighter, and will often escape over the roof.

Hotels and Motels. The hotel or motel burglar is more often than not a professional. Entry may be made by slipping the lock or using a master key. In many cases the burglar will rent a room in the hotel and make a key, to be used at a later time. This type of burglar often works alone, and is interested only in currency and other small valuables.

Vacation Homes. Burglaries of vacation homes are generally committed by juveniles, and obviously there is a higher incidence during off-season months. In some cases the burglary may be accomplished for no more than a desire to use the home for parties.

Within the nonresidence burglary category are the following.

Warehouses and Factories. Entry is gained through some accessible point, such as a skylight or window. In many instances the crime is well planned, and large amounts of property may be removed. Generally, more than one person is involved, and an analysis of the scene will often indicate whether or not the job was a professional one. Employees of the company may be recruited, or may initiate the burglary with others. Merchandise stolen is usually easily disposed of to legitimate dealers, and includes such items as liquor, cigarettes, drugs, clothing, appliances, and the like.

Retail Stores. Retail stores are often the target for both juveniles and professionals. Juveniles are more likely to throw a trash can or other object through the plate glass window and remove items from the display. Entry may also be made through the roof or from an adjoining store or building. The professional is interested in stealing any merchandise that can be marketed easily.

Business Offices. The business office burglar is more often a professional. Entry is gained through slipping the lock, a master key, or force. This type of thief is interested in stealing cash, which is usually in a safe, or office equipment, such as typewriters and adding machines. Generally, more than one person is involved, and the crime is likely to be planned. Safe burglars present a special problem to be discussed in a later section.

The *modus operandi* of burglars varies with the type of crime and the individual peculiarities of the perpetrator. It may be classified according to time, location, entry, search, property, removal and escape, and unique characteristics.

Time. The time of day is often significant in developing M.O. patterns. Most residence burglaries are committed during the day, whereas nonresidence burglaries are usually committed at night or during the early morning hours. A pattern analysis by time will often disclose the number of burglars or burglary teams operating in a particular location.

Location. In addition to the type of crime, the geographic location is also important. A determination should be made as to mobility, accessibility, and proximity to other locations. An analysis of this information may enable the investigator to determine whether the crime was committed by professionals or by juveniles.

Entry. The location and method of entry is important in terms of both developing M.O. and discovering physical evidence. Entry can be classified initially according to front, side, rear, roof, or floor. The means used to effect entry will be by force, open door or window, key, or other. In commercial and business thefts, the perpetrator may conceal himself inside the building before closing time. A further description of method of entry should include, if possible, the type of force employed, such as breaking windows, using a crowbar to jimmy the door, slipping the lock with acetate, or picking the lock, to name a few. The manner in which entry is effected may enable a determination of the type of criminal to be sought.

Search. The method used by the suspect to search for property is likely to be of value to the investigator. Was it accomplished systematically and with care, or was it a hasty, sloppy undertaking? Did the thief appear to have a particular goal in mind, such as looking for a safe or cash? The professional house burglar will often empty each drawer out onto the bed, look through the contents, push them to the floor, and proceed on to the next drawer. His approach is methodical. If large property is to be removed, it will often be stacked near a door or window before removal. Search by a juvenile or nonprofessional is more likely to be haphazard, and not systematic. He is more likely to overlook common hiding places, such as kitchen cabinets. A careful analysis of the method of search and a full written description may make it possible to develop a list of suspects at a later time.

Property. The type of property stolen offers a number of investigative clues. In addition to tracing property, the investigator may also be able to develop his picture of the perpetrator by combining and comparing this information with previous crimes. While it may be difficult to classify the more common thief by the type of property he steals, the professional has usually developed a patterned approach to theft, and focuses on specific kinds of property. If property other than cash has been taken, the perpetrator is faced with the problem of disposal, either to a fence, a legitimate businessman, or some other source. Working backward, the investigator may be able to locate stolen property and develop information leading to the suspect.

Removal and Escape. The investigator should also concern himself with the way in which property was removed from the scene, and the manner in which the perpetrator escaped. Was an auto or truck necessary to carry the goods? Was the property small and capable of being concealed on the person? Was any special equipment such as a forklift or winches, necessary to accomplish the task? The escape route used by the perpetrator may provide clues as to technique and may assist in the follow-up investigation. The professional burglar will often unlock a rear or front door once inside the premises as a means for quick escape if discovered. The assumption should not be made, however, that because one or more doors are open they were left open by the occupant. If the suspect escapes through a window or over a roof, there are likely to be traces of physical evidence on the suspect's clothing, as well as along the escape route.

Unique Characteristics. Here the investigator is concerned with anything that might distinguish the perpetrator. Some activities of burglars may include eating in the residence, changing clothes and wearing the victim's, defecating on the scene, or leaving a message for the victim. Anything that is unusual should be considered and included in the report, for such information may provide a vital link at some future time. Quite often a burglar will be given a nickname by the police or the media, based on some specific characteristic.

PROPERTY IDENTIFICATION AND RECOVERY

Earlier the use of records, pawn shops, secondhand dealers and other sources of information was discussed. Frequently these may be the only leads an investigator has to pursue. Use of the computer is becoming more common, and will continue to grow in importance insofar as property recovery is concerned.

Cooperation with the police departments of neighboring cities is of paramount importance, especially when larger cities abut, for it is not unlikely that stolen property will be moved from city to city. In some cases property may be moved hundreds or even thousands of miles before it is finally disposed of. This is especially true when organized crime is involved.

Informants may be of value in determining where property is turning up, and in providing further information; the investigator should make every effort to develop this source. The patrol force may provide leads; thus, investigators would do well to publish lists of stolen property for dissemination. Finally, in cases in which it is known specifically what has been stolen, it is wise to circulate flyers to businessmen. Such items as cameras, television sets, and other appliances may be offered by the burglars to legitimate businessmen.

PATTERN ANALYSIS

Although the investigator is not likely to be involved in pattern analysis, he should develop a close liaison with the crime analysis division, or other units responsible for criminal data. Most departments continue to use the pin map system, but recent advances in computer technology have resulted in computer mapping, which is rapidly being adopted by the departments in larger cities. Using this approach, an investigator may be able to determine crime patterns according to numerous variables, such as location, time of day, frequency, and crime type. Such information, when combined with M.O. data, will aid the investigator in determining the mobility of the burglar, frequency, specific typology analysis of various burglaries, and other factors. If the use of computer mapping has been thoroughly developed, the investigator may make inquiries concerning a particular crime. For example, he may ask for a printout of all burglaries involving a roof break, committed between the hours of midnight and 8:00 A.M., either during a particular week, month, or year, or in a particular geographical location, and in which property valued at over $1000 was taken. Figure 10.4 illustrates a computer map of homicide reports. This type of information can also be used for burglaries, will aid the investigator greatly, and, as the systems become more developed, will provide data heretofore virtually unavailable.

PRIMARY AND SECONDARY WITNESS INFORMATION

Primary witnesses (victims) are rare in burglary cases. However, secondary witnesses, persons who may have observed the perpetrator, are more common if they are sought out. Secondary witnesses are often reluctant to come forward, but it is not unlikely that someone in the neighborhood observed either the burglar, his car, or something else that may aid in the investigation.

A thorough canvass of the vicinity should be undertaken. If not initiated immediately after the burglary, it is often wise to recanvass the next day during the hours in which the burglary was committed, because witnesses may have left for work or other engagements in the meantime.

PHYSICAL EVIDENCE

Chapters 3, 4, and 5 discussed in detail initial investigation at the crime scene and the use of physical evidence. Nevertheless, because physical evidence is of the utmost importance in burglary investigations, some discussion is warranted here. In addition to latent fingerprints, the burglary scene is likely to provide a wealth of trace evidence. Each of these subjects shall be handled separately.

Fingerprints. As technology improves, latent fingerprints will be increasingly more important to investigators. A workable single digit classification system, which makes it possible to classify individual fingerprints for retrieval purposes, is close to reality, and this in itself should revolutionize burglary investigations. In areas where single digit classification is not a reality, combining M.O. and physical descriptions may result in a list of suspects, which can then be checked by fingerprint comparisons.

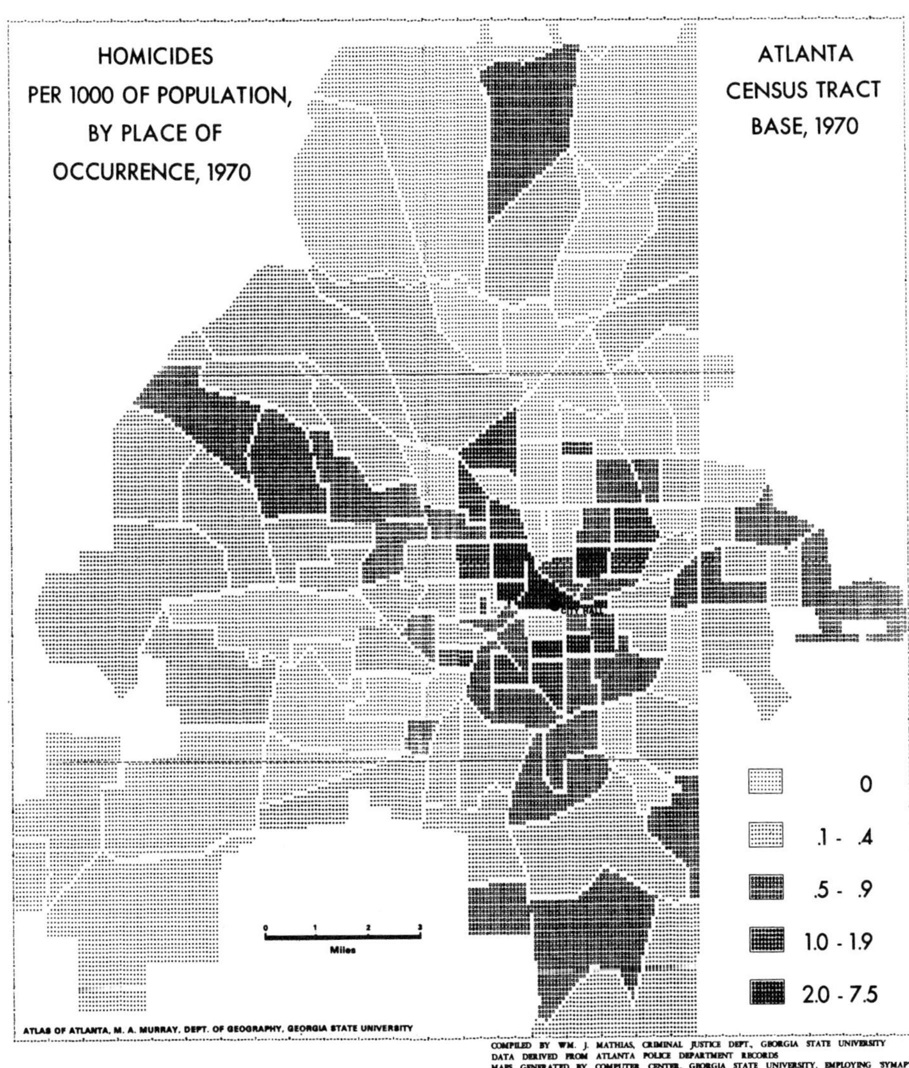

FIG. 10.4 Computer map of homicide reports. (Reprinted from *Atlas of Atlanta, the 1970's* by Malcolm A. Murray. Copyright 1974 by the University of Alabama Press. Used by permission.)

In searching for latent prints at the crime scene, careful attention should be given to out-of-the-way places, such as inside drawers, beneath chairs or tables that might have been moved, and on objects that may have been handled. In addition, surfaces immediately outside the entry point may prove valuable.

Finally, it is often worthwhile to dust recovered property for latent prints, especially if there is a suspect in the case. A positive identification here may result in a link between the suspect and the crime scene.

Trace Evidence. In addition to fingerprints the investigator should carefully examine the scene for trace evidence such as fibers, blood, footprints, tool marks, and other forms of residue that may have been imparted to the scene by the perpetrator. These forms of evidence may later be invaluable in linking the suspect to the scene. All too often the investigator is careless in this regard, and fails to make use of the technology available to him.

If a suspect has been apprehended, a review of the report and recognition of what physical evidence was collected will provide leads for examining property in his possession. For example, if tool marks were recorded, an examination of tools in the suspect's possession may result in an identification. Keep in mind that the perpetrator is not likely to discard his tools after each crime. Some subjects even wear the same clothes to each burglary.

An examination of clothing or shoes may reveal traces of residue imparted from the scene, which when compared by the laboratory could result in a positive link. Plaster, paint, tar, glass fragments, or other building compounds often adhere to shoes or clothing, and may remain for a period of time. The investigator's ingenuity in discovering such evidence can make the difference between success and failure.

BURGLARY OF SAFES

Because of its unique characteristics some mention should be made of the burglary of safes. Generally, this crime is committed by the professional.

Popular mythology to the contrary, the average safe is not designed so much to prevent burglary as it is to safeguard the contents from fire. Most safes are constructed of layers of steel with some form of fireproof insulation between them. The professional safe burglar is adept at gaining entrance to most safes with relative ease, especially if they are placed in a hidden location in which he can work with little fear of discovery.

The M.O. of the safe burglar usually takes one or more of the following forms:

Touch or "Open" Combination. Contrary to popular belief, the safecracker who can open a safe by listening to the tumblers fall is virtually nonexistent. If this appears to be the case, the thief has usually found the combination under a drawer, behind a calendar, or in some other seemingly obscure place. Carelessness in failing to properly secure a safe, or laziness in only turning the dial a few numbers away also contribute to the safecracker's success.

Rip. In this instance, the safecracker drills a hole in one corner of the safe, inserts a crowbar, and rips the door off. This is a common technique and may take a variety of forms. Some burglars use what appears to be a large can opener; a hole is punched or drilled in the side of the safe, and the tool is used to cut an entrance in the steel.

Punch. Requiring some skill, this technique involves knocking off the dial of the safe, and punching out the spindle, which will usually release the lock. Some safes are susceptible to this form of entry, and a moderate degree of luck is necessary for success.

Chop. Using this method, the safecracker merely hacks his way into the safe with a sledgehammer or other heavy tool. Generally entry is through the bottom of the safe, which is the weakest point.

Burning and Blowing. The use of explosives or an acetylene torch is rare, and accomplished only by the skilled safecracker. In such cases entry is gained by removing the dial.

Removal. In some instances the safe will be removed to another location where it can be opened at ease by one of the above methods. Obviously this approach is limited to smaller safes, and requires more than one man, as well as transportation.

If an attempt has been made to crack a safe, the floor will be covered with a white powder that is part of the fire insulation. Often this powder will reveal footprints, and care should be taken to safeguard the area for laboratory examination. Also, this powder will adhere to the clothing of the perpetrator; thus it should be examined for comparison if a suspect is turned up.

SUMMARY

The more frequent crimes against property, burglary and larceny, have been discussed in this chapter. The various types of larceny and burglary were analyzed, with a view toward familiarizing the investigator with the unique characteristics of these crimes. Investigative approaches and the use of physical evidence were discussed, and the legal elements of each crime spelled out. The large volume of larcenies and burglaries reported each year necessitates the investigator's development of a thorough and comprehensive approach to their investigation.

NOTE

1. The Part I crimes as listed by the Federal Bureau of Investigation include Murder and Non-negligent Manslaughter, Manslaughter by Negligence, Forcible Rape, Aggravated Assault, Burglary, Larceny $50 and over, Larceny over $50, and Auto Theft. While auto larceny accounts for an initial loss greater than burglary, the recovery rate is much higher.

QUESTIONS FOR DISCUSSION

1. Define and discuss the legal elements of larceny and burglary.

2. What are the various types of larceny and the M.O. involved in each?

3. What are the various types of burglary and the M.O. involved in each? Is it possible to determine whether or not the thief was a professional? How?

4. What are the various methods used in safe burglaries?

CHAPTER 11

legal aspects of the investigative function

In addition to identifying and arresting the perpetrator, the investigator must prepare the case for court. Unlike the patrolman, whose case is generally less complicated because the suspect has been apprehended either during or shortly after the crime, the investigator is faced with the problem of building a case upon witness descriptions, physical and circumstantial evidence, and other tangible results of his investigation. The task is not an easy one, as evidenced by the large number of dismissals, hung juries, and verdicts of "not guilty" each year throughout the country. A thorough understanding of the laws that set the parameters of the legal aspects of criminal investigation is mandatory.

The investigator must also be aware of his moral responsibility to both the citizen and his department. The investigator has the responsibility of upholding the highest traditions of law enforcement in protecting the public and seeing that justice is served.

CRIMINAL LAW AND THE INVESTIGATOR

Obviously there is a great deal more that the investigator should know about criminal law than can be adequately covered in one chapter. Indeed, Herbert Jenkins, former police chief of Atlanta, Georgia, has postulated that we may soon see the day when a law degree will be required for detectives.[1] The emphasis here, then, shall be on familiarizing the investigator with some of the major Supreme Court decisions affecting the investigative process. Among the areas of interest are cases involving admissions and confessions, wiretapping and eavesdropping, searches and seizures, informants and information, search warrants, and lineups. The focus will be on decisions as they affect the investigator, although they will be important to the patrol officer also. Ours is a dynamic legal system, changing constantly to meet the needs of society. In recent years the Supreme Court has come under increasing attack for its liberal interpretation of the Constitution. Undoubtedly, many of these decisions have placed restrictions on law enforcement, and their impact on the investigative process is often seen as being too restrictive. Nevertheless, it is the investigator's responsibility to abide by these decisions, whatever his personal feelings might be.

ADMISSIONS AND CONFESSIONS

In 1966 the Supreme Court, in the case of *Miranda* v. *Arizona,* held that "a warning at the time of interrogation is indispensible to overcome its pressures and to insure that the individual knows he is free to exercise the privilege (of remaining silent) at that time."[2]

Under this ruling a suspect must be told the following:

1. You have the right to remain silent and refuse to answer any questions.
2. Anything you do or say may be used against you in a court of law.
3. You have the right to consult an attorney before speaking and to have an attorney present during any questioning.
4. If you cannot afford an attorney, one will be provided to you without cost.

The police officer must also show that the subject understood all questions asked of him.

The *Miranda* ruling thus placed specific restrictions on the police insofar as custodial interrogation is concerned. Custodial interrogation occurs when an individual in police custody believes that his freedom has been restrained in any significant manner. The circumstances under which the questioning takes place will be used to determine the degree of restraint, and among the factors the court will consider are:

1. Whether or not the admission or confession was given freely and voluntarily.
2. The time and location of questioning.
3. Whether or not force or threats were used.
4. The degree of psychological stress exerted.
5. The length of time involved, which includes the time in custody as well as time spent under interrogation.

In all cases the investigator must show that the admission or confession was voluntary, that the suspect knew what he was saying, and that he was intelligent enough to recognize the consequences of his statement. Some of the more common defenses against the accuracy of confessions include the suspect's limited I.Q., a language difficulty, his age, the use of coercion, and the suspect's being under the influence of drugs or alcohol. If children are involved the investigator should see that a parent or guardian is present during the questioning.

Given the above requirements by the law, many investigators assume that no statements are admissible. To the contrary, as the Supreme Court noted in *Miranda:*

> In dealing with statements obtained through interrogations, we do not purport to find all confessions inadmissable. Confessions remain a proper element in law enforcement. Any statement given freely and voluntarily without any compelling influence is, of course, admissable in evidence. The fundamental import of the privilege while an

individual is in custody is not whether he is allowed to talk to the police without the benefits of warnings and counsel, but whether he can be interrogated. There is no requirement that police stop a person who enters a police station and states that he wishes to confess to a crime, or a person who calls the police to offer a confession or any other statement he desires to make.[3]

Essentially, interrogation begins when the investigator focuses suspicion on an individual, and before he asks any question he must advise the suspect of his rights. If an officer enters the scene and says nothing, other than perhaps, "What happened?" and the suspect says, "I killed him," the statement is inadmissible. The fine line that has been drawn between an admissible and inadmissible confession places the burden of proof on the officer.

SEARCHES AND SEIZURES

The Fourth Amendment of the Constitution states:

> The right of people to be secure in their persons, houses, papers and effects, against unreasonable searches and seizures, shall not be violated, and no Warrants shall issue, but upon probable cause, supported by oath or affirmation, and particularly describing the place to be searched, and the persons or things to be seized.

Despite this provision, it was not until 1961 that the Supreme Court, in *Mapp* v. *Ohio,* held that evidence obtained in violation of the Fourth Amendment was inadmissible.[4,5] This decision placed greater emphasis on the use of search warrants (the subject of a later section) and restricted searches conducted without a warrant.

There are, however, certain instances in which a police officer may conduct a search without a warrant. These include:

1. Searches incidental to a lawful arrest.
2. Waiver of Constitutional rights.
3. Search of a moving vehicle.
4. Seizure in which no search is required.
5. Search by a private citizen.
6. Search after lawful seizure or impoundment.
7. Frisking a suspect.

The legality of searches incidental to lawful arrests has been upheld by the Supreme Court.[6] Thus, it is imperative that the officer be familiar with the laws of arrest, for any evidence discovered after an illegal arrest is inadmissible. The type of article seized after a lawful arrest will have a bearing on its admissibility in court, and the arrest upon which the search is based must be made in good faith. An arrest made in order to conduct a search is not admissible. The area involved and the length of time between the arrest and a search also help to determine the admissibility of evidence. Essentially, the arresting officer does not have *carte blanche* to search wherever he wants; the search should be limited to the immediate area surrounding the suspect, unless there is a specific reason to justify a wider search. The amount of time permitted to conduct a search varies according to such factors as the size of the article, the size of the area to be searched, and the condition of the place to be searched.

If an automobile is involved, there is likely to be some disagreement as to whether or not the trunk of the car is under the driver's control. As a general rule, the officer may not search the trunk of an automobile if a minor traffic arrest occurs. However, in more serious offenses the trunk may be searched.

The courts have held that if an individual consents to a search, any evidence discovered is admissible. However, the courts will closely scrutinize cases in which the person waives his rights and permits a search, and *any* doubt will be resolved in favor of the defendant. In order to establish a legal waiver the officer must show that the consent was voluntary, the search was limited to the exact area of consent, and the person giving permission had the capacity to consent. A landlord may not permit the search of a tenant or roomer's residence. If more than one person share the premises, either may give permission to conduct a search, although it is unlikely that evidence recovered in searching personal property, such as a bureau or cabinet, used solely by the other person, would be admissible. Although a spouse may give permission to conduct a search, the search is not valid against a mate who refuses to permit the search.

If a vehicle is involved in the case, and there is a strong possibility that the vehicle contains contraband material, a search may be upheld by the courts. The investigating officer must establish probable cause for the search; this must be substantially more than a whim or hunch. Thus, it is important that the circumstances leading to the search be recorded, and developed at the hearing or trial. However, persons traveling aboard airplanes or ships are subject to search without a warrant and without the need for probable cause. The increasing number of skyjackings and bomb threats indicates that such searches will become more common in the future. If contraband goods are discovered during this type of search, the individual is subject to arrest, although the particulars of the case are likely to have a bearing on the acceptance of this evidence in court.

In cases where no search was necessary to effect a seizure evidence has been deemed admissible. Thus, if an officer observes contraband in plain view he may make an arrest. In the *United States* v. *McDaniel* case, the Supreme Court held that if there is no illegal search and entry is not unlawful, "the police are not required to close their eyes and need not walk out and leave the (illegal) article where they saw it."[7] In *Lee* v. *United States* the Supreme Court also held that the use of field glasses or a telescope by the investigator does not amount to a trespass.[8]

Frequently the circumstances surrounding seizure of material in plain view will be called into question. This is particularly true in narcotics cases. The large number of police officers testifying in various cases that they observed the defendant throw the contraband to the ground has led these to be called "dropsy" cases in some cities, and caused the courts to take a jaundiced view of such testimony.

In those cases in which a private citizen has conducted a search and discovered evidence, the courts have upheld the conviction of the suspect. However, such a search must be made without official knowledge, and any indication that an officer was involved, either in assisting or advising the citizen, is likely to lead to a dismissal.

If property has been lawfully seized or impounded and the officer discovers illegal property while preparing a property voucher, the owner may be subject to arrest. This form of search usually occurs when vehicles have been impounded; items such as trunks, handbags, and suitcases may yield contraband. "Apparently most courts will admit evidence which is illegally possessed where the impounding and search are in good faith."[9]

In *Terry* v. *Ohio* the Supreme Court held that "where a police officer observes unusual conduct which leads him reasonably to conclude in light of his experience that criminal activity may be afoot and that the persons with whom he is dealing may be armed and presently dangerous; where in the course of investigating this behavior he identifies himself as a policeman and makes reasonable inquiries; and where nothing in the initial stages of the encounter serves to dispel his reasonable fear for his own or other's safety, he is entitled for the protection of himself and others in the area to conduct a carefully limited search of the outer clothing of such persons in an attempt to discover weapons which might be used to assault him."[10]

As a result of the ruling of the Supreme Court on this case an officer may conduct a frisk of a suspect for a weapon. However, if other contraband (such as narcotics) is discovered, this evidence may be inadmissible. Admissibility will depend in large measure on the circumstances of the case, as evidenced by two companion cases handed down with the *Terry* case. In *Sibron* v. *New York* the Supreme Court overturned a marijuana conviction based on a "stop and frisk," and in *Peters* v. *New York* upheld a conviction for a burglary tool discovered during a stop and frisk situation.[11]

The investigator is less likely to conduct a search without a warrant than the patrolman, although frequently the investigator acts too hastily and fails to secure a search warrant when one is required. The result is often dismissal of the case; for this reason a thorough knowledge of the search warrant procedure is necessary.

SEARCH WARRANTS

A general rule to follow concerning search warrants is "When in doubt, get one." Obviously there are situations in which the procurement of a search warrant may be infeasible or impossible. On the other hand, experience has shown that many cases might have been strengthened by the use of a warrant.

A search warrant is an order in writing, issued by a judge or magistrate, requiring a police officer to search a particular location for particular property. As Klotter and Kanovitz point out,* the following is necessary in order for a warrant to be valid:

1. "The proper official must issue the warrant." The Code of Criminal Procedure or its equivalent in each state specifies who has the authority to issue a search warrant.

2. "The warrant may only be issued for authorized objects." While the laws vary among states, most states place some restrictions on the articles for which a search is to be conducted. For example, it is generally unacceptable to request a search for mere evidence without some further description, although the courts have not been completely clear in their delineations in this area.

3. "The warrant must be issued on probable cause." Something other than hunch or suspicion must accompany the petition for a search warrant. However, the Supreme Court, in *Jones* v. *United States,* noted that the statement of an informant may be used to secure a search warrant.[12] Hearsay evidence, then, is generally acceptable, although the circumstances surrounding the case and information concerning the reliability of the allegation will be considered. In addition, search warrants may be issued on the observations of a police officer if the probability of illegal property being present can be shown.

4. "The warrant must be supported by oath or affirmation." If a search warrant is issued the officer must swear that, to the best of his knowledge, its information is the truth. The officer should be sure that this requirement is carried out, since failure to do so may invalidate the warrant.

5. "The place to be searched and the things to be seized must be particularly described." The place to be searched must be described within reasonable limits, and the officer should ensure that there can be no confusion at a later date as to the exact location to be searched. The extent of the search, whether it be for a room or a whole house, will depend in large part on the circumstances of the case. The property in question must be described as accurately as possible under the circumstances. A blind search is not permissible.

EXECUTING A SEARCH WARRANT

Once the warrant has been secured it must be executed by the officer named to carry out the search. The warrant must be executed within a reasonable time, although this period may not be clearly indicated in some states. Federal rules require that a warrant be executed within ten days after the date of issuance, although some states require an earlier execution.

---

*John C. Klotter and Jacqueline R. Kanovitz, *Constitutional Law for Police,* © 1973, pp. 117–125. Reprinted by permission of W. H. Anderson Publishing Co., Cincinnati, Ohio.

The use of *necessary* force to execute the warrant is permissible; if an officer is denied entrance he may break down an outer or inner door after giving notice of his authority and the purpose for which he is seeking entrance. Once entry has been gained the occupant should be informed of the proposed search and, if possible, given a copy of the search warrant.

In carrying out a search the officer must comply with the limitations specified in the warrant. He cannot extend his search to a wider area, nor can he search for articles that are not listed in the warrant. Once the article or articles in question have been found the search must cease. If property other than what is spelled out in the warrant is discovered, its admissibility as evidence will generally depend on the circumstances surrounding its discovery. If possession of the property is illegal (as in the case of narcotics or counterfeit bills), an arrest should be made. If it appears that the property may be the proceeds of another crime that is not the subject of the search warrant, the investigator should confer with the prosecutor's office. While the officer is not expected to overlook a crime, there is a thin line insofar as search warrants are concerned, and the courts are apt to frown on the seizure of any evidence that was not listed in the warrant. Once the warrant has been executed it must be returned to the issuing court, and an account of the action taken and results recorded.

The search warrant is an extremely effective tool in the hands of the investigator who uses it properly. However, ignorance of procedures and, in many of the larger cities, time constraints in securing such warrants inhibit their use. Nevertheless, the investigator must make every effort to familiarize himself with the procedures involved, and recognize that the loss of a few hours in securing a warrant may save days in court at a later time, and the embarrassment of being asked by the defense why a warrant was not secured.

ELECTRONIC SURVEILLANCE AND WIRETAPPING

Technological advances in the areas of electronic surveillance and wiretapping make it possible to monitor a person's conversation from miles away, with relatively little fear of discovery. Needless to say, the dangers to personal liberty and freedom are great when technological surveillance is used. On the other hand, used properly and with adequate safeguards these advances can enhance the investigative process. Before beginning a discussion of electronic surveillance and wiretapping, a cautionary note is in order; under no circumstances is the investigator justified in the illegal use of monitoring equipment to carry out an investigation. The ends do not justify the means!

Wiretapping may be defined as the interception of a telephone conversation, either by use of a listening device or, in federal cases and some states, by listening on an extension. It is not usually an illegal interception unless neither party in the conversation is aware that a third party is listening, or has given him permission to do so. The Federal Communication Act passed by Congress in 1934 made wiretapping illegal, although this law applied only to federal courts and jurisdictional matters. Thus, under federal law evidence gained as the result of an illegal wiretap is inadmissable.

Because wiretap laws vary significantly from one state to another and are often vague at best the investigator should familiarize himself with the particular laws of his jurisdiction. Section 605 of the Federal Communications act states that:

> . . . (N)o person not being authorized by the sender shall intercept any communication and divulge or publish the existence, contents, substance, purport, effect or meaning of such intercepted communication to any person.[13]

Despite this law both federal and state agencies continue to conduct wiretaps, although in federal courts a case may be dismissed if it can be proven that the wiretap led either directly or indirectly to the charge for which the defendant is being prosecuted.[14] The Court was not as strict regarding state prosecutions. In *Schwartz* v. *Texas,* the Supreme Court held that Section 605 was applicable to the states insofar as divulging information gained through a wiretap is concerned, but that leads developed through a wiretap which led to an arrest, were permissible.[15] For example, if as the result of a wiretap officers learn that one of the parties in the conversation committed a crime, and they subsequently make an arrest based on evidence other than the wiretap, the case would be upheld in the state court under federal law. In the federal court the case would be dismissed under the "fruit of the poisonous tree doctrine."

The one exception to the use of wiretap evidence in federal courts involves cases in which a third party is involved. If two parties implicate a third party who is not part of the telephone conversation, and an arrest is subsequently made on the basis of information gained from a wiretap, the third party cannot claim a violation of his rights under Section 605. In *Goldstein* v. *United States* the Court held that, although a violation of Section 605 occurred, Goldstein had no redress under the wiretap provision, since he was not a party to the conversation overheard by federal officers.[16]

As noted earlier the laws surrounding wiretaps are often unclear, and with the recent technological developments in this area it may be some time before adequate guidelines are developed. In general, the thought of wiretapping brings to mind the use of spliced wires or a hookup to a relay box. However, it is now possible to execute a wiretap without touching any of the telephone wires. While a Supreme Court decision on the legality of electromagnetic or inductive wiretapping has not yet been made, it is generally assumed that the use of such equipment constitutes an illegal wiretap.

Eavesdropping involves surreptitiously listening in on a conversation, be it over a telephone or between two persons at the same location. In 1942 the Court held that it is not illegal to overhear one side of a telephone conversation so long as there is no physical trespass by the police.[17] However, in a subsequent decision the Court held that a law enforcement agency does not have the exclusive right to eavesdrop at will, and must obtain a warrant in order to place an eavesdropping device.[18] Furthermore, the police are required to state the allegations of the specific criminal offense in order to obtain the warrant.

Court-ordered wiretapping and electronic surveillance is allowed in most states, even though evidence may have been obtained in violation of Section 605. However, a number of states, notably New York, Illinois, Rhode Island, Maryland, Nevada, Texas, Delaware, and Pennsylvania, have some restrictions on either wiretapping, eavesdropping, or both.

Some mention should be made of the use of hidden recorders or transmitters, either on the person or in the room, where at least one party has knowledge of their presence. As a general rule, if there has been no illegal trespass and one of the parties is either a law enforcement agent or is working in cooperation with the law enforcement agency, recorded evidence is admissible.[19]

INFORMANTS

The use of an informant to effect an arrest has been upheld by the Supreme Court,[20] although his reliability is extremely important for prosecution. Regarding the informant, the investigator must be prepared to provide evidence of his character, reputation, past dealings, accuracy of tips, and the circumstances surrounding his use (paid or voluntary). If an informant's character is in question the investigator should be ready to provide information concerning his reliability in the past, and the number of times he was previously used. If there is some indication that the informant may be harboring a grudge or vendetta against the suspect, an attempt to develop ancillary evidence should be made.

In *Hoffa* v. *United States* the Supreme Court held that "the use of secret informers is not *per se* unconstitutional."[21] In this particular case the informant was thought to be a friend, when in reality he was providing information to the government. Although the informant could be shown to have ulterior motives for cooperating with authorities (he was himself under indictment), he was placed on the witness stand and was subject to cross-examination, the credibility of his testimony to be determined by the jury.

SURVEILLANCE

Much of the investigator's work involves visual surveillance; thus, some understanding of the laws involved in this area is necessary. Generally, police may conduct a surveillance of any location that is visible to the naked eye or through the use of technical equipment (such as binoculars or an infrared scope) so long as they do not commit a physical trespass in carrying out the observation. Police may also enter any public place to conduct a surveillance, and it is not against the law to look through the windows or doors of a private location.

An officer may also make observations of the interior of a residence if he is standing at the door. On the other hand, the Supreme Court has held that visual surveillance through a keyhole or other aperture (such as a peephole or crack) or entry of an apartment to look around without permission is illegal.[22]

The Court has also held that the police may enter an open field owned by the suspect in order to conduct surveillance.[23]

Surveillance of an individual may take one of two forms. In the first instance observations are maintained in a clandestine manner, without the subject's knowledge. There is no legal problem here so long as the laws against trespass are maintained. In the second instance the individual is aware that he is being watched. While this is not illegal, any unnecessary harassment of the subject may result in an injunction against this form of surveillance.

LINEUPS AND IDENTIFICATION

Identification of a suspect through the use of a lineup or other means such as photographs, is likely to raise a number of legal problems. Identification may also be established through the use of fingerprints, for example, of which there is no legal question as to acceptance, or voiceprint, which has not been conclusively determined as an acceptable means of identification.

If identification of the suspect is made at the scene or shortly after the crime has been committed, there is generally no legal problem, at least insofar as the admissibility of testimony. However, if a suspect is confronted or observed by a witness at a later time, procedural irregularities may prejudice the case. The use of a lineup is more acceptable than is identification on a one-to-one basis, although the Supreme Court has established certain guidelines that should be followed. The following rules summarize recent decisions in this area:

1. A suspect is not immune from participating in a lineup for identification purposes, and may be required to do so at any time.
2. The lineup is a critical stage in the criminal proceeding and the suspect should be advised that he has a right to counsel.
3. The right to counsel may be waived.
4. Failure to have a lawyer at the lineup does not totally rule out identification of the suspect in court, and the prosecution can attempt to show that the lineup identification did affect the identification in court.
5. If a police department formulates rules that guarantee a fair lineup the presence of a lawyer may not be necessary.

6. Exhibiting a suspect on a one-to-one basis is not an acceptable procedure, although it may be permissible in exceptional circumstances, e.g., the possibility that the suspect may die.
7. A suspect may be asked to exhibit himself in a certain way, e.g., wear certain clothing, make a gesture, or take a stance, and he may be asked to say certain words. However this should be required of all persons in the lineup. Samples of the individual's hair, clothing, blood, or handwriting may be taken; this is not a violation of the rights given by the fifth Amendment.[24]

Care must be taken during the lineup not to present the suspect in some manner that might be deemed prejudicial. This includes dressing or exhibiting him in such a way as to make him stand out from others. Obviously, the investigator should not make any statements that might lead the witness, such as, "How about the guy on the left?" If an identification is made, the position of the subject should be recorded, e.g., the third person from the left in a lineup of eight. Also, the names of the persons participating in the lineup should be recorded. The author has observed cases in which the defense was successful in developing inconsistencies because there was uncertainty in the mind of a witness or the investigator as to a suspect's position or the number of persons in the lineup.

The use of photographs for identification purposes was upheld by the Supreme Court in *Simmons* v. *United States.*[25] However, once again the danger of prejudicing the witness' recollection was discussed in detail, and if an officer provides but one photograph or points out the suspect in any way, there may be grounds for dismissal.

The use of a voiceprint for identification of a suspect, a mechanical invention designed to distinguish different patterns in speech, has not been decided by the Supreme Court. However, voiceprint identification has been used in several cases in the United States.

SUMMARY

Knowledge of the law is of prime importance to every police officer. However, because of his function the investigator's expertise must often go far beyond that required of the patrolman. The preceding chapter represents but a small part of the legal problems affecting the investigative function, and it is not meant to be all-inclusive. The purpose here has been to provide a basic knowledge of the laws that affect an investigation the most. Throughout the discussion, the reader has been encouraged to familiarize himself with the individual laws of his own jurisdiction. This cannot be overstated.

In addition to discussing the holdings of Supreme Court decisions, each case was cited for reference purposes, and the reader is encouraged to pursue these for further insight into the circumstances surrounding them and the reasoning behind the Court's decisions.

NOTES

1. Herbert Jenkins, *Keeping the Peace: a Police Chief Looks at His Job.* New York: Harper and Row, 1970.

2. *Miranda* v. *Arizona,* 384 U.S. 436, 86 S.Ct. 1602.

3. *Ibid.*

4. *Mapp* v. *Ohio,* 367 U.S. 643, 6 LEd (2d) 1081, 81 SCt 1684 (1961).

5. Prior to the *Mapp* decision, federal officers were prohibited from using illegally seized evidence as a result of *Weeks* v. *United States,* but would turn this evidence over to local officers for use in state courts. This was known as "The Silver Platter Doctrine."

6. *United States* v. *Rabinowitz,* 339 U.S. 56, 70 S.Ct. 430. In this case federal officers executing an arrest warrant apprehended the subject at his place of business, and thereupon searched his safe and file cabinets. Some 573 stamps with forged overprints were found. This evidence was introduced and its use upheld by the Court.

7. *United States* v. *McDaniel,* 154 F. Supp. 1 (1957). Cited in John C. Klotter and Jacqueline R. Kanovitz, *Constitutional Law for Police.* Cincinnati, Ohio: W. H. Anderson, 1968, p. 132.

8. *Lee* v. *United States,* 343 U.S. 747, 96 LEd 1273, 72 SCt 967 (1952).

9. John C. Klotter and Jacqueline R. Kanovitz, *Constitutional Law for Police.* Cincinnati, Ohio: W. H. Anderson, 1968, p. 138.

10. *Terry* v. *Ohio,* 392 U.S. 1, 88 SCt. 1868, 20 L.Ed. 2d 889 (1968).

11. *Sibron* v. *New York* and *Peters* v. *New York,* 392 U.S. 40, 88 S.Ct. 1889, 20 L.Ed. 2d 917 (1968).

12. *Jones* v. *United States,* 362 U.S. 257, 4 LEd (2d) 697, 80 SCt 725 (1960). Cited in Klotter and Kanovitz, *op. cit.*

13. Cited in Klotter and Kanovitz, *op. cit.,* p. 146.

14. In two landmark decisions, both involving the same defendant, the Court held that both direct and indirect evidence gained through wiretapping was inadmissible and under the "Fruit of the poisonous tree doctrine" this was cause for dismissal. See *Nardone* v. *United States,* 308 U.S., 60 SCt 266 (1939).

15. *Schwartz* v. *Texas,* 344 U.S. 199, 97 LEd 231, 73 SCt 232 (1952).

16. *Goldstein* v. *United States,* 316 U.S. 114, 86 LEd 1312 62 SCt 1000 (1942).

17. *Goldman* v. *United States,* 316 U.S. 129, 86 LEd 1322, 62 SCt 993 (1942).

18. *Katz* v. *United States,* 389 U.S. 347, 88 SCt 507 (1967).

19. See *Lee* v. *United States,* 343 US 747, 96 LEd 1270, 72 SCt 967 (1952); and *Lopez* v. *United States,* 373 US 427, 10 LEd (2d) 462, 83 SCt 1381 (1963).

20. *Draper* v. *United States,* 358 US 307, 3 LEd (2d) 327, 79 SCt 329 (1959).

21. *Hoffa* v. *United States,* 385 U.S. 293, 87 SCt 408 (1966).

22. See *McDonald* v. *United States,* 335 US 451 93 LEd 153, 69 SCt 191, (1948); and *Morrison* v. *United States,* 262 F(2d) 449 (DC Cir. 1958). Cited in Klotter and Kanovitz, *op. cit.,* p. 174.

23. *Abel* v. *United States,* 362 US 217 4 LEd (2d) 668, 80 SCt 683 (1960).

24. See *United States* v. *Wade,* 388 US 218, SCt 1926 (1967); and *Gilbert* v. *California,* 388 US 263, 87 SCt 1951 (1967).

25. *Simmons* v. *United States,* 390 US 377, 88 SCt 967 (1968).

QUESTIONS FOR DISCUSSION

1. What constitutes the *Miranda* warning? What kind of an impact does this have on criminal investigation?

2. What types of search may be carried out without a warrant? Why is it advisable to secure a warrant whenever possible?

3. Discuss the laws regarding wiretapping and eavesdropping. What is permissible under Section 605 of the Federal Communication Act?

EXERCISES

1. Using a role-playing situation, develop a short case for investigation. Conduct an interrogation on the basis of this. How can the case be handled if the suspect refuses to talk?

2. Develop a set of procedures for lineups that would be consistent with the Supreme Court's position concerning adequate guidelines to ensure fairness.

SUGGESTED READINGS

Eldefonso, Edward, Alan R. Coffey, and James Sullivan, *Police and the Criminal Law.* Pacific Palisades, Calif.: Goodyear, 1972.

George, B. James, Jr., *Constitutional Limitations on Evidence in Criminal Cases.* New York: Practicing Law Institute, 1969.

Klein, Irving, *Law of Evidence for Police.* St. Paul, Minn.: West Publishing Co., 1973.

Klotter, John C., and Jacqueline R. Kanovitz, *Constitutional Law for Police.* Cincinnati, Ohio: W. H. Anderson, 1968.

LaFave, Wayne R., *Arrest: the Decision to take a Suspect into Custody.* Boston, Mass.: Little, Brown and Co., 1965.

Legislation and Special Projects Section Criminal Division, Department of Justice, *Handbook on the Law of Search and Seizure.* U.S. Government Printing Office, January, 1968.

McKinney, William, *Criminal Procedure Law.* St. Paul, Minn.: West Publishing Co., 1971.

Prince, Jerome, *Cases and Materials on Evidence.* Mineola, N.Y.: Foundation Press, 1963.

SPECIAL INVESTIGATIVE TECHNIQUES AND PROBLEMS

part III

Obviously no two investigative operations are completely alike and their diversity can be attributed to such factors as the size of the police department and its geographical location, selection and promotion procedures, the political climate of the community, the training of investigators and the particular investigative orientation, such as specialization or generalization and decentralization or centralization.

There is little doubt that attitudes of the police chief and his immediate subordinates will have an impact on the investigative function, just as the spirit and morale of individual members in the department affect performance. On a more basic level, the operations of particular units will vary constantly depending on their mission, and some understanding of the unique aspects and special problems of the investigative function is worth discussion. Among these are:

1. Undercover and surveillance operations.
2. Narcotics and dangerous drugs.
3. Investigations in the ghetto or inner city.
4. Organized crime.
5. Relations with other agencies.

While the problems discussed in the following chapters are not all-inclusive, they should serve to highlight some of the many facets of criminal investigation, and provide the reader with a basic understanding of the techniques involved in handling them.

CHAPTER 12

undercover and surveillance operations

UNDERCOVER OPERATIONS

While the focus of this book is on the investigation of a crime after it has occurred, some discussion must be made of surveillance techniques. There are times when an undercover operation may be necessary to gather evidence either concerning a past crime, or in anticipation of a future crime.

Undercover operatives are probably used most frequently in the investigation of narcotics cases, although this approach has also become increasingly effective in cases involving organized crime and militant groups. In certain instances an undercover operative may be used on a particular case in order to develop information.

Simply defined, an undercover operative is a law enforcement agent who attempts to develop the confidence of an individual or to infiltrate a group or operation for the purpose of developing information concerning criminal activity. The advantages of using an undercover investigator generally outweigh those of the informant, although there are often drawbacks that preclude their use. Generally, an undercover operation will take more time to mount because the officer must gain the confidence of an individual or the group. Not only are the manpower costs relatively high, but there is also the danger of discovery and possible harm to the officer. On the other hand, an undercover operative is usually more reliable than an informant, and may be in a position to develop leads of which the informant is unaware. In some cases he may be the only means to a successful investigation.

The nature of an undercover assignment will have a bearing on the individual chosen to attempt it. Among the considerations in selecting undercover operatives are age, race and ethnic factors, social background, personality, previous occupation, and contacts. In addition, the type of assignment and the information needed may have a bearing on the individual chosen. It would not be wise, for example, to assign a novice to an important case unless absolutely necessary. Certain types of assignments will require that the assigned be "street-wise," whereas some assignments may require a particular skill, such as having had experience in accounting. Each department should maintain a skills inventory listing all relevant criteria for instances in which a particular skill is needed.

Obviously not all investigators will make effective undercover operatives. The primary considerations in choosing an undercover agent are usually a desire to participate and a gregarious personality, as well as the ability to adapt to various roles. In preparing for an assignment the investigator should gather as much information as he can about the persons involved, the locale, the particular allegations, and the operations of other units or agencies that might also be conducting a similar or parallel investigation. Information on the suspect or suspects should include biographical data, character traits, hangouts, associates, and family relationships. Knowledge of the area should include a general description of the neighborhood, locations that are frequented or used by the suspect, and places where contacts or telephone calls can be made in safety.

Role preparation is extremely important, and should include a background history, consideration of attire, attitude to be presented, and the means to be used in gaining confidence. The number of lies fabricated to carry out the role should be limited, and elaborate stories avoided. Whenever possible the same or a similar name should be used, and an attempt made to keep in character (leave the dramatic acting to the actors!). The background story should be believable and some cover established in case it is questioned or checked. The author is familiar with one instance in which the undercover operative claimed that he had been away in prison, but could not provide the names of the warden, any of the guards, or a description of the facility. Needless to say, he did not get far in his investigation.

Gaining the confidence of an individual or infiltrating a group is difficult, and care should be taken not to appear overanxious. Frequently an informant may be used to make introductions. If this is not possible the investigator should attempt to develop a friendship with someone close to the suspect or within the group. Another approach is to move into a house, apply for a job in the vicinity, and frequent the hangouts of the suspect. When a contact is made the contact will frequently test the undercover man before bringing him into his confidence. Asking many questions or being too curious will arouse suspicion, and the undercover man should avoid this.

Once contact has been made the investigator should let the natural course of events take place. Under no circumstances should he suggest or initiate a criminal act, since this is entrapment. Although he can lead the suspect along and indicate that he will participate, he should not take part in any criminal activity without the specific authorization of his superiors. In some cases the undercover man may be permitted to participate in or overlook minor crimes in order to develop information on a more important case. The danger of an entrapment defense is always present, and many cases have been lost in court because an overzealous undercover operative became too involved in planning the crime.

In communicating with superiors or police contacts, the undercover man should take care not to make any action that might create suspicion. Telephone calls should not be made through a central switchboard and, if possible, a "dummy" number should be established, which when answered does not reveal itself as a police number. Written reports should be made at a location where there is no possibility of discovery, and the investigator should not keep copies in his possession. Once the report has been written it should be mailed in a plain envelope. Meetings with police contacts should be avoided unless necessary, and if one has been set up, adequate safeguards to avoid being followed or discovered should be taken.

For the investigator's protection various signals can be worked out beforehand, both for telephone and visual communication. Visual signals may indicate that the investigator needs assistance, or that a particular event is about to take place. Drawing a blind, placing something in a window, blowing a horn, or the display of clothing in a particular way are but a few visual signals that might be effective. Code words in a telephone call may also be used to signal the contact man. Examples might be the names of persons, the use of numbers in conversation, or particular words. The investigator should keep in mind that all too frequently codes are missed or misinterpreted, and care should be taken to plan them adequately beforehand.

Frequently the investigator's actions or familiarity with a saying, location, or event will arouse suspicion. Care should be taken to avoid slang that is common in police work or some other aspect of life with which the individual is not supposed to be familiar. Obviously, he should avoid carrying anything that might link him with the police department or his actual background. This includes pictures of a wife and children, membership cards in organizations, police identification, and other articles. Possession of a weapon will depend on the assignment. If a weapon is carried it is often advisable not to carry one that is associated with police work, such as a .38 caliber. This also holds true for the holster, many types of which are in common use by police officers. Some assignments may require carrying a weapon without the suspect being aware of it. In such instances the weapon should be easily concealable, and should be kept somewhere other than on the hip, such as the crotch, leg, or small of the back.

Transmitting and recording equipment are extremely valuable tools in undercover work. Once again, though, care must be taken to see that they are secreted properly. If a tape recorder has been used the tape should be mailed or placed in a drop where it can be picked up as soon as possible after the contact in order to avoid discovery. The same holds true of film if photographs are taken by the undercover man.

SURVEILLANCE

Surveillance is the observation of a person, place, or thing, usually surreptitiously. Surveillance operations are conducted either to obtain evidence of a crime, to locate a suspect or to obtain information about a suspect's activities, to check on informants, to protect a victim or witness, or to apprehend the perpetrator of a crime in the act. The latter is usually called a stakeout.

The two general types of surveillance are the stationary, known as a plant, and the moving, known as a tail. The various forms used may be classified as close surveillance, loose surveillance, rough surveillance, and progressive surveillance. In close surveillance the suspect is to be kept under watch at all times and the surveillant will risk being discovered before losing a suspect. In loose surveillance secrecy is important and the goal is to develop a familiarization with the suspect's activities without taking a chance on being discovered. Rough surveillance is used if there is no need for secrecy and the suspect is aware that he is being followed. This type of surveillance is common in investigating prominent figures involved in organized crime. Progressive surveillance is developed in stages, proceeding from loose, casual surveillance to almost constant surveillance.

Preparation for surveillance should include the development of a thorough plan of operation; various alternatives and strategies should be considered. Personnel chosen should be given specific assignments, and it is generally more effective to work in teams. Equipment needs should be considered at the outset, as it may be too late once the operation has begun. This may include communications equipment, cameras and binoculars, automobiles or vans, attire, cover material (including specific types of equipment if the agent is impersonating someone, such as a laborer or mailman). An attempt should be made to anticipate any unforeseen problems; an example might be to ensure that tokens are carried in case the subject decides to use public transportation.

Before the operation everyone involved should be briefed, at which time the particulars of the case and the reason why surveillance is necessary should be explained. Guidelines should be established for particular situations, such as the discovery of the surveillance by the suspect. A thorough description, including photographs of the subject, should be given to those involved. Surveillance operations often suffer from a lack of coordination, and proper initial preparation can reduce the chance of error.

Stationary surveillance may be conducted from either an inside location or the street. If a long period of waiting is anticipated arrangements should be made to use an inside location that affords good observation and cover. Street surveillance may be as simple as using an auto or van with a two-way mirror or as complex an operation as using borrowed equipment and pretending to be working in the street. Because word travels fast it is often as important to deceive residents of the neighborhood as it is to fool the subject. If an inside location is used care should be taken to avoid coming and going frequently or at specific hours. When outside the surveillant should attempt to look inconspicuous and appear to be doing whatever he is supposed to be doing. For example, if he is meant to be working on a stalled auto he should not just stand around. If an auto is used for surveillance, the driver's seat should be left vacant, in order to create the impression that the occupants are waiting for someone.

The reason for surveillance must be considered. If it is a stakeout in anticipation of a robbery the location should provide visibility, cover, and a clear line of sight in case the subject is armed. If the purpose is to develop information concerning persons coming and going at a particular location, the observation point should permit the use of binoculars and a camera equipped with a telephoto lens. Frequently this can be accomplished from a relatively distant point.

The moving surveillance, or tail, presents numerous problems, not the least of which is maintaining surreptitious contact with the subject. The one-man tail is the simplest and yet the most difficult and ineffective of approaches. In addition to a high probability of discovery, it is easy for the suspect to shake or elude a one-man tail. The team approach, involving anywhere from two to five men, is generally a more effective method, although in some cases it may be necessary to use several teams in order to carry out an effective surveillance. There are a number of variations that can be used and choice will depend on the particular situation as well as the expertise of the surveillants. The more popular tail is executed with three persons working behind and across from the subject. One man works from across the street, maintaining visual contact, while the second and third man work behind the subject, one keeping him in view and the other acting as backup (see Fig. 12.1). Through a prearranged signal, or if the subject appears to become suspicious, the number-one man or the backup man may move up (see Fig. 12.2). It is often advisable for the agents to switch places when the subject enters a building or turns a corner. The type of building will determine whether or not the subject is to be followed inside. The leap frog method is a variation on the method of following the suspect, but only one man maintains visual contact, while the rest are behind him, exchanging positions at various intervals. The contact man drops to the rear as the number-two man moves into position behind the subject.

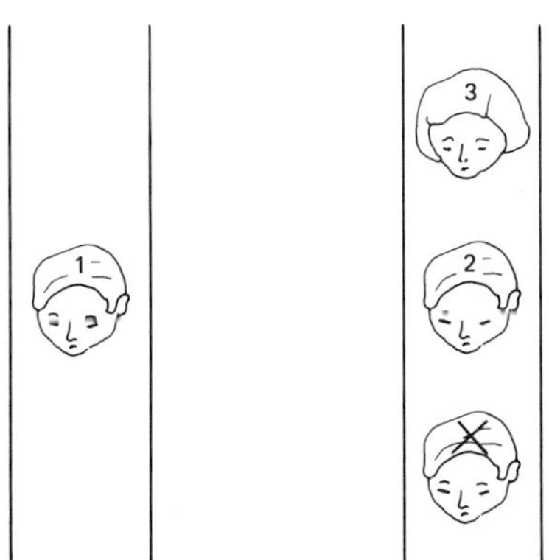

FIG. 12.1 Team surveillance: following.

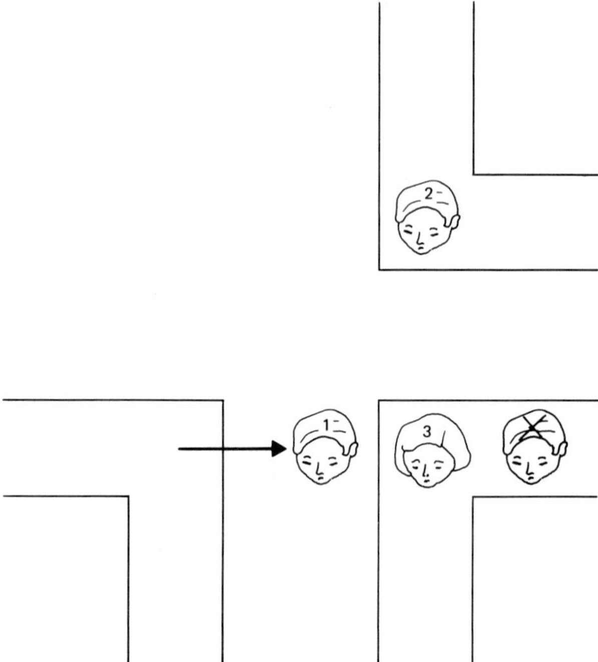

FIG. 12.2 Team surveillance: following with position exchange.

The lead surveillance requires more skill and preparation, but can be more effective if the suspect is suspicious. Using this approach the subject is virtually surrounded. This method is more effective in busy areas where pedestrian traffic is heavy. The lead man operates a short distance in front of the subject, observing him in the reflection of store windows or from the side. The second man works somewhat further behind and the third man works from across the street. The third man should act as a control, signalling when a switch should be made. (See Fig. 12.3.) A careful set of signals should be worked out beforehand to ensure coordination. In any of the above approaches an automobile may be used to pick up the surveillants if the subject enters a cab or car. However, it may be inadvisable to pick up all the surveillants, because this may tip the subject if he is already suspicious. A central telephone number should be established which surveillants can call if they are separated during the operation. In most operations it is advisable to use communications equipment, although care must be taken to avoid discovery.

Automobile surveillance is also difficult and it is advisable to use two or more cars in this type of operation. The advantage of radio contact increases coordination, although heavy traffic may make it difficult to keep the subject in sight. The

FIG. 12.3 Team surveillance: lead.

approaches used are similar to those mentioned above, with one exception. In light traffic it may be more advisable to use parallel surveillance with a car in each block parallel to the block the subject is on. The surveillance autos should take turns beating the subject to the next intersection (see Fig. 12.4). This method is most effective if the subject's travel pattern is similar each day; it also lessens the probability of discovery. The use of lead cars at key locations to pick up the subject as he passes or to lead him for a predetermined distance is also effective.

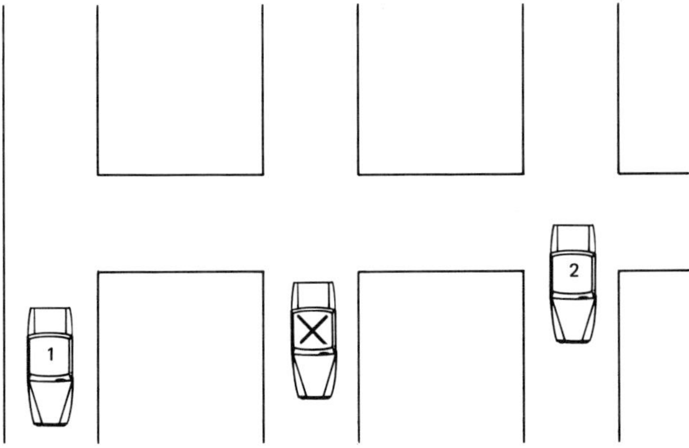

FIG. 12.4 Parallel automobile surveillance.

During the course of an operation the surveillants are likely to encounter specific problems. Preplanning should account for most of the actions the subject might take. If the subject enters a building he should only be followed if it can be accomplished with a slight chance of discovery; the number of persons entering will depend on the type of building. For example, everyone may move into a department store or large hotel, whereas only one or two men should enter an apartment house or small store. Should the subject enter an elevator the surveillant should board with him and get off at the same floor or the one above, if possible. One person should remain in the lobby in case the subject returns immediately. In an apartment house the surveillant may be forced to ring someone's doorbell to avoid suspicion. If this should happen the surveillant should have some story worked out in case the occupant is home. He might identify himself as a salesman or indicate that he has the wrong address. Should the subject enter a small store or a restaurant one or two men may follow him, although it is probably wiser to wait outside and cover the entrances.

If the subject enters public transportation, at least two of the surveillants should attempt to board with him and sit behind him, if possible. If the subject appears suspicious one of the surveillants may alight two or three stops later. When the stops are relatively close only one surveillant should alight with the subject and the second should proceed to the next stop and quickly work his way back. Once he has made contact the surveillant who followed the subject from the bus should drop back. On a train the subject may be observed from an adjoining car if it is not too crowded. If the subject has the habit of getting on a bus or train and then getting off before it starts one person should follow him aboard and the rest stay behind. If he enters a car or taxi the registration should be recorded; then if he is lost, a check with the cab company may reveal his whereabouts.

During the course of surveillance care should be taken to act naturally and avoid doing anything that might arouse suspicion. It is common for inexperienced investigators to think that they have been discovered. Frequently this is no more than an overactive imagination. However, if the subject appears to be taking evasive action, perhaps moving quickly through a department store or using public transportation in some unlikely pattern, there is a greater probability that he is aware or at least suspects that he is being followed. In such cases the more surveillants used the less the probability of discovery. Female surveillants can be extremely effective and should be used whenever possible.

While it is advisable not to look directly at the subject, eye contact should not be obviously avoided. Surveillants should wear clothing which can be rearranged to avoid discovery. Examples are removing a jacket or hat, switching clothing, and carrying objects, such as a newspaper, briefcase, or package, that can be discarded. It may also be advisable to carry a paperback book that can be taken out while on a bus or while waiting in a lobby. At all times the surveillant should look as though he knows what he is doing, even if he is attempting to appear confused about a location. If the subject appears convinced that he is being followed by a particular person, suspicion may be drawn off by walking up and asking a question, such as how to find a particular location. Once this is done, however, the surveillant should be taken off the operation for a few days or kept out of sight.

During the course of a surveillance, surveillants should avoid breaking laws or regulations, such as running a red light or parking in unauthorized zones, unless it is absolutely necessary.

A written record of surveillance operations should be maintained for both the relieving team and possible later use in court. The oncoming team should be briefed concerning the subject's activities during the previous 24 hours. Most people follow a relatively similar pattern in their everyday movements, and an understanding of this pattern may aid investigators in picking up the subject if he is lost. The author is familiar with one case in which the subject, a numbers runner, developed an intricate pattern in order to avoid being followed each day. However, his intricate pattern was virtually the same each day; thus if he were lost the surveillants merely had to move to a subsequent contact point and pick him up again.

In recent years the use of helicopters in surveillance operations has become increasingly popular. This form of surveillance is most effective in suburban areas, or in areas in which light traffic is anticipated. Before beginning the operation a plan for coordination should be developed. In some instances it may prove worthwhile to mark the surveillance autos with plastic tape for easy recognition. Unless this is done in a nondescript way, such as creating racing stripes, the surveillance cars should not operate in sight of the subject.

Surveillance operations require more than the ability to walk behind a subject, and should be viewed as an art that can be developed to a high degree of perfection. A thorough understanding of the techniques involved, adequate coordination, and experience will enhance the operation.

SUGGESTED READINGS

Adams, Thomas F., *Police Patrol: Tactics and Techniques.* Englewood Cliffs, N.J.: Prentice-Hall, 1971.

CHAPTER 13

narcotics and dangerous drugs

The narcotics investigator is usually a special breed of individual who must have an above average dedication to his work. In many respects narcotics investigation is a specialized operation that requires much more knowledge than can be covered within the scope of this book. It cannot be classified within the definition of criminal investigation discussed in this book, since most narcotics investigations involve an attempt to gather evidence to prove the existence of a criminal act, rather than to conduct an investigation after the act has occurred. Nevertheless, the interrelationship of narcotics violations and other forms of crime is so close as to justify some discussion here.

The problem of narcotics and dangerous drugs is not unknown to the police or the American populace; indeed, it has been characterized by some as a national epidemic. Because the abuse of narcotics and dangerous drugs affects primarily the young, it has become a growing source of concern. Unfortunately, too little is known about preventive and causative factors of narcotic and dangerous drug abuse. Indeed, our knowledge of treatment is woefully limited.

The investigator should have some familiarity with the definitions concerning narcotics and dangerous drugs, as well as some knowledge of those most commonly abused, and an understanding of the terminology used in the drug culture (see Figs. 13.1 through 13.6). The following definitions are taken from *A Federal Source Book: Answers to the Most Frequently Asked Questions About Drugs*:[1]

Drug. A drug is a substance that has an effect upon the body or mind.

Drug dependence. Drug dependence is a state of psychological or physical dependence, or both, that results from chronic, periodic, or continuous use. Many kinds of drug dependence exist; they all have specific problems associated with them.

FIG. 13.1 Terms and symptoms of drug abuse. (This chart and other photographs in this chapter courtesy of the Bureau of Narcotics and Dangerous Drugs, United States Department of Justice.) ▶

Terms & Symptoms of Drug Abuse

This chart indicates the most common symptoms of drug abuse. However, all of the signs are not always evident, nor are they the only ones that may occur. Any drug's reaction will usually depend on the person, his mood, his environment, the dosage of the drug and how the drug interacts with others drugs the abuser has taken or contaminants within the drug.

Drug	Terms	Drowsiness	Excitation & Hyperactivity	Irritability & Restlessness	Belligerence	Anxiety	Euphoria	Depression	Hallucinations	Panic	Irrational Behavior	Confusion	Talkativeness	Rambling Speech	Slurred Speech	Laughter	Tremor	Staggering	Impairment of Coordination	Dizziness
MORPHINE	M, dreamer, white stuff, hard stuff, morpho, unkie, Miss Emma, monkey, cube, morf, tab, emsel, hocus, morphie, melter	○		●		● ○	○	●	○	●		●			○		●		○	
HEROIN	Snow, stuff, H, junk, big Harry, caballo, DooJee, boy, horse, white stuff, Harry, hairy, joy powder, salt, dope, Duige, hard stuff, schmeek, shit, skag, thing	○		●		● ○	○	●		●		●			○		●		○	
CODEINE	Schoolboy	○		●		● ○	○	●		●		●			○		●		○	
HYDROMORPHONE	Dilaudid, Lords	○		●		● ○	○	●		●		●			○		●		○	
MEPERIDINE	Demerol, Isonipecaine, Dolantol, Pethidine	○		●		● ○	○	●	○	●		●			○		●		○	
METHADONE	Dolophine, Dollies, dolls, amidone	○		●		● ○	○	●		●		●			○		●		○	
EXEMPT PREPARATIONS	P.G., P.O., blue velvet (Paregoric with anti-histamine), red water, bitter, licorice	○		●		●	○	●		●		●					●		○	
COCAINE	The leaf, snow, C, cecil, coke, dynamite, flake, speedball (when mixed with Heroin), girl, happy dust, joy powder, white girl, gold dust, Corine, Bernies, Burese, gin, Bernice, Star dust, Carrie, Cholly, heaven dust, paradise		○	○		○	○		○				○				○			
MARIHUANA	Smoke, straw, Texas tea, jive, pod, mutah, splim, Acapulco Gold, Bhang, boo, bush, butter flower, Ganja, weed, grass, pot, muggles, tea, has, hemp, griffo, Indian hay, loco weed, hay, herb, J, mu, giggles-smoke, love weed, Mary Warner, Mohasky, Mary Jane, joint sticks, reefers, sativa, roach	○	○	○		○	○	○	○	○			○			○			○	

	SLANG TERMS																			
AMPHETAMINES	Pep pills, bennies, wake-ups, eye-openers, lid poppers co-pilots, truck drivers, peaches, roses, hearts, cartwheels, whites, coast to coast, LA turnabouts, browns, footballs, greenies, bombido, oranges, dexies, jolly-beans, A's, jellie babies, sweets, beans, uppers		●	●		●	●		●	●			●				●			●
METHAMPHETAMINE	Speed, meth splash, crystal, bombita, Methedrine, Doe		●	●		●	●		●	●			●				●			●
OTHER STIMULANTS	Pep pills, uppers		●	●			●		●				●				●			
BARBITURATES	Yellows, yellow jackets, nimby, nimbles, reds, pinks, red birds, red devils, seggy, seccy, pink ladies, blues, blue birds, blue devils, blue heavens, red & blues, double trouble, tooies, Christmas trees, phennies, barbs	●		◍ ●	●	◍	●	●	◍		●	●			●	●	◍	●	●	
OTHER DEPRESSANTS	Candy, goofballs, sleeping pills, peanuts	●		◍ ●	●	◍	●	●	◍		●	●			●		◍	●	●	
LYSERGIC ACID DIETHLAMIDE (LSD)	Acid, cubes, pearly gates, heavenly blue, royal blue, wedding bells, sugar, Big D, Blue Acid, the Chief, the Hawk, instant Zen, 25, Zen, sugar lump		●			●	●	●	●	●	●			●			●			
STP	Serenity, tranquility, peace, DOM, syndicate acid						●	●	●		●			●			●			
PHENCYCLIDINE (PCP)	PCP, peace pill, synthetic marihauna	●				●				●		●				●			●	●
PEYOTE	Mescal button, mescal beans, hikori, hikuli, huatari, seni, wokowi, cactus, the button, tops, a moon, half moon, P, the bad seed, Big Chief, Mesc		●	●		●			●					●						
PSILOCYBIN	Sacred mushrooms, mushrooms		●	●		●	●	●	●		●			●						
DIMETHLTRYPTAMINE (DMT)	DMT, 45-minute psychosis, businessman's special		●			●	●	●	●		●			●						

● SYMPTOMS OF ABUSE ◍ SYMPTOMS OF WITHDRAWAL

	HYPERACTIVE REFLEXES	DEPRESSED REFLEXES	INCREASED SWEATING	CONSTRICTED PUPILS	DILATED PUPILS	UNUSUALLY BRIGHT SHINY EYES	INFLAMED EYES	RUNNY EYES AND NOSE	LOSS OF APPETITE	INCREASED APPETITE	INSOMNIA	DISTORTION OF SPACE OR TIME	NAUSEA AND VOMITING	ABDOMINAL CRAMPS	DIARRHEA	CONSTIPATION	PHYSICAL DEPENDENCE	PSYCHOLOGICAL DEPENDENCE	TOLERANCE	CONVULSIONS	UNCONSCIOUSNESS	HEPATITIS	PSYCHOSIS	DEATH FROM WITHDRAWAL	DEATH FROM OVERDOSE	POSSIBILE CHROMOSOME DAMAGE	ORALLY	INJECTION	SNIFFED	SMOKED
MORPHINE		●	●	●	●			●	●		●		●	●	●	●	●	●	●	●	●	●			●			●		
HEROIN		●	●	●	●			●	●		●		●	●	●	●	●	●	●	●	●	●			●			●	●	
CODEINE		●	●	●	●			●	●		●		●	●	●	●	●	●	●			●			●		●	●		
HYDROMORPHONE		●	●	●	●			●	●		●		●	●	●	●	●	●	●		●	●			●		●	●		
MEPERIDINE		●	●	●	●			●	●		●		●	●	●	●	●	●	●		●	●			●		●	●		
METHADONE		●	●	●	●			●	●		●		●	●	●	●	●	●	●		●	●			●		●	●		
EXEMPT PREPARATIONS		●	●	●	●			●	●		●		●	●	●	●	●	●	●			●					●	●		
COCAINE	●				●				●		●							●		●		●			●			●	●	
MARIHUANA							●			●		●						●									●			●

AMPHETAMINES	○		○		○	○			○		○							●	●			●	●		●		◍	◍		
METHAMPHETAMINE	○		○		○	○			○									●	●			●	●		●		◍	◍		
OTHER STIMULANTS	○				○													●	●			●			●		◍	◍		
BARBITURATES		○	○	○							◍		◍	◍			●	●	●	●	●	●		●	●		◍	◍		
OTHER DEPRESSANTS		○									◍		◍	◍			●	●	●	●		●			●		◍	◍		
LYSERGIC ACID DIETHLAMIDE (LSD)			○		○							○						●	●				●			●	◍			
STP					○							○						●				●					◍	◍		
PHENCYCLIDINE (PCP)																		●			●	●					◍	◍		
PEYOTE					○								○					●	●			●					◍	◍		
PSILOCYBIN			○		○							○						●	●								◍			
DIMETHLTRYPTAMINE (DMT)			○		○							○						●	●			●						◍		◍

● DANGERS OF ABUSE

◍ HOW TAKEN

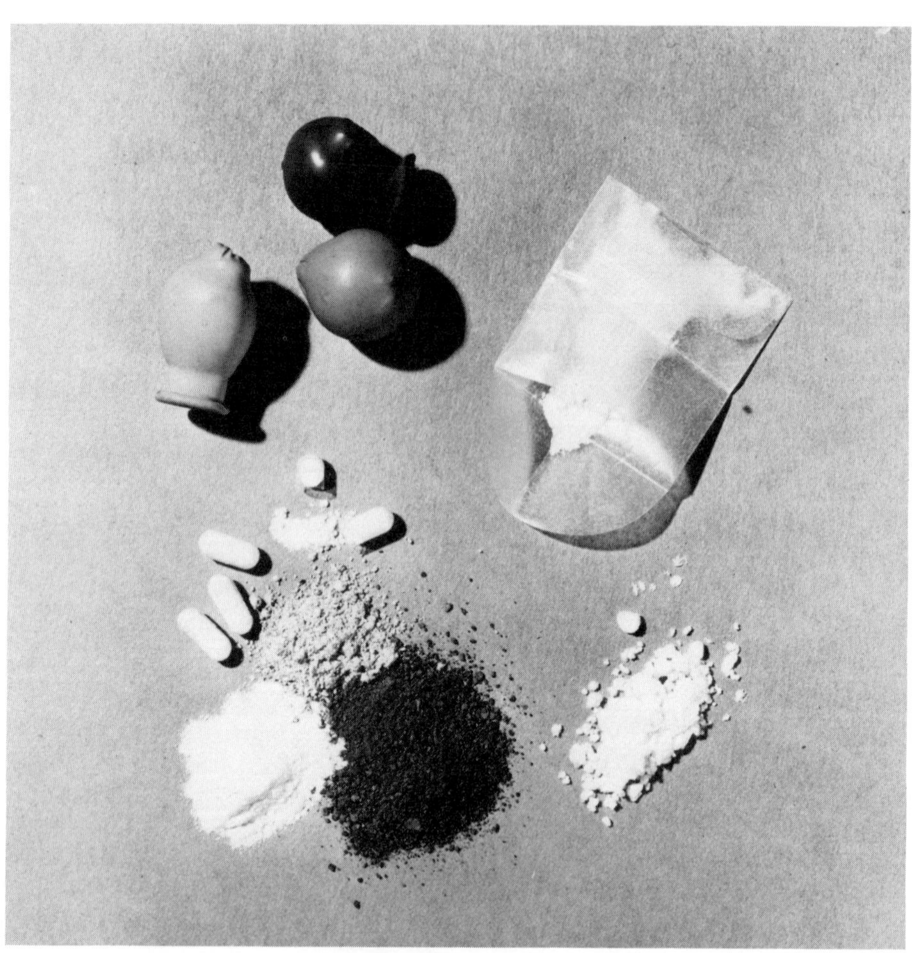

FIG. 13.2 Forms of heroin.

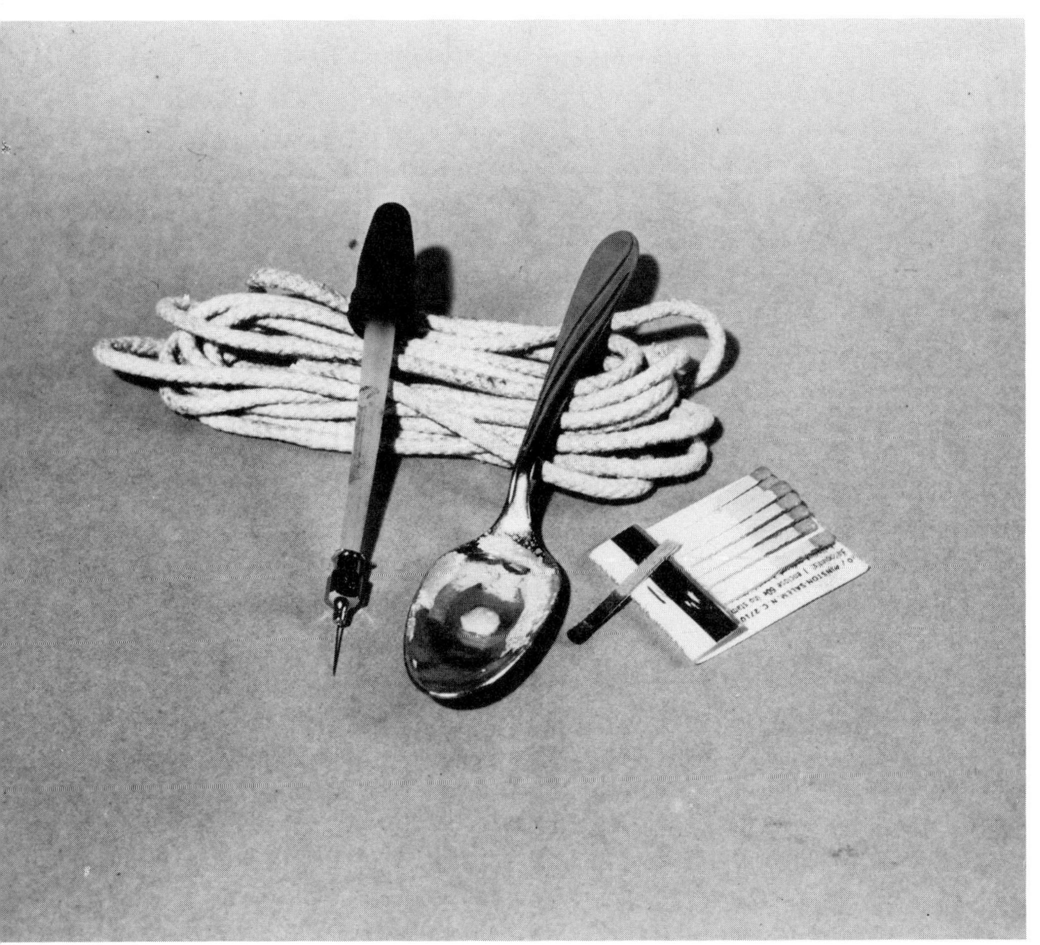

FIG. 13.3 An addict's equipment.

FIG. 13.4 Coca leaves and illicit forms of cocaine.

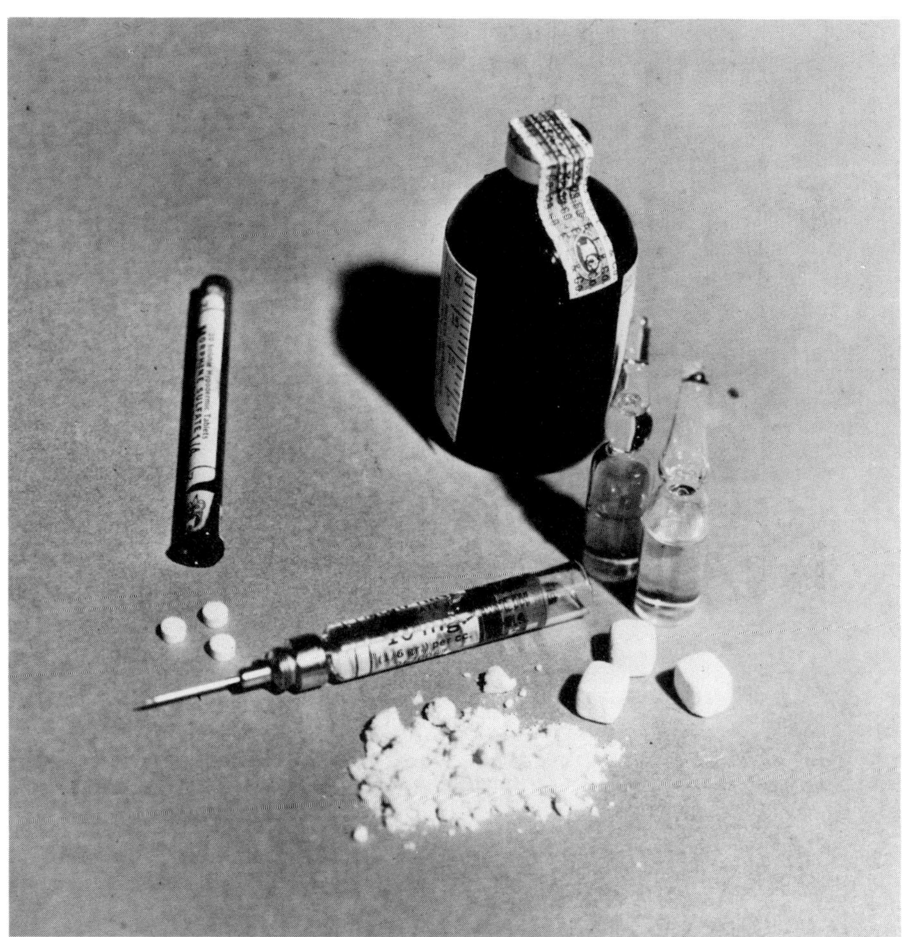

FIG. 13.5 Illicit forms of morphine.

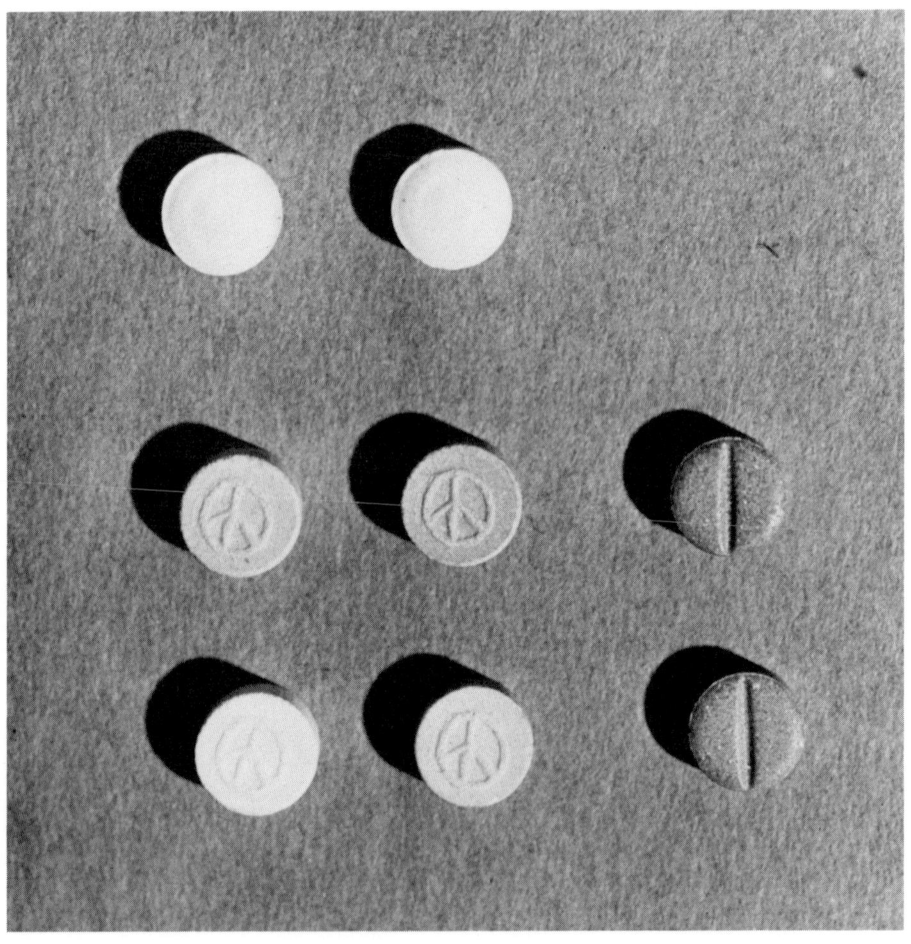

FIG. 13.6 LSD (peace pills).

Habituation. Habituation is the *psychological* desire to repeat the use of a drug intermittently or continuously because of emotional reasons. Escape from tension, dulling of reality, euphoria (being "high") are some of the reasons why drugs come to be used habitually.

Addiction. Addiction is a physical dependence upon a drug. Its scientific definition includes the development of tolerance and withdrawal. As a person develops tolerance, he requires larger and larger amounts of the drug to produce the same effect. When use of the addicting drug is stopped abruptly, the period of withdrawal is characterized by such distressing symptoms as vomiting and convulsions. A compulsion to repeat the use of the addicting drug is understandable because the drug temporarily solves one's problems and keeps the withdrawal symptoms away.

Drug culture. A drug culture or subculture is a group of people whose lives are committed to drugs. The members of any subculture may congregate in a particular geographic area such as the Haight-Ashbury district in San Francisco. Marihuana is almost invariably smoked in such communities, but hallucinogens, sedatives, stimulants, and narcotics are also used. It has been demonstrated that these subcultures are transient in nature; only a minority of the members remain for more than a year.

Marihuana. Marihuana is Indian hemp (*Cannabis sativa*). The parts with the highest tetrahydrocannabinol (THC) content are the flowering tops of the unfertilized female plant. The leaves have a smaller amount. The stalks and seeds have little or none. The male plant has a lesser amount of THC than the female plant. THC is believed to be the active ingredient in marihuana. Many other compounds are present in marihuana, but they do not produce the mental effects of the drug.

Hallucinogens. Hallucinogens (also called psychedelics) are drugs capable of provoking changes of sensation, thinking, self-awareness, and emotion. Alterations of time and space perception, illusions, hallucinations, and delusions may be either minimal or overwhelming depending on the dose. The results are very variable; a "high" or a "bad trip" ("freakout or bummer") may occur in the same person on different occasions. LSD is the most potent and best-studied hallucinogen. Besides LSD, a large number of synthetic and natural hallucinogens are known. Mescaline from the peyote cactus, psilocybin from the mexican mushroom, morning glory seed, DMT, STP, MDA and dozens of others are known and abused. Along with its active component THC, marihuana is medically classified as a hallucinogen.

Stimulants. Stimulants are drugs, usually amphetamines, that increase alertness, reduce hunger, and provide a feeling of well being. Their medical uses include the suppression of appetite and the reduction of fatigue or mild depression. Many stimulants are known, including cocaine, amphetamine (benzedrine "bennies"), dextroamphetamine (Dexidrine "dexies") and methamphetamine (Methadrine). The latter drug is commonly called "speed" or "crystal" stimulants.

In conducting the narcotics investigation the use of undercover operatives and informants is of prime importance. In recent years there has been a shift in law enforcement, and the focus has been on the dealers and traffickers in narcotics and dangerous drugs, rather than on the user. Because of the various levels of operation involved in this activity, it is difficult to reach the financial supporters and key figures, many of whom are also actively involved in other forms of organized crime. Cooperation between local, state, and federal agencies is probably the only effective way of conducting thorough investigations involving narcotics and dangerous drugs. Although such cooperation has generally been poor in the past, there are increasing signs that agencies are willing to pool their resources in working toward a common goal. The implementation of joint Strike Forces made up of local and federal officers has been most effective in dealing with organized crime.

On the local level the investigator may be faced with the investigation of cases at a particular location or in a specific area. Such cases are most likely to come about through the receipt of information from a variety of sources: residents of the area, informants, patrolmen, and arrested persons. Some central information unit should be responsible for collating all information and determining significant relationships.

If narcotics trafficking or sales are suspected, surveillance operations should be undertaken to determine the *modus operandi.* If street sales are involved, the common practice is for the pusher to meet the buyer at a particular location, take his order and money, retrieve the narcotics or drugs from some hidden location known as the "stash," or from his residence. This makes it difficult for the police to apprehend the suspect with a large amount of drugs on his person. In some cases the pusher may establish several stashes to avoid detection. Because the street pusher is the last man in the network of illegal traffic an attempt should be made to discover his source of supply. This may be accomplished through surveillance, the use of undercover operatives or informants, or apprehension of the suspect, inducing him to cooperate with authorities, through either the offer of a lesser charge or suspended prosecution. If an arrangement is made with anyone involved in illegal activity of this nature the prosecutor should be advised and made aware of the circumstances. Under no circumstances should the investigator take it upon himself to make a promise or deal without notifying his superior. This is for his own protection.

Undercover operations are dangerous in themselves, but even more so when narcotics are involved. Discovery may lead to serious injury or death, and extreme precautions must be taken to offer the undercover man as much protection as possible under the circumstances. Frequently he must pose as an addict, and in order to do so must be familiar with the actions and slang of the narcotics user. In making a "buy," an attempt should be made to have a witness present, or to have someone film the transaction from a surveillance location. Obviously, such methods are often difficult or nearly impossible; thus, the narcotics investigation is characterized by a "play-it-by-ear" approach.

In all narcotics investigations an attempt should be made to develop information concerning suppliers. Arresting the addict unfortunately does little to stop the supply of narcotics.

NOTE

1. *A Federal Source Book: Answers to the Most Frequently Asked Questions About Drugs.* Washington, D.C.: Government Printing Office, 1970, pp. 1–3, 9, 17, 23.

SUGGESTED READINGS

Susman, Jackwell, ed., *Drug Use and Social Policy.* New York: AMS Press, 1972.

CHAPTER 14

ghetto or inner-city investigations

Unfortunately, many investigators fail to recognize the various problems associated with working in different geographical locations. Frequently the investigator must carry the investigation beyond his general area of assignment into a neighborhood with which he is unfamiliar. In some cases this is likely to go beyond the city or county to which he is assigned. In this chapter the focus is on conducting an investigation in the inner city, or ghetto, as the slums of our cities have come to be called.

The investigator who believes that one single approach to his task will work is not only deluding himself, but is likely to be ineffective in situations with which he is unfamiliar. While such situations are as diverse as every city in the United States, the focus here is on investigating crime in the inner city, for it is in such situations that there is a wide range of misunderstanding and distrust, on the part of both the public and the police. Too frequently, for example, the investigator assumes that because his constituency is of a minority group (black, Puerto Rican, or Mexican-American), there will be no cooperation. It is true that hostility toward the police is likely to be greater, although this feeling is frequently overrated. Virtually all studies undertaken of minority attitudes toward the police indicate that the vast majority show positive attitudes toward the police.[1]

Second, the investigator is generally looked on more favorably by the public, and this holds true insofar as minorities are concerned. This, of course, is not to say that there are no problems, but an understanding of these problems can help to establish more effective approaches.

Finally, the problems of the ghetto are not restricted to blacks, Puerto Ricans, or Mexican-Americans, but to all those living in poverty or substandard conditions. Experience has shown that the close-knit association among immigrant groups residing in various sections of the city is likely to prohibit an investigation. The inner city, as defined here, may be viewed as those geographic areas inhabited by the poor, transients, disadvantaged, and, in many instances, ethnic and racial minorities. Frequently the police are viewed by inner-city residents as outsiders, and their actions are viewed with skepticism and hostility.

The Report of the National Advisory Commission on Civil Disorders noted that "Negroes firmly believe that police brutality and harassment occur repeatedly in Negro neighborhoods. This belief is unquestionably one of the major reasons for intense Negro resentment against the police."[2]

There is little doubt that this sense of resentment and hostility has an impact on the investigative function, for without citizen cooperation the investigator is more likely to be unsuccessful in solving crimes.

APPROACHING THE PROBLEM

Perhaps the most important aspect of conducting an investigation in the inner city is the recognition that it is likely to be more difficult than the average case in another locality. Too often the investigator assumes that all investigations can be handled in a similar manner, that there is no difference in general citizen attitudes toward the police, and that intensive investigative techniques will outweigh problems inherent to a neighborhood. This is simply not the case, for the more familiar an investigator is with the locality and its citizens, the better are his chances of success. Thus, in approaching the problem an investigator should make every attempt to understand the culture and mores of the community.

Second, the investigator should understand human behavior and the underlying motivation that causes people to react in various ways. This also involves an understanding of sociological and psychological factors influencing the community. Frequently the investigator's background and upbringing have not prepared him for diverse assignments. While police departments have begun to adapt their training programs toward a more humanistic approach, such efforts are frequently too little and too late. Furthermore, human relations programs are often general and do not take into account the individual differences between neighborhoods.

One of the most effective ways to learn about a neighborhood is to meet its residents. In addition to developing knowledge about individuals, it is possible to develop an overview of community attitudes, and to meet those persons who are most likely to be helpful during an investigation. A common mistake lies in paying too much attention to the attitudes and opinions of other police officers assigned to a community. Cynicism is a natural commodity in most police departments, and it is not uncommon for another officer to lead an investigator astray by telling him that there is no cooperation between the police and a particular individual, or the community in general. In most instances the investigator can develop ties, and it is not unlikely that there are some citizens who would be willing to help. The problem is to find them. One should not rule out the impact of the personal approach.

The investigator should also make it a point to meet community leaders, and to assure them of his interest in the community. Community leaders are important sources of information, and frequently their interests run parallel to those of the investigative function. However, the investigator must recognize that political pressures may inhibit cooperation, and he should be aware of the political ramifications involved in any particular case. He cannot afford to be aloof and fail to consider the implications of his actions. To expose a community leader to unfavorable publicity is to lose a friend, and probably a good contact. In developing a working relationship the investigator should also maintain regular contact with community spokesmen.

The news media are also an important asset; thus the investigator should make it a habit to read local newspapers, keep abreast of local affairs and, in general, be familiar with events in the neighborhood. He should also get to know local reporters and should not alienate them, as so often happens, by failing to cooperate within the bounds of department policy.

MINORITIES AND INVESTIGATION

There is a general feeling within law enforcement agencies that members of a minority group are likely to be more effective within their own communities. While this is no doubt true in some instances, it is probably overstated. Racial conflict has had a deleterious effect on law enforcement, and police departments are not immune to such conflict within their own organization. While this appears to be less true insofar as investigative units are concerned, it is a feeling of which all personnel must be aware. Racial slurs, hostility, and bad feelings only exacerbate an already difficult problem. Because the investigative function is one of the more adequately defined areas of the police role, there is more often a spirit of camaraderie among investigators that does not exist in other units. This should result in greater cooperation. Nevertheless, it should also be recognized that role conflict may be greater if the police officer is a member of a minority group.[3]

One cannot categorically state that a black or Puerto Rican investigator will be more effective in the ghetto, but there is little doubt that they can move about more freely than their white counterparts can. Thus, the black or Puerto Rican investigator may be able to develop information in specific areas more effectively. In such instances cooperation is paramount, and the police mission requires a thorough understanding of mutual problems and goals. Obviously, this is not limited to blacks and Puerto Ricans, but cuts across all racial and ethnic backgrounds.

The lack of adequate minority group representation in urban police departments throughout the country does have an impact on the investigative function. Until such time as this deficiency is alleviated, investigative units will frequently find their effectiveness limited. Nevertheless, the reader should not assume that all investigations in the ghetto are impossible, or that any investigation cannot be pursued. Statistics continuously indicate that ghetto residents are more likely to be the victims of crime.[4] There is no doubt that for this reason residents of the inner city are as concerned with crime as the police, if not more so. Unfortunately, the artificial barriers frequently existing between the community and the police do serve to hamper communication. It is the investigator's responsibility to work toward removing the barriers of fear and mistrust.

THE INNER-CITY INVESTIGATION

There is often a difference between an investigation in the inner city and that being conducted in the suburban or middle-class neighborhood. The difference, however, lies not so much in technique as in attitude. The rules of evidence collection, interviewing, interrogation, and general investigative techniques change little, for in all cases the investigator is expected to adapt to the particular situation. For one reason or another adaptation appears to be less common in the inner city. There is likely to be a general attitude among investigators that the community is getting what it deserves. Frequently the investigator is less motivated, or has given in to the unique problems confronting him. There is little doubt that handling a case in the inner city is likely to be more challenging, but this should be a reason for striving rather than cynicism.

One should not assume that because a case is difficult it is impossible. The key to cooperation is understanding. Thus, the investigator should make every effort to illustrate his interest in the case. In some measure he must work harder to develop information, and he should not hesitate to seek it out. Sources of information are as varied as the city itself. While experience will help, it is also possible to educate oneself to the problems of individual and group attitudes. Here again it is important to be honest and aggressive in understanding human behavior.

Cooperation within the investigative unit is also extremely important, and the various talents and backgrounds of individual investigators should be utilized to the fullest. The investigator who has been raised in the inner city is more likely to provide greater insight than one who has not. This continues to hold true throughout all levels of the department; thus the investigator should also familiarize himself with members of the patrol force, who are in closer contact with the community and who are more likely to know cooperative citizens.

SUMMARY

In some measure it is difficult to put one's finger on the problems that prohibit effective investigations in the inner city, yet there is no doubt that problems exist. This chapter provides but a glimpse of the needs, and the reader is encouraged to become more familiar with the literature that abounds on police community relations and citizen cooperation. A key word here is attitude; in the past the police attitude toward social problems has been poor at best. Fortunately, there is a growing recognition of the problem, but it cannot be cured merely by a training program, for the real impetus must come from within the individual. Perhaps it is a sign of the weakness of our society that a chapter such as this must be written, for one may rightfully ask why there even exists a difference in investigative approach insofar as communities are concerned. Unfortunately, the problem is a real one, and can only be handled individually. Until such time as the problem is recognized by the investigator, little will be accomplished.

NOTES

1. See, for example, Robert Steadman, ed., *The Police and the Community.* Baltimore: The Johns Hopkins University Press, 1972.

2. *Report of the National Advisory Commission on Civil Disorders.* New York: Bantam Books, 1968), p. 302.

3. *Op. cit.,* pp. 37–39.

4. See, for example, The President's Commission on Law Enforcement and Administration of Justice. The Challenge of Crime in a Free Society. Washington, D.C.: Government Printing Office, 1967; *Report of the National Advisory Commission on Civil Disorders, op. cit.*

SUGGESTED READINGS

Coffey, Allan, Edward Eldefonso, and Walter Hartinger, *Human Relations: Law Enforcement in a Changing Community.* Englewood Cliffs, N.J.: Prentice-Hall, 1971.

CHAPTER 15

organized crime

The President's Task Force on Organized Crime noted:

> In many ways organized crime is the most sinister kind of crime in America. The men who control it have become rich and powerful by encouraging the needy to gamble, by luring the troubled to destroy themselves with drugs, by extorting the profits of honest and hardworking businessmen, by collecting usury from those in financial plight, by maiming or murdering those who oppose them, by bribing those sworn to destroy them. Organized crime is not merely a few preying on a few. In a very real sense, it is dedicated to subverting not only American institutions, but the very decency and integrity that are the most cherished attributes of a free society.[1]

The impact of organized crime on the United States is immeasurable, both in dollar costs and in human suffering. It is only in recent years that the nature and extent of organized crime has been publicized, and an alarmed public has become concerned about the menace it represents. Nevertheless, there are still some, both within and outside the area of law enforcement, who deny the existence of even a loosely defined structure of organized criminal activity. The evidence just does not bear this out.

The nebulous activities that make up organized crime, and mark it as different from our common concept of crime, make it difficult to define the term adequately. Donald Cressey, an expert on organized crime, notes that:

> There are at least two aspects of organized crime that characterize it as a unique form of criminal activity. The first is the element of corruption. The second is the element of enforcement, which is necessary for the maintenance of both internal discipline and the regularity of business transactions.[2]

Whether one uses the term Mafia, Cosa Nostra, Crime Confederation, or Syndicate, there should be a recognition that certain forms of criminal activity are organized and controlled by groups of individuals. These activities are multitudinous and vary from nickel-and-dime gambling to murder. It is unlikely that some aspect of an investigator's caseload is not related in some way to organized crime.

While a thorough discussion of organized crime is beyond the scope of this book, the investigator should be familiar with the more important aspects of organized criminal activity, and would be wise to supplement his knowledge by reading available literature.

THE STRUCTURE OF ORGANIZED CRIME

Although the focus of this chapter is on the more common definition of organized crime, it should be recognized that organized crime is not limited to one ethnic or racial group, nor should it be seen as operating over a wide geographic area. In many urban areas relatively lower-level organized criminal activities have developed, especially in the ghettos, where criminal activity may be controlled by local groups rather than by a national organization.

The Mafia, or Cosa Nostra, is no doubt the largest criminal organization in the United States, and operates in virtually all the larger cities. While each of these operations is somewhat autonomous, there is a national hierarchy with a set of established rules and guidelines. Failure to comply with the organization's policy can, and often has, resulted in gang wars and the death of criminal participants as well as innocent victims.

Cressey has illustrated the positions in a Cosa Nostra family organization, and points out that members of the organization infiltrate virtually all levels of society. The general organizational structure of organized criminal activity follows a similar pattern, whether it be the Cosa Nostra or an independent organization; only the titles are different.

Despite popular belief, members of organized crime do not belong to one ethnic group.

> Organized crime syndicates or groups are composed of people representing a wide variety of backgrounds. Taking into account outerfringe personnel who are associates, though not members, and including political organizations, unions, businesses, and other groups directly or indirectly under the thumb of organized crime, the manpower available to the organized underworld could conceivably number in the hundreds of thousands.[3]

COMBATTING ORGANIZED CRIME

Unless he is assigned to a unit directly involved in the investigation of organized crime, the average investigator may not be aware of its relationship to his function. For this reason it is important to have some understanding of organized criminal activity; the investigator should not hesitate to request or provide information when he encounters a case related to such activity. Frequently the bit of information supplied by a patrol officer or an investigator provides the link that may be needed by the special unit in charge of the case.

Organized criminal activity encompasses a wide range of crime, but certain crimes are more likely to be controlled or run by the syndicate. These include gambling, loan sharking, narcotics, prostitution, hijacking, fencing, racketeering, counterfeiting, and infiltration of legitimate businesses.

Gambling. Gambling activities, in the form of bookmaking, numbers and policy, account for the greatest organized crime revenues. These monies are frequently used to fund other illegal operations. Bookmaking involves taking bets on horse races or other sports events. Policy and numbers are a form of lottery in which the bettor chooses a number based on some regularly published number, such as the daily handle at a particular race track or the Treasury balance. There are numerous variations on a similar theme, and the investigator should familiarize himself with the common gambling forms in his district.

Loan Sharking or Shylocking. This activity is often financed from gambling revenues, and involves loaning money over a short period of time at exorbitant rates, ranging anywhere from five percent to as much as twenty percent a week, depending on the victim's need for the loan. It is not uncommon for a gambling debt to be turned over to a loan shark, wherein the victim finds himself at the mercy of organized crime. If he is a businessman he may find his business taken over by organized crime, and if he is unable to pay his debt the outcome may be a severe beating or even death.

Prostitution. Most of organized crime in prostitution appears to have declined considerably over the past decade, although there are still cities in which call girls are controlled by the syndicate. In such cases there are usually several "middle men" to protect the hierarchy of the organization.

Narcotics. Organized criminal activity in the narcotics area varies considerably. In recent years there has been a trend away from narcotics especially in urban centers, although there are still strong indications that organized crime is responsible for providing funds to purchase large quantities of narcotics abroad. Infiltration of legitimate businesses has also made it possible for organized crime to secure dangerous drugs from suppliers and manufacturers for illegal distribution.

Hijacking. Hijacking activities have become more popular in recent years, and frequently such activities are the result of organized crime. The need for an extensive network to dispose of goods is well suited to organized criminal activity, and the use of larger trucks and containers makes this a highly profitable operation.

Fencing. Frequently the goods obtained through hijacking and other thefts find their way into the organized criminal network, and it is not unusual to find property moved hundreds of miles before it is finally distributed, often through connections with syndicate-controlled stores. Cigarettes, meat, automobiles, and appliances are common items fenced by organized crime.

Racketeering. Organized crime has been involved in the internal operations of several labor unions throughout the country, and continues to be a major threat. The syndicate is also active in settling labor disputes through the use of force or fear.

Business Infiltration. The infiltration of legal businesses has become a prime goal of organized crime, with the result in mind of either recycling illegally obtained funds or running the businesses into bankruptcy for the profits involved. This approach, known as a "scam," involves placing orders for merchandise on credit, then selling it and not paying the bills, forcing the business into bankruptcy.

The investigator, in familiarizing himself with the operations of organized crime, is in a better position to recognize illegal activity. The following examples, cited from the *Police Guide on Organized Crime,* illustrate some of the activities which may lead to a recognition of organized criminal activity.

1. A candy store, grocery store, drug store, or other retail establishment seems to be doing a brisk business—many customers coming and going. But the customers do not remain in the store very long and do not leave with packages or other evidence that purchases were made. The store may have a meager selection of merchandise, which raises the question of how it can attract so many customers day after day. This could indicate the presence of a policy operation at the writer level or the place of business of a bookmaker's commissionman.

2. At about the same time each day, a package is delivered to a newsstand, bar, or other location. Later the package is picked up by another individual. The newsstand or whatever could be a policy drop—the place to which a policy writer sends his slips and/or day's receipts.

3. A number is chalked on a street lamp pole. The same number is observed in other locations. It might be the winning number for the day's policy play.

4. You are called to investigate a beating in a bar or at a location near a factory or other place of employment. The incident may occur on a payday or within a couple of days thereafter. The beating may have resulted from the impatience of a loan shark who has not been paid on schedule.

5. A parked car—often double parked—is observed daily at the same location and at the same time. The driver remains in the vehicle while a number of "friends" come up to say hello. Such a situation may indicate bet-taking activity.

6. A well-dressed individual is often seen driving an expensive model car in the area. No one seems to know what his occupation is. One patrolman pursued observations similar to this and found out that the individual was a policy operator—and had been for 21 years—without so much as an arrest. On the basis of this information and further investigation a special squad of detectives made a case against the operator and his employers.

7. A shopkeeper complains about poor business and notes that as a result he had to borrow money recently. A few comments by the patrolman about the high interest rates and the shopkeeper might disclose the imposition of an interest rate above the legal maximum. If so, the shopkeeper may have been dealing with a loan shark. If the shopkeeper advises that he cannot keep up with the payments, the officer might find an opportune time to ask for the identity of the shark. Depending on the desperation and temperament of the victim, the suggestion to cooperate may bring positive results.

8. After arriving at the scene of an assault, a patrolman learns that the victim is a union official. This information should be noted because if there have been other similar assaults in the city, the overall total, when analyzed by an organized crime intelligence unit, may strongly indicate an attempt by racketeers to gain control over a union local.

9. Merchants complain about another price rise by the cartage company that removes their garbage or trash. They also mention that there is either no competitor to deal with or if there is one, it will not accept their business. Not infrequently, this is an indication that an organized crime group is trying to monopolize the cartage business or limit competition through territorial agreements.

10. During a routine check of a restaurant, a patrolman recognizes several organized crime figures at a table, or many double-parked cars are spotted in front of a bar that is either known or suspected as a meeting place for racketeers. The patrolman should jot down the license plate numbers and phone in his observations immediately, so that investigators can be dispatched to the scene. Such signs indicate that underworld figures are meeting for one reason or another. However, they also may be indicia of hidden ownership of the bar or restaurant by organized crime. In some instances, bars can be closed down if they are frequented by criminals.

11. A new set of vendors begins to service a business—a restaurant, for example. The linen supplier is new, as are the meat provisioner, fuel oil company, and cartage firm. Perhaps new vending machines or jukeboxes are observed being installed. Some of these suppliers are recognized as enterprises run by organized crime. These are fairly solid indicators that organized crime figures have purchased, or have otherwise secured, a degree of control in the business being serviced.

12. A rash of vandalism strikes a number of establishments engaged in the same type of business, such as dry cleaning. Racketeers may be trying to coerce reluctant owners into joining an association or into doing business with mob-controlled vendors.

13. Appliances are seen being loaded into the storeroom of a sporting goods store. Scams or bankruptcy frauds frequently involve the ordering of goods (on credit, of course) unrelated to the customary line of the business.

14. Determining who the bettors are in your area can be as important as knowing who the bookmakers are—indeed, many times the identification of a bettor leads to the identification of a bookie. Patrolmen have identified bettors through conversations with those on their posts—sometimes even by observing who buys racing forms. In some instances, you may even get close enough to a bettor to observe the number dialed when

a bet is placed. Observations such as these could trigger an investigation leading to the prosecution of the upper echelon of organized crime's gambling hierarchy.

15. Just as identification of the bettor is important, so also is identification of addicts and loan shark customers. In two separate incidents, an arrested burglar revealed, under questioning by a patrolman, that he was stealing to finance his heroin purchases; while another arrested thief said he had to raise money to keep up with his loan shark payments. This information led to the arrest of a pusher in one case and the loan shark in the other.

16. Make a habit of checking out new businesses that set up shop in the area. If the enterprise is one that requires a license—such as a bar—ask to see it if for no other reason than to observe who the owners are, ascertain the identity of the company which distributes or services the jukeboxes, et cetera. If, for example, the distributor of the jukeboxes or vending machines is a company controlled by the organized underworld, so also might be the bar in which they are located.

17. You note pickets outside one or two stores in the same line of business. The picketing may be a perfectly legitimate tactic, or it may represent an attempt by organized crime to coerce employers into doing business with an underworld firm, to extort payments in return for labor peace, to convince employers to join an "association" and pay substantial dues, or to demonstrate the advisability of hiring a "labor consultant" who is able to resolve such troublesome activities as picketing.

18. A cheap hotel appears to be doing a reasonably brisk business. Its patrons travel light—many do not carry luggage. A bar has a reputation for being a clip joint; charges of watered-down liquor are frequent. These signs indicate a possible call-girl operation at the hotel and B-girl activity at the bar.

19. A truck is loaded at a location other than a depot or shipping dock. Goods are transferred from a truck of a well-known company to an unmarked truck or vehicle. A warehouse that is almost always empty is now full. Unusual activity at an unusual time occurs in a warehouse area. Merchandise is transferred from a truck to the garage of a residence. Any of these activities could point to a hijacking. License numbers, locations, times and other facts should be noted.

20. A group begins to congregate at a certain street location at certain times during each day. The group could be composed of addicts waiting for a pusher to make his rounds.

21. A business establishment suspected of being mob-controlled burns to the ground. One possibility is that arson was committed to collect the insurance.

22. Certain individuals always seem to frequent a certain bar although none of them live in the neighborhood. Perhaps they use the bar as a bet-taking center.

23. A club shuts down at irregular times—sometimes early in the afternoon, other times at mid-evening. Do these times coincide with the completion of racing or when the results of other sporting events become available? If so, the club may be a base for gambling operations.

24. A known racketeer frequently meets with certain unidentified individuals. If possible, note the license plate numbers of the vehicles of these individuals as well as the time and location of the conversations. Racketeers, like most everyone else, are victims of habit and associate with each other.

25. Many cars pull up and park in front of the suburban home of a suspected racketeer, who is ostensibly throwing a party for friends. Jot down license plate numbers and call in the information promptly. The party may be bona fide or the real purpose of the gathering may be to conduct underworld business, as was the case at the famed Apalachin meeting, where an alert officer noted unusual activity at a country estate and blew the whistle on what turned out to be a nationwide assembly of high-ranking members of the organized underworld. Knowledge of who associates with whom is highly important —whether the occasion is a bona fide social activity or otherwise.

SUMMARY

The subject of organized crime is one that should be uppermost in every investigator's mind, for such activities strike at the fabric of our society. The investigator's role places him in a unique position with respect to organized crime, and he should not hesitate to collect and report information that may be of value. Furthermore, he should be familiar with local syndicate figures, their hangouts, and their activities. The very nature of this activity breeds further crime and corruption, which can only be eliminated through recognition and action.

NOTES

1. The President's Commission on Law Enforcement and Administration of Justice, *Task Force Report on Organized Crime.* Washington, D.C.: Government Printing Office, 1967.

2. Donald Cressey, *Theft of the Nation.* New York: Harper and Row, 1969, p. 319.

3. *Police Guide on Organized Crime.* Washington, D.C.: Law Enforcement Assistance Administration, p. 6.

SUGGESTED READINGS

Cressey, Donald R., *Theft of the Nation.* New York: Harper and Row, 1969.

Godfrey, Drexel, and Don R. Harris, *Basic Elements of Intelligence: A Manual of Theory, Structure and Procedures for Use by Law Enforcement Agencies Against Organized Crime.* Washington, D.C.: Government Printing Office, 1971.

Salerno, Ralph, and John S. Tompkins, *The Crime Confederation.* New York: Popular Library, 1969.

CHAPTER 16

relations with other agencies and organizations

Frequently the success of an investigation depends on information in the possession of another agency or organization. In an earlier chapter the subject of information sources was discussed, and the reader should have some general familiarization with the various types of information each agency might provide. However, it should be noted that for several reasons an agency may be reluctant or unwilling to cooperate. Some of these reasons include jealousy, professional rivalry, bureaucratic red tape, and poor interagency relations.

In some measure the relationship between agencies is one that must be cultivated and solidified through the administration. Nevertheless, the investigator should be aware that his actions are likely to be extremely important, in terms of both maintaining good cooperation and developing specific information. It is not unusual to find within an investigative operation those persons who have good contacts with other agencies and those who cannot seem to develop any outside contacts. Obviously, personality is an important factor, and the investigator who continuously brags about his own agency and derogates others is likely to find cooperation poor. On the other hand, an investigator who does not hesitate to say thank you and give credit where it is due is likely to be more successful.

Although one would think that interagency cooperation is a matter of common sense, there are too many instances in which poor relations do exist. The following is a brief description of some of these problems and some of the ways in which an investigator might cope with them. Perhaps the key word in all situations is "enthusiasm." If the investigator can elicit a feeling of commonality and a shared problem, he has gone a long way toward knocking down the walls of suspicion and hostility that are likely to exist.

JEALOUSY

Frequently there exists between agencies or organizations a sense of jealousy with regard to the mission of each. This exists at both the federal and local levels, and one cannot assume that because the ultimate goals are the same, people will work together. At the local level there is sometimes a feeling of inferiority when dealing with a federal agency, and this can result in strained relationships, especially if one of the agencies appears to take on a superior attitude.

In attempting to cope with the problem of jealousy, an investigator should not take on a superior attitude and should always be willing to cooperate in return. All too often the information process becomes a one-way street, and it is not long before the channels begin to close up. Obviously, it is important to develop a rapport with the personnel of other agencies, and showing an interest in their operation frequently helps to reduce conflict. Knowing the names of individuals within the agency is also important, and the investigator would do well to keep a record of those persons with whom he comes in contact.

PROFESSIONAL RIVALRY

Closely related to jealousy is professional rivalry; only in this instance there is frequently an explicit hostility. Unfortunately, such rivalry is frequently cultivated by the head of an agency in his public or private statements. Overcoming such a problem is often difficult for the individual investigator; it is something that can rarely be alleviated on a personal level, for it operates as an integral part of the organization.

Professional rivalry, as opposed to jealousy, is an attitude of which most people in the organizations are aware, and in some instances there may be unwritten rules concerning cooperation. In such cases an investigator must develop his own contacts within the agency, and should recognize that there may be times when he has to protect his source. He should also recognize the need for displaying a willingness to cooperate, and be willing to assist in return.

If, for one reason or another, there is a strained relationship between agencies, the investigator should maintain communication and make it a point to meet on a regular basis with his contact. This is especially true if there is some common purpose or need to share information. Frequently more information can be gained through a meeting over coffee than can be developed through interdepartmental correspondence.

BUREAUCRATIC RED TAPE

Perhaps the most annoying aspect of an investigation is the abundance of bureaucratic red tape. A request for information can result in a long list of memorandums or endless telephone calls, with the investigator winding up with little relevant information. While it may be impossible to eliminate all the problems of bureaucracy, it is not impossible to learn the techniques of coping with them. Once again, the most effective resource is personal contact, knowing someone within the agency. A personal telephone call or visit is usually much more effective than an impersonal letter, even when the investigator does not know anyone in the agency.

It is more difficult to say no to a person's face than it is in a letter or on the telephone. If a personal visit is impossible or infeasible, a telephone call will often set the stage for assistance. A follow-up letter of appreciation can also be valuable, and helps maintain continuity for further requests.

Some knowledge of the organizational structure of other agencies can also be invaluable, and when an investigator has frequent dealings with a particular department he should familiarize himself with its structure and personnel. One should not assume that the telephone operator or a secretary is familiar with all the operations of a particular agency, and an attempt should be made to contact the unit that has specific responsibility for the area with which you are concerned. Most large agencies are subdivided in numerous ways, with varying levels of responsibility, some of which overlap and some of which do not.

POOR INTERAGENCY RELATIONS

In some cases it may be necessary to communicate with an agency or organization that is not a common source of information for the police department, and that may not have a policy for providing information or assistance to law enforcement. Such agencies may include schools, newspapers, the Social Security Administration, credit bureaus, public service agencies, and the like. While some agencies may have strict rules concerning providing particular kinds of information, most are willing to cooperate if the right contact is made. Keep in mind that it is much easier for a clerk to refuse, than to give, assistance. Contact should be made initially with someone at the middle management level who has the authority to make decisions. Obviously, if it is against the law for an agency to divulge information, as is the general rule with the Social Security Administration, the investigator should not press for it. In those areas where policy is not defined it may be important for the investigator to ensure the confidentiality of the source, or to provide legitimate reasons for the request.

SUMMARY

One need not proceed very far into the world of criminal investigation before a recognition of the importance of cooperation between agencies and organizations is realized. Despite this, too few investigators are aware of the efforts necessary to cement good relationships, and perhaps even fewer make any strong effort to create strong interagency ties. Like so much of the material in this text, this chapter serves only to offer a glimpse at the problem and some of the minimal points that should be pursued if good cooperation and communication are to be initiated. However, the investigator who pursues this subject and develops a thorough understanding of bureaucracy and organizational style is more likely to be successful than the individual who chooses to operate in the vacuum of his own system.

On another level, the investigator who recognizes the need for cooperation and who can identify those agencies and organizations that can provide assistance, opens a whole new source of information, one that is not fully recognized by most of his contemporaries. The need for information in criminal investigation is paramount, and it is not usually something to be developed without hard work and effort.

One may reasonably ask about the time involved in developing good interagency contacts, and it is a reasonable concern. It is not something that can be answered easily, but it can be worked out through knowledge and experience. Obviously, if an investigator uses a source infrequently or only once, he will not put as much time into maintaining contacts as he would in an agency that is used frequently. Keep in mind also that contacts need not be every week, nor every month in some cases, but an occasional telephone call or the volunteering of information that may not have been asked for often goes a long way toward maintaining harmony. No one likes to feel they are being used, yet this is probably the most common mistake made by investigators. They only call when they want information.

Understanding the particular agency or organization you are dealing with is also extremely important. It might be said that every bureaucracy has an organizational philosophy; understanding its philosophy helps in formulating and asking the right kinds of questions. One finds, for example, that the philosophy of a school administrator is likely to be different from that of a law enforcement official. The manner in which each is approached for information will often have a bearing on the outcome. One could argue for ages why such discrepancies exist; the fact is that they do, and it is something the investigator should recognize. Despite differences in opinion, ideology, and philosophy, it is possible to secure cooperation between agencies, and the investigator should keep this in mind at all times.

SUGGESTED READINGS

Ahern, James F., *Police in Trouble: Our Frightening Crisis in Law Enforcement.* New York: Hawthorn Books, 1972.

Parker, Brian, and Vonnie Gurgin, *The Role of Criminalistics in the World of the Future.* Stanford, Calif.: Stanford Research Institute, July, 1972.

CHAPTER 17

the role of the criminal investigator in contemporary society

The focus of this book has been on the techniques and fundamentals of criminal investigation. By now the reader has some rudimentary knowledge of those factors that will aid him in conducting an investigation. However, this is only a beginning, for the serious practitioner has a long way to go if he is to become a professional investigator. One need not look very far into the future to see tremendous changes on the horizon in the field of criminal investigation. Furthermore, one cannot expect to be an expert by reading one book, just as experience is not the result of one case.

Criminal investigation, like so many other aspects of the criminal justice field, is entering a new era, one in which new breakthroughs are occurring every day. The concept of single digit classification and search is now being applied in several police departments; the use of computers as an investigative aid has only begun to be accepted, and will continue to grow over the next decade; techniques of interviewing and interrogation are being studied and refined in light of recent Supreme Court decisions; application of the behavioral sciences is rapidly becoming an important tool for the investigator; and we have only begun to witness the birth of a technological revolution that will no doubt have a tremendous impact on the field.

Despite all the breakthroughs and advances, the investigative function still depends largely on the capabilities of the individual assigned to a case. Ultimately, the decision to arrest lies with an investigator, and the necessity for making the right decisions has never been greater, for as our society becomes more complex the possibility of error increases. Thus, it becomes paramount that the criminal investigator be a true professional, versed in the art and science of his calling. Society can ill afford to depend on the unskilled and untrained investigator of the past, for too much is at stake.

Obviously, selection and training of investigators must be given close scrutiny, but beyond this must come the recognition that a good arrest record and forty hours of training does not make a good investigator. The professional investigator must keep abreast of the literature in his field; he must be familiar with recent court decisions, and be well grounded in the area of criminal law; he must understand and be able to use the technology available to him; and his dedication to the pursuit of justice must be unquestioned.

In reviewing the previous chapters one comes to realize the importance of information in criminal investigation. Virtually all that has been discussed involves the means used to develop information and to utilize it in making decisions. The reader has been encouraged to go beyond the bounds of this book and pursue the suggested readings, but this is only a beginning, for he must keep abreast of the happenings of our time. He must learn to question his ideas and opinions, and he must be willing to admit that he can make mistakes, for they are inevitable. Today we are faced with an information explosion that makes it impossible to be aware of, much less synthesize, all that is relevant. In some measure this can be overcome through the development of a higher order of reasoning, and by conditioning oneself to the environment. One cannot possibly retain all that is important, nor can he possibly analyze all data at once. He can, however, learn to use the tools that are available to him, and he can develop an expertise in information collection, storage, and processing. This may be as simple as a card index or as complex as computer application. The key is in knowing how to do it.

A major portion of this book has been devoted to the crime scene and physical evidence. Here again, the investigator's approach is crucial. Earlier we discussed the internal and external aspects of criminal investigation. Knowing when to call for assistance can frequently be the difference between success and failure. If the investigator does not know what the crime laboratory can do for him he is more likely to overlook a crucial point. If he is not aware of how photographs and sketches will aid him, he cannot possibly use them to their fullest potential.

The importance of interviewing and interrogation cannot be overstated, for not only is most of an investigator's time expended here, but it is in such activity that the average case is often solved or lost. An understanding of human psychology and an ability to handle a wide range of personality types are paramount. Too frequently cases are lost because the investigator failed to ask the right question, or engendered hostility in the subject. And all too often a case is lost because the investigator failed to follow up a clue or was too apathetic in his approach to the case. Good interviewing techniques are the result of experience and knowledge; they are not something with which one is born. Unfortunately, too little consideration is given to this aspect of the investigative function, at least from a scientific viewpoint.

From society's standpoint, criminal investigation is fraught with misconception and myth. The investigator is frequently looked on as a super sleuth whose ability to solve a crime is virtually without question. The average investigator knows that most crimes go unsolved, and this frequently leads to cynicism and dismay, which in turn results in even fewer crimes being solved. Nevertheless, if one recognizes the problems and drawbacks of criminal investigation, it becomes possible to deal with them. The investigator must realize that much of the glamor is lost in the everyday work, and most of his cases will not be as exciting or interesting as he might have imagined, but he should also recognize that each case is a challenge, and that through proper preparation, dedication, and effort, he is likely to have more success than his unenthusiastic counterpart.

bibliography

bibliography

Adams, Thomas F., *Police Patrol: Tactics and Techniques.* Englewood Cliffs, N.J.: Prentice-Hall, 1971.

Ahern, James F., *Police in Trouble: Our Frightening Crisis in Law Enforcement.* New York: Hawthorn Books, 1972.

Allen, A. L., *Personal Descriptions.* London: Butterworth, 1950.

Allison, Harrison C., *Personal Identification.* Boston, Mass.: Holbrook Press, 1973.

Armitage, Gilbert, *The History of the Bow Street Runners.* London, 1932.

Arons, Harry, *Hypnosis in Criminal Investigation.* Springfield, Ill.: Charles C. Thomas, 1967.

Beveridge, W. I. B., *The Art of Scientific Investigation.* New York: Random House, 1957.

Bonner, John W., *Homicide Analysis.* N.Y.C.P.D., Office of Programs and Policies, Crime Analysis Division, New York, 1972.

Brussel, James A., *Casebook of a Crime Psychiatrist.* New York: Bernard Beis, 1968.

Byrnes, Thomas, *1886 Professional Criminals of America.* New York: Chelsea House Publishers, 1969.

Camps, Francis E., *Medical and Scientific Investigations in the Christie Case.* London: London Medical Publications, 1953.

Ceccaldi, Pierre-Ferdinand, *La Criminalistique,* 1st ed. Paris: Presses Universitaires de France, 1962.

The Change Process in Criminal Justice. Criminal Justice Monograph, U.S. Department of Justice. LEAA/NILE & CJ, 1973.

Clark and Marshall: A Treatise on the Law of Crimes, 7th ed. Chicago: Callaghan and Co., 1967.

Coffey, Allan, Edward Eldefonso, and Walter Hartinger, *Human Relations: Law Enforcement in a Changing Community.* Englewood Cliffs, N.J.: Prentice-Hall, 1971.

Conklin, John E., *Robbery and the Criminal Justice System.* New York: J. B. Lippincott, 1972.

Cordella, Robert, *The Detective Division: New York City Police Department.* Unpublished Master's thesis. Bernard M. Baruch School of Public Administration, the City College, City University of New York, June, 1960.

Cressey, Donald R., *Theft of the Nation.* New York: Harper and Row, 1969.

Criminal Investigation and Physical Evidence Handbook. State of Wisconsin Department of Justice, Crime Laboratory Division, 1968.

Davis, John E., *Tool Marks, Firearms, and the Striagraph.* Springfield, Ill.: Charles C. Thomas, 1958.

Dewey, John, *How We Think.* Boston, Mass.: D.C. Heath, 1933.

Dieckman, Edward A., *Practical Homicide Investigation.* Springfield, Ill.: Charles C. Thomas, 1961.

Duncan, J. H., *An Introduction to Fingerprints.* London: Butterworth, 1942.

Edwards, Ward, and Amos Tversky, *Decision Making.* Baltimore: Penguin Books, 1967.

Eiseman, James S., *Elements of Investigative Techniques.* Bloomington, Ill.: McKnight and McKnight, 1949.

Eisenberg, Terry, Deborah Ann Kent, and Charles R. Wall, *Police Personnel Practices in State and Local Governments.* Washington, D.C.: International Association of Chiefs of Police and the Police Foundation, 1973.

Eldefonso, Edward, Alan R. Doffey, and James Sullivan. *Police and the Criminal Law.* Pacific Palisades, Calif.: Goodyear, 1972.

Ellis, Havelock, *The Criminal.* New York: AMS Press, 1973.

Else, Walter Martyn, *The Detection of Crime.* London Publishers at the office of the Police Journal, 1934.

Felkenes, George T., *The Criminal Justice System: Its Functions and Personnel.* Englewood Cliffs, N.J.: Prentice-Hall, 1973.

Ferguson, Robert J., Jr., *The Scientific Informer.* Springfield, Ill.: Charles C. Thomas, 1971.

Fisher, Jacob, *The Art of Detection.* New York: Carlton Press, 1963.

Fisher, Jacob, *Faces of Deceit.* New York: Carlton Press, 1963.

Flinn, John J., *History of the Chicago Police.* Chicago: Police Book Fund, 1887.

Forrest, A. J., *Interpol.* London: A. Wingate Publishers, 1955.

Frankel, Harold A., *Homicide Investigator.* Philadelphia: Gainor Press, 1931.

Frecon, André, *Des Empreintes en Général et de leur application dans la pratique de la médecine judiciaire.* Paris: Lyon A. Storck, 1889.

Fricke, Charles William, *Criminal Investigation.* Los Angeles: O. W. Smith, 1933.

Gaynet, Jean, *Manuel de Police Scientifique.* Paris: Payet, 1961.

George, B. James, Jr., *Constitutional Limitations on Evidence in Criminal Cases.* New York: Practicing Law Institute, 1969.

Gerber, Samuel R., *Criminal Investigation and Interrogation.* Cincinnati, Ohio: W. H. Anderson, 1962.

Goddefroy, E., *Manuel de Police Technique.* Brussells: Ferdinand Larcier, 1931.

Goddefroy, E., *Manuel Elémentaire de Police Technique.* Brussels: Ferdinand Larcier, 1922.

Greenwood, Peter W., *An Analysis of the Apprehension Activities of the New York City Police Department.* New York City Rand Institute, 1970.

Gross, Hans, *Criminal Psychology.* Montclair, N.J.: Patterson Smith (reprint), 1968.

Gross, Hans, and Adolf Gustav, *Criminal Investigation.* London: Sweet and Maxwell, 1924.

Hale, Charles D., *Police Community Relations.* Albany, N.Y.: Delmar Publishers, 1974.

Hammond, W. H., and Edna Chayen, *Persistent Criminals.* London: Her Majesty's Stationery Office, 1963.

Harris, Raymond I., *Outline of Death Investigation.* Springfield, Ill.: Charles C. Thomas, 1962.

Heffron, Floyd Nicholas, *Evidence for the Patrolman.* Springfield, Ill.: Charles C. Thomas, 1958.

Hoover, John E., *Criminal Investigation and the Function of the Identification Division.* Washington, D.C.: U.S. Federal Bureau of Investigation, 1937.

Horan, James D., *The Pinkertons: Detective Dynasty That Made History.* New York: Crown Publishers, 1967.

Houts, Marshall, *From Evidence to Proof.* Springfield, Ill.: Charles C. Thomas, 1956.

Hunt, Morton, *The Mugging.* New York: Anteneum, 1972.

Hutnick, Melroy B., *Criminal Law and Court Procedures.* Albany, N.Y.: Delmar Publishers, 1974.

Inbau, Fred E., Andre A. Moenssens, and Louis R. Vitullo, *Lie Detection and Criminal Interrogation.* Baltimore: Williams and Wilkins, 1948.

Inbau, Fred E., Andre A. Moenssens, and Louis R. Vitullo, *Scientific Police Investigation.* New York: Chilton, 1972.

Innovation in Law Enforcement. Criminal Justice Monograph, U.S. Department of Justice. LEAA/NILE & CJ, 1973.

International Association of Chiefs of Police, *Criminal Investigation.* Library of Congress, 1968.

Irwin, John, *The Felon.* Englewood Cliffs, N.J.: Prentice-Hall, 1970.

Jenkins, Herbert, *Keeping the Peace: A Police Chief Looks at His Job.* New York: Harper and Row, 1970.

Kerper, Hazel P., *Introduction to the Criminal Justice System.* St. Paul, Minn.: West Publishing Co., 1972.

Kessler, William Frederic, *The Detection of Murder.* New York: Arco Publishing Co., 1953.

Kirk, Paul Leland, *Crime Investigation.* New York: Interscience Publishers, 1953.

Klein, Irving, *Law of Evidence for Police.* St. Paul, Minn.: West Publishing Co., 1973.

Klotter, John C., and Jacqueline R. Kanovitz, *Constitutional Law for Police.* Cincinnati, Ohio: W. H. Anderson, 1968.

LaFave, Wayne R., *Arrest: The Decision to Take a Suspect into Custody.* Boston, Mass.: Little, Brown and Co., 1965.

Lane, Roger, *Policing the City: Boston 1822–1885.* Cambridge, Mass.: Harvard University Press, 1967.

Langford, Nathaniel Pitt, *Vigilante Days and Ways.* New York: AMS Press, 1973.

Legislation and Special Projects Section Criminal Division, Department of Justice, *Handbook on the Law of Search and Seizure.* U.S. Government Printing Office, January, 1968.

Leonard, V. A., *Criminal Investigation and Identification.* Springfield, Ill.: Charles C. Thomas, 1971.

Leonard, V.A., ed., *Lie Detection.* Springfield, Ill.: Charles C. Thomas, 1957.

Leonard, V. A., *Police of the Twentieth Century.* Brooklyn: The Foundation Press, Inc., 1964.

Lichem, Arnold, *Die Kriminalpolizei.* Graz, Leykan, 1935.

Liebers, Arthur, and Carl Vollmer, *The Investigator's Handbook.* New York: Arco Publishing Co., 1962.

Loth, David Goldsmith, *Crime Lab: Science Turns Detective.* New York: J. Messner, 1964.

Lundquist, Frank, and A. S. Curry, eds., *Methods of Forensic Science.* New York: Interscience Publishers, 1962–1965.

McCormick, Mona, *Who-What-When-Where-How-Why-Made Easy.* New York: The New York Times Co., 1971.

McCreedy, Kenneth R., *Theory and Methods of Police Patrol.* Albany, N.Y.: Delmar Publishers, 1974.

McKinney, William, *Police Edition: Criminal Procedure Law.* St. Paul, Minn.: West Publishing Co., 1970.

Merkeley, Donald K., *The Investigation of Death.* Springfield, Ill.: Charles C. Thomas, 1957.

Misner, Gordon E., and William F. McDonald, *Reduction of Robberies and Assaults of Bus Drivers: Volume II: The Scope of the Crime Problem and its Resolution.* U.S. Department of Transportation Demonstration Project, 1970.

Mitchell, Charles Ainsworth, *The Expert Witness and the Application of Science and Art to Human Identification, Criminal Investigation Civil Actions and History.* Cambridge, England: W. Heffer and Sons, Ltd., 1923.

Mitchell, Charles Ainsworth, *Science and the Criminal.* London: Sir I. Pitman and Sons, Ltd., 1911.

Moenssens, Andre A., *Fingerprint Techniques.* Philadelphia: Chilton, 1971.

Morland, Nigel, *The Conquest of Crime.* London: Cassell, 1937.

Morland, Nigel, ed., *Crime and Detection.* Oxford, England: Tallis Press, 1966.

Nelson, John G., *Preliminary Investigation and Police Reporting: A Complete Guide to Police Written Communication.* Beverly Hills, Calif.: Glencoe Press, 1970.

Nickolls, Lewis C., *The Scientific Investigation of Crime.* London: Butterworth, 1956.

Nimmer, Raymond T., *Diversion the Search for Alternative Forms of Prosecution.* Chicago: American Bar Foundation, 1974.

O'Brien, Kevin P., and Robert C. Sullivan, *Criminalistics: Theory and Practice.* Boston, Mass.: Holbrook Press, 1972.

O'Hara, Charles E., *Fundamentals of Criminal Investigation.* Springfield, Ill.: Charles C. Thomas, 1956.

O'Hara, Charles E., *An Introduction to Criminalistics: The Application of the Physical Sciences to the Detection Of Crime.* New York: MacMillan, 1949.

Osterburg, James W., *The Crime Laboratory: Case Studies of Scientific Investigation.* Bloomington, Ind.: Indiana University Press, 1968.

Parker, Brian, and Joseph Peterson, *Physical Evidence Utilization in the Administration of Criminal Justice.* National Institute of Law Enforcement and Criminal Justice, March, 1970.

Parker, Brian, Joseph Peterson, and Vonnie Gurgin, *The Role of Criminalistics in the World of the Future.* Menlo Park, Calif.: Stanford Research Institute, July, 1972.

Pinkerton, Allan, *Professional Thieves and the Detective.* New York: AMS Press, 1973.

Police Guide on Organized Crime. Washington, D.C.: Government Printing Office, Law Enforcement Assistance Administration, 1972.

President's Commission on Law Enforcement and Administration of Justice, *The Challenge of Crime in a Free Society.* Washington, D.C.: Government Printing Office, 1967.

Prevention of Violence in Correction Institutions. Criminal Justice Monograph, U.S. Department of Justice. LEAA/NILE & CJ, 1973.

Prince, Jerome, *Cases and Materials on Evidence.* Mineola, N.Y.: Foundation Press, 1963.

Radin, Edward D., *12 Against Crime.* New York: Putnam, 1950.

Reik, Theodor, *The Compulsion to Confess: On the Psychoanalysis of Crime and Punishment.* New York: Farrar, Straus and Cudahy, 1959.

Reik, Theodor, *The Unknown Murderer.* New York: International Universities Press, 1945.

Report of the National Advisory Commission on Civil Disorders. New York: Bantam Books, 1968.

Rhodes, Henry Taylor Fowkes, *Clues and Crime: The Science of Criminal Investigation.* London: J. Murrary, 1936.

Ribeiro, Leonidio, *Policia Scientifica.* Rio de Janeiro: Editora Guanabara, 1934.

Richardson, James R., *The New York Police: Colonial Times to 1901.* New York: Oxford University Press, 1970.

Richardson, James R., *Scientific Evidence for Police Officers.* Cincinnati, Ohio: W. H. Anderson, 1963.

Riis, Jacob, *The Making of an American.* New York: Macmillan, 1901.

Rizer, Conrad, *Police Mathematics: A Textbook in Applied Mathematics for Police.* Springfield, Ill.: Charles C. Thomas, 1955.

Salerno, Ralph, and John S. Tompkins, *The Crime Confederation.* New York: Popular Library, 1969.

Sansone, Sam J., *Modern Photography for Police and Firemen.* Cincinnati, Ohio: W. H. Anderson Co., 1971.

Saudek, Robert, *Anonymous Letters. A Study in Crime and Handwriting.* London: Methuen and Co. Ltd., 1933.

Schneickert, Hans, *Kriminaltaktik und Kriminaltechnik.* Lubek: Deutscher PolizieVerlag, 1933.

Schultz, Donald O., and Loran A. Norton, *Police Operational Intelligence.* Springfield, Ill.: Charles C. Thomas, 1968.

Schur, Edwin M., *Our Criminal Society.* Englewood Cliffs, N.J.: Prentice-Hall, 1969.

Snyder, LeMoyne, *Homicide Investigation: Practical Information for Coroners, Police Officers and other Investigators.* Springfield, Ill.: Charles C. Thomas, 1944.

Soderman, Harry, *Modern Criminal Investigation.* New York: Funk and Wagnalls, 1962.

Susman, Jackwell, ed., *Drug Use and Social Policy.* New York: AMS Press, 1972.

Svensson, Arne, *Crime Detection: Modern Methods of Criminal Investigation.* New York: Elsevier, 1955.

Svensson, Arne, and Otto Wendel, *Techniques of Crime Scene Investigation.* New York: American Elsevier, 1965.

Thorwald, Jurgen, *The Century of the Detective.* New York: Harcourt, Brace and World, 1965.

Thorwald, Jurgen, *Crime and Science: The New Frontier in Criminology.* New York: Harcourt, Brace and World, 1967.

Thorwald, Jurgen, *Proof of Poison.* London: Thames and Hudson, 1966.

Tobias, J. J., *Against the Peace.* London: Ginn and Co., Ltd., 1970.

Turner, William W., *Invisible Witness: The Use and Abuse of the New Technology of Crime Investigation.* Indianapolis: Bobbs-Merrill, 1968.

Turrou, Leon G., *Where My Shadow Falls: Two Decades of Crime Detection.* Garden City, N.Y.: Doubleday, 1949.

Ullyett, Kenneth, *Crime Out of Hand.* London: M. Joseph, 1963.

Walls, Henry James, *Forensic Science: An Introduction to the Science of Crime Detection.* New York: Praeger, 1968.

Weston, Paul B., and Kenneth M. Wells, *Criminal Evidence for Police.* Englewood Cliffs, N.J.: Prentice-Hall, 1971.

Whisenand, Paul M., and Tug T. Tamaru, *Automated Police Information Systems.* New York: John Wiley and Sons, 1970.

Willmer, M.A.P., *Crime and Information Theory.* Edinburgh: University Press, 1970.

index

index

Admissions, 190–191
Alcohol, 76–77
Anthropometry, 8-9
Assault, 151–152
Auto theft, 177–178

Ballistics, forensic, 11
Bertillon, Alphonse, 8-9
Bertillon method, 8-9
Beveridge, W.I.B., 130, 132, 134, 136
Blood, 63–74
Boone, Allan, 5
Bow Street Runners, 4
Bureau of Investigation, 8, 10–11
Burglary, 179–187
  apartments, 181
  business offices, 181
  factories, 181
  hotels or motels, 181
  pattern analysis, 183–184
  physical evidence, 184–186
  private homes, 180
  property identification and recovery, 183
  retail stores, 181
  safes, 186–187
  typology, 180–183
  vacation homes, 181
  witness information, 184

Burns, William J., 8
Burns Detective Agency, 8
Business infiltration, by organized crime, 238–241
Business larceny, 167–168
Byrnes, Thomas, 6–7

Casts, 61-63
Chemical analysis, 63–77
  alcohol, 76–77
  blood, 63–74
  fibers, 75–76
  narcotics, 76–77
  paint, 76
  poisons, 76–77
  semen, 75
  stains, 75
  trace evidence, 76
Child molestation, 162
Commerical larceny, 167–168
Confessions, 190–191
Confidence games, 174–176
Confidential informant, 116–118
Corpus delecti, 17, 25
Counterfeiting, 170–174
Credit card and check thieves, 169–170
Cressey, Donald, 235, 236
Crime report, 28–32
Crime scene, 20, 32–39

Crime scene photography, 43-51
Crime scene search, 38-39
  grid, 34-35
  link, 37
  spiral, 36
  strip, 35
  wheel, 37
  zone, 35-36
Crime scene sketching, 51-55
Criminal law and the investigator, 189-199

Documents, 77-79

Electronic surveillance, 194-195
Embezzlement, 178-179

Faulds, Henry, 9
Faurot, Joseph A., 10
Federal Communications Act, 196
Fencing, 237
Fielding, Henry, 4
Fingerprints, 9-10, 79-86, 184-186
  dusting for, 79-82
  latent, lifting of, 82-84
  photographing, 82
  special techniques, 82
  use of, 85-86
Firearms, 87-92
  cartridges and shells, 89-90
  investigation of, 90-92
  types of, 87-88
Fisher, John, 11
Flinn, John, 5
Forensic medicine, 11
Forgery, 170-174

Galton, Francis, 9
Gambling, 237
Goddard, Calvin, 12
Goldstein v. *United States*, 196
Gravelle, Philip, 11-12
Gross, Hans, 4

Hijacking, 237
Hoffa v. *United States*, 197
Homicide, criminal, 146-153
  establishing a case, 147-148
  murder during commission of a crime, 150-151
  murder as result of physical assault, 151-152
  and physical evidence, 146-147
  premeditated murder, 148-150
Hoover, J. Edgar, 8, 10-11

Identification of suspects, 198-199
Informants, 115-121, 160, 197
  confidential informant, 116-118
  involuntary informant, 120
  management of confidential, 118-119
  "one-time," 119-120
  verification of statements by, 120-121
Information, 19-20, 121-126
  government sources, 122-123
  private sources, 123-124
  public sources, 124-125
  utilization of, 125-126
Information analysis, 129-138
  chance, 130-131
  imagination, 131-133
  intuition, 133-134
  observation, 136-137
  reason, 134-136
  strategy, 137-138
Inner-city investigation, 229-233
Instrumentation, 92-93
Interagency relations, 243-246
Interrogation, 18-19, 108-113
  clientele, 110-111
  language, 111
  method, 111-113
  setting, 109-110
  situation, 109
Interviewing, 18-19, 100-108
  clientele, 103-106

language, 107
method, 107-108
setting, 102-103
situation, 100-102
Involuntary informant, 120

Kanovitz, Jacqueline R., 194
Kerper, Hazel, 165
Klotter, John C., 194

Larceny, 165-179
auto theft, 177-178
commercial and business, 167-168
confidence games, 174-176
embezzlement, 178-179
pickpockets, 176
Lee v. *United States*, 192
Lineups, 198-199
Loan sharking, 237

Mapp v. *Ohio*, 191
Metropolitan Police Act, 4
Microscopes, 92
Minorities and investigation, 231-232
Miranda v. *Arizona*, 19, 95, 109, 190-191
Murder, 146-153
during commission of a crime, 150-151
premeditated, 148-150
as result of physical assault, 151-152

Narcotics, 215-227, 237
National Auto Theft Bureau, 124, 177-178
New York City Police Department Robbery Manual, 153-158

"One-time informant," 119-120
Organized crime, 235-241
business infiltration, 238-241
fencing, 237
gambling, 237
hijacking, 237
loan sharking or shylocking, 237
narcotics, 237
prostitution, 237
racketeering, 238
structure of, 236

Pattern analysis, 183-184
"Peoria Kid," 6
Photography of crime scene, 43-51
fingerprints, 82
measurements and markings, 49-50
objects, 49
persons, 47
places, 48
special problems, 50-51
videotape and motion pictures, 51
Physical evidence, collection of, 33, 58-95, 146-147
at burglary scene, 184-186
casts, 61-63
chemical, 63-77
documents, 77-79
fingerprints, 79-86
firearms, 87-92
instrumentation, 92-93
photographic, 93
physical matches, 93-94
tool mark comparison, 93
weapons, 92
Physical matches, 93-94
Physical search, 34
"Piano Charley," 6
Pickpockets, 176
Pinkerton, Allan, 5
Poisons, 76-77
Police Guide on Organized Crime, 238-241
Polygraph, 93
President's Task Force on Organized Crime, 235

Professional rivalry, 244
Property identification and recovery, 183
Prostitution, 237

Racketeering, 238
Rape, 160–161
Records, *see* Reports
Relations with other agencies, 243–246
  bureaucratic red tape, 244–245
  jealousy, 243–244
  professional rivalry, 244
Report of the National Advisory Commission on Civil Disorders, 230
Reports, 21–22
  crime reports, 28
  function of records, 26–28
  initial complaint, 28–29
  maintenance of the case, 29–32
  supplementary investigative reports, 29, 31
Richardson, James, 6
Robbery, 153–160
  armored cars, 154
  bank messengers, 153–154
  banks, 154
  chain stores, 156
  clubs, 157
  delivery trucks, 157
  drugstores, 157
  gambling games, 157
  gasoline stations, 156–157
  jewelry stores, 155
  payrolls, 154–155
  physicians and dentists, 158
  private cars, 158
  private homes, 157
  rapid transit lines, 157–158
  restaurants and luncheonettes, 156
  salesmen, 155
  taxicabs, 157
  theaters, 156
  warehouses, 158
Robbery investigation, 158–160
"Roundsmen," 5

Schur, Edwin, 136
Schwartz v. *Texas*, 196
Scientific evidence, utilization of, 20–21
Scotland Yard, 4–5
Search warrants, 193–195
  execution of, 194–195
Searches, 191–193
Secret Service, 170
Seizures, 191–193
Sex crimes, 160–162
Sexual deviation, 161
Shylocking, 237
Simmons v. *United States*, 199
Sketches of crime scene, 51–55
  measured field sketch, 52–53
  scaled sketch, 54
  special techniques, 54
  use of, 54–55
Spectrograph, 92
Spectrophotometer, 92
Stone, Harlan Fiske, 8
Surveillance, 197–198, 207–213
  electronic, 195–196
  moving, 209–213
  stationary, 208–209
Suspects, 21

Terry v. *Ohio*, 193
Theft, 168–169
Theory building, 39–40, 139–142
"Thief Takers," 4
Thorwald, Jurgen, 3, 11
Tool mark comparison, 93
Trace evidence, 76, 186

Undercover operations, 205–207
United States v. *mcDaniel*, 192

Victims, 21
Videotape, 51
Vidocq, Eugene Francois
Vucetich, Juan, 9

Waite, Charles E., 11–12
Weapons, 92
Wiretapping, 195–196
Witnesses, 21, 184
  children, 103
  elderly, 104
  middle-aged, 104
  primary and secondary, 184
  young adults, 104
  youngsters or teenagers, 103–104